Church Stretton through the ages

Church Stretton
through the ages

Tony Crowe and Barrie Raynor

Church Stretton through the ages

Copyright © Tony Crowe and Barrie Raynor, 2011.

All rights reserved.

No part of this publication may be produced, stored in a retrieval system or transmitted in any form or by any means, electronic, mechanical, photocopying or otherwise, without permission in writing from the authors.

Published by Greengates, High Street, Church Stretton, Shropshire, SY6 6BY, England.

A catalogue record for this book is available from the British Library.

ISBN 978-0-9568018-0-7

Printed by Cambrian Printers, Aberystwyth.

Foreword

From Cllr. Bob Welch, Chairman and Mayor, Church Stretton Town Council.

Church Stretton is a small market town near the Welsh border, located in a beautiful wooded valley beneath the Long Mynd. So it is perhaps not surprising that more attention has been paid in the past to the scenery rather than to the town itself. Church Stretton is the only town in the Shropshire Hills Area of Outstanding Natural Beauty and, as such, the natural hub from which to explore this wonderful landscape. This book is a timely reminder that the town has a story of its own, which should not be overlooked, as it gives fascinating insights into its past.

The town is attracting an ever increasing number of visitors. Some years ago a survey was taken to find out what was needed to make the town an even more attractive place to visit. While most visitors were very satisfied with their visit, there was a recurrent plea for more information about the heritage of the area, especially as there is no museum in the town.

In response, a small working group was formed to research and create explanatory plaques to be fixed to historic buildings around the town. This was followed shortly afterwards by an Illustrated Historical Time Line, telling the history of the town and area from 650 million years ago to the present day, set out in panels running the length of the external wall of the Antiques Centre. These enhancements have attracted much positive comment, not only from visitors but also from residents, who value a deeper understanding of the roots of the community in which they live and which commands such a strong sense of loyalty.

Key members of that small working group were the two authors of this book, Tony Crowe and Barrie Raynor. They have done a great service to the town by drawing together, in both words and pictures, much that is known about the people, places and events which have shaped local history. A former librarian who has lived here for over forty years, Tony Crowe has amassed a very large private collection of pictures and documents relating to Church Stretton's past, providing much of the source material for this book. He has generously shared elements of this material in the innumerable history lectures that he has given locally over many years but it is invaluable that they have now been drawn together into one publication. That achievement owes much to the diligent research and presentational skills of Barrie Raynor, resulting in the same effective partnership as made such a noteable contribution to the contents of the plaques and Historical Time-line.

For all those, whether resident or visitor, who wish to find out more of Church Stretton's past, this book is a veritable treasure trove.

Preface

This book sets out to tell the story of Church Stretton in words and pictures from the time of the first settlement in Anglo Saxon times until the present day. It is not meant to be a comprehensive history but to give the reader a flavour of how and why the town has grown to the size and shape it is today. The inspiration for the book comes from a series of talks on Church Stretton history which Tony Crowe gave in 2009.

Over the last thirty five years Tony has amassed a substantial collection of postcards, photographs and printed material which has formed the basis of this book. Other illustrations have been provided by individuals whose help we have acknowledged in the text. Members of the staff of Shropshire Archives have helped with the necessary research and we are very grateful for this and their permission to reproduce a number of illustrations from material in the County collection.

In writing this book we have drawn on existing written sources, in particular the series of articles written by David Bilbey published from 1981 to 1991 in *Stretton Focus*. His original research also provided the basis for his books *Church Stretton* (1985, Phillimore) and *Church Stretton Walkabout* (1987, The Stretton Society). The *Victoria County History of Shropshire* (volume 10, 1998) has many pages devoted to the Parish and has provided essential material. Another book, *A History of the Church of St Laurence, Church Stretton,* by Douglas Grounds (2002, Logaston Press) provided an excellent account of the interaction of the developing local community with the church and is still available.

Some smaller publications, namely *The Strettons, Scenes from the past* (1979, Shropshire Libraries) and *Our Memories of Church Stretton* (about 1998, Mayfair Community Centre) have also provided information. An interesting article entitled 'Church Stretton of yore' written by Eliza Jones which appeared in the journal *Bye-Gones* (1st February 1911) describes in detail the town in the nineteenth century. Other sources include the many trade directories from 1797 to 1941, guide books such as *Church Stretton Illustrated* (1903 - 1937) and many others issued pre and post-war and George Windsor's *A Handbook to the Capabilities, Attractions, Beauties and Scenery of Church Stretton* (1885).

Information has been gathered from the tithe apportionment maps of 1838 and associated field name maps, the decennial census returns from 1841 and the Ordnance Survey 25″ map of 1883. By combining information from the 1838 tithe lists and the 1841 census, detailed information about family individuals, their occupations, houses and lands can be obtained for the first time. This information has been given in the belief that it provides the human interest which brings to life what it was like to live in the town in the nineteenth century.

We are especially grateful to the following individuals who have provided much useful additional information: Reg and Dorothy Beasley, Tony Bloor, Linda Campbell, Eileen Deakin, Ian Dormor, Lesley Forbes, Douglas Grounds, Anne Halliburton, Christine Harvey, Hilary Jones, Tim Jones, Sheila Martland, Mike Morris, David and Sheila Newbrook, Jane Norwich, Oonagh O'Neill, Bill Reynolds, Peter and Angela Ridge, Ivar Rømo, Peter and Anne Stafford, Paul Stamper, Paul Stephens, Percy Tarbuck, Tony Thomson, Ray Tipton, Dominic and Sally Wilson, David and Sylvia Witting and Stuart Wright.

Whilst we have tried to mention everyone who has helped by providing information or images, we are bound to have forgotten someone - to any such person, our sincere apologies.

A number of images we have reproduced remain the copyright of the owner, in particular those from the Shropshire Archives [SA], English Heritage National Monuments Record, Lion Television Limited (2010), Simon Madin (Abbeycolour), The Imperial War Museum, Shropshire Magazine and the Shropshire Star. We are grateful for their kind permission to reproduce their material.

Finally, thanks are especially due to our wives who, like us, have lived with this book throughout its preparation.

The Early Stretton Township

Early Settlement

The earliest evidence of human activity in the vicinity of Church Stretton occurs on the Long Mynd in the form of the Port Way, a well established route running north - south along the ridge. Worked flints of the Stone Age period have been found near the Port Way and a Neolithic (late Stone Age, *c.* 5,000 - 2,400 BC) axe head has been found in the Carding Mill valley.

There is much evidence of Bronze Age (*c.* 2,500 - 800 BC) activity on the Long Mynd in the form of barrows (burial mounds), earthworks and artifacts. Also, on the top of Caer Caradoc hill to the east, there is a large Iron Age (*c.* 800 BC - 43 AD) fortification. Bodbury Ring, another prominent hill fort on the north side of the Carding Mill valley, is also probably Iron Age. Originally the Long Mynd was covered with forest but was progressively cleared by Bronze Age farmers.

The Roman Road

There is no evidence of Roman settlement despite the military road they built through the Stretton gap, though a couple of Roman coins and a brooch have been found beside the road.

The Roman road is a spur off the main Watling Street which runs from Dover via London to Wroxeter (near Shrewsbury), which became the fourth largest city in Roman Britain. This spur, originally called Botte Street and from about 1580 called Watling Street, runs south from Wroxeter through the Stretton gap at the foot of the Lawley, Caer Caradoc and Ragleth Hills, so avoiding the marshy valley bottom, to Leintwardine, Kenchester (near Hereford) and on to Caerleon in South Wales. The Stretton gap is a strategic corridor linking these major towns and garrisons.

The Anglo Saxon Settlement

The name Stretton is Saxon meaning a tun or township by the 'street' or Roman road. It is possible that the original Stretton was located between the site of the present church and the Town Brook valley. Since the end of the last Ice Age some 12,000 years ago the Town Brook has deposited a terrace of sand and gravel on top of the hard Long Mynd shale. The Town Brook emerges from the hill in the vicinity of Pryll Cottage on its way to the valley bottom in the Stretton gap. By 1858 the stream was channelled on a fairly straight course down Brook Street (now Burway Road) and Lake Lane (now Sandford Avenue) before running south to join the river Onny.

This location was a good place to establish a settlement since it was on the well drained western side of the valley hidden from the Roman road, sheltered from storms and with a clean stream running through it. Beyond, in the main valley, there was easily cultivated soil spreading out across the valley floor which contrasted with the surrounding areas of heavy boulder clay. This area was originally marsh land but a simple drainage scheme provided excellent water meadows which yielded a good crop of hay to provide winter feed for the cattle and for the oxen which were particularly valuable draught animals for ploughing the fields.

The Norman Manor

The purpose of the great survey which William I made in 1086 of all the land in England was to find out who owned what before and after the Conquest and how much it was worth. It provided a detailed insight into what Stretton looked like that year.

The entry for Stretton in the Domesday Book, as it became known, was written in very abbreviated Latin.

> Ipse com ten *Stratvn*. Eduin tenuit cu . iiii . bereuuich. Ibi . viii . hidæ   In dnio sunt . iii . car . 7 vi . serui . 7 ii . ancillæ . 7 xviii . uilli 7 viii . bord cu pbro hntes . xii . car . Ibi moliñ 7 æccta . 7 in silua . v . haiæ . 7 vi . car adhuc possuñ . ee. T.R.E. ualb . xiii . lib . Modo . c . solid.

In English, it reads

The Earl himself holds Stratun. Earl Edwin held it with four berewicks. Here eight hides. In demesne are three ox teams. Six male and two female serfs and 18 villeins and eight bordars with a priest have 12 teams. Here a mill and a church and in the wood five hayes. There might be six more teams. In the time of King Edward was worth £13. Now 100 shillings.

It was therefore a demesne manor, that is it was held by Roger de Montgomery, the Norman Earl of Shrewsbury himself and not granted to a vassal. Before the Conquest it had been held by Earl Edwin, the Saxon Earl of Mercia (who kept it until his death in 1071) and was an area still largely forested. The manor of Stretton included, in 1086, four berewicks (outlying hamlets) which can probably be identified as All Stretton, Little Stretton, Minton and Whittingslow. It contained eight hides. (A hide was the amount of land a team of eight oxen could plough in a year, equivalent to about 120 acres.)

On the demesne land, which produced directly for the lord of the manor, there were three ploughs and six male and two female slaves, the males probably serving as three plough teams, so reducing the labour services of the villeins. The two females may have been maidservants, implying that the Earl may have had an occasional residence within the circuit of the manor where he stayed when hunting in the Long Mynd forest.

The community also included 18 villeins who held a landed stake in the village fields, eight bordars (the smallholders and craftsmen) and a priest. Between them they had twelve ploughs. With 35 males specifically mentioned, the total population could have been between 140 and 175. There was a mill and a church and in the woodland five hayes (hedged enclosures) for the capture of game, usually roebuck, for royal hunting. The mill may have been Brooks Mill, the later Carding Mill. It was reckoned that there was sufficient land for a further six ploughs. The fall in value since the Conquest was striking: from £13 to £5, presumably the result of Welsh raids and the punitive devastation of 1070.

To the south of the town there was, for a time, an impressive castle, sited to dominate the Stretton gap. Called Brocards or Brockhurst, it was probably built during the early 12th century to guard the route through the Stretton valley. It consisted of an inner bailey surrounded by a massive stone wall and an outer bailey. There were also fishponds, a mill bank and a sluice crossing the valley forming an access to the castle. However by 1255 the castle had all but collapsed and the fishponds drained. Camden, writing 350 years later, said 'near Stretton in a valley are yet to be seen the rubbish of an old castle called Brocards castle and the same set amidst green meadows that before time were fishponds'.

The manor was held by successive Earls of Shrewsbury until 1102 when it reverted to the King and mostly remained so until 1336.

Stretton in the Middle Ages

The period around 1200 saw great changes to the settlement at Stretton as it emerged from obscurity; it was a time of peace and increasing prosperity. The population had increased to such an extent that the church needed to be considerably enlarged; a new chancel, two transepts and a tower were built. The centre of gravity of the town moved to the area around what is now the Market Square. The town assumed the basic layout that can still be seen today, that is with a single wide market street from which long narrow burgage plots ran at right angles, with premises fronting the street while the gardens or yards had access from a back lane. Church Street is one such back lane that still exists.

Until 1285 markets were held in the churchyard but this was stopped by Edward I with the result that markets were held on the other side of the churchyard wall. Thus in most towns, including Church Stretton, the market place is typically found next to the church.

In 1214 King John ordered the Sheriff of Shropshire to announce the holding of a weekly market on Wednesdays at the King's manor of Stretton-en-le-Dale and a yearly fair on the Feast of the Assumption (15th August).

King John, Lord of the Manor

By 1253 the market had been moved to Tuesday and the fair to a four-day event from the 2nd to 5th of May. This was changed again in 1337 when Edward III, having given the manor to the Earl of Arundel, granted him a charter which moved the weekly market to Thursdays with another yearly fair on the three days 13-15th September, the Feast of the Exaltation of the Holy Cross. The name *chirlestretton* was recorded for the first time in 1250.

Church Stretton's market place was planned and laid out adjacent to the churchyard probably as long ago as 1214 when the first market was ordered by the Lord of the Manor, King John. The market place then was a long wide open space which, on the prescribed day of the week, was filled with pens of livestock and stalls for produce.

The market area was surrounded by the houses of the wealthier inhabitants, merchants, artisans and traders. The building plots, known as burgage plots, on which they built their houses and workshops were leased from the the lord of the manor and like any modern developer he fitted in as many as possible along the sides of the market place to maximise his rental income. Burgage rents were for the empty plot and no extra charge was made whether buildings were erected on only part or along the whole length of the plot. The further the plot from the centre of the town the lower the rent.

Burgage holders had often migrated from nearby country areas in order to ply their trades and set up workshops and businesses. Thus once a market was established the population grew rapidly and the town prospered. It is no coincidence that this was the time when there was a major extension to the parish church.

The wide streets or market places of medieval towns were often colonised by later buildings recognisable by their lack of yards or gardens. The map on the next page shows how the town may have looked in the 13th century with the original market street as wide as the market place is today but much longer. The west side of today's Market Square is probably the line of the original wide street of the planned medieval town. If this were so, then 2 The Square, 10 High Street (formerly *The Plough Inn*),

The front of Ashlett Cottages (left side of photo A) in a narrow alley behind Ashlett House may lie on the boundary of the original wide main street. Similarly, 2 The Square (centre of photo B) is not a natural site for a building and suggests that 10 High Street, formerly the Plough Inn (right in photo B) is a later intrusion into the original market place. The straight building line of the west side of the present Square, the churchyard wall and the front of Ashlett Cottages suggests it is the western edge of the original market place.

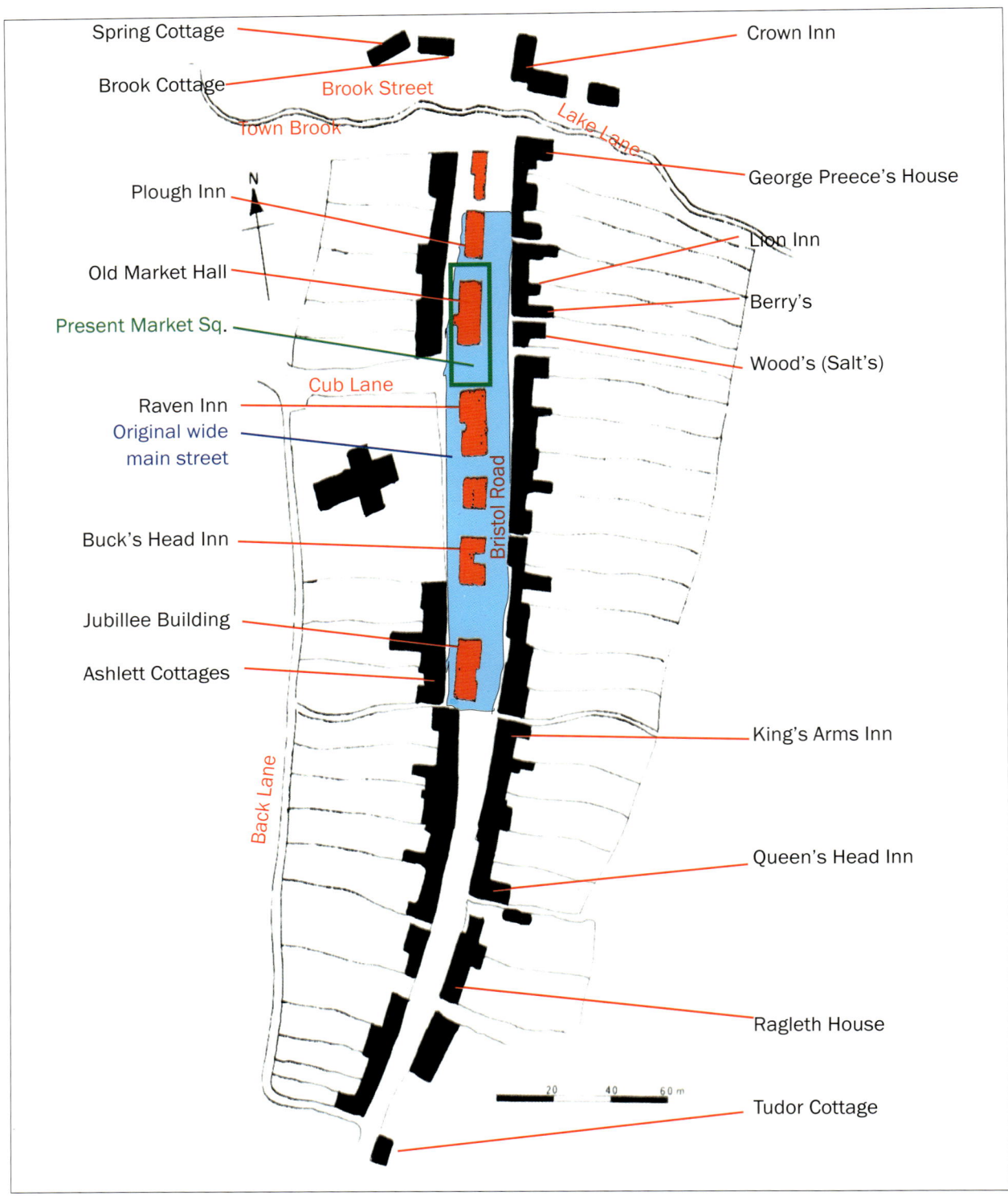

Conjectured plan of Church Stretton at the beginning of the 13th century. It shows the long narrow burgage plots on either side of the main street and suggests how the original wide main street, shaded blue, was encroached upon by subsequent buildings (shown in red) which ultimately formed the west side of the Bristol Road (High Street). The naming of the buildings is to help place the map in a modern context.

The Raven Inn, The Buck's Head Inn and as far as Jubilee Buildings are later intrusions into the original market street. This was a common feature of many medieval towns such as Ludlow, Chipping Norton, Bury St Edmunds and St Albans. This also explains why the church seems to be separated from the centre of the town; in medieval times the churchyard would have formed one edge of the market area.

Royal Visitors

Watling Street was a strategic north-south artery through the Welsh Marches, an area which needed constant military defence to prevent incursions by the Welsh princes. In a bitter war in 1233 the Marches were desolated and insurgents penetrated as far as Stretton. On the 26th and 27th August 1278 Edward I, *en route* from Gloucester to Rhuddlan Castle (Denbighshire), stayed for two days in Stretton, presumably as the guest of the steward of the manor and, as a devout Christian, may well have attended mass in the parish church.

King Edward I

In 1322 his son Edward II stayed briefly in Stretton while campaigning against Roger Mortimer who was plotting to overthrow him. Another important visitor may have been Henry Bolinbrooke who in 1399 could well have stopped here as he marched from Ludlow to Shrewsbury one month before deposing Richard II and becoming King as Henry IV.

The growing importance of Stretton as a town on the main north-south highway was shown by the granting in 1309 of permission to take a toll on all carts passing through it. This yielded 20 shillings each year. That year the value of the manor was assessed at £20 per annum (a substantial sum) from rents, pasture, timber, mill, fisheries and the profits from justice.

Although Stretton has had many distinguished lords of the manor, they were invariably absentee rulers and no great family has ever made its home here. Consequently there was no grand residence, although there was the Hall, the residence of the stewards of the manor. The Hearth Tax returns for 1672 showed only three buildings with more than one hearth. The largest was the home of Thomas Powell, the steward at the Hall, with eleven hearths, then the Rector, Henry Clayton, at the Rectory and Edward Brooke at Bank House, each with six hearths.

The Fire of 1593

Fire was an ever present hazard in all towns because of the close-packed nature of properties which were built of such inflamable materials as timber and thatch. The use of fire in so many trades such as smithies and by wheelwrights, as well as the domestic hearths in every house, made towns highly vulnerable to conflagrations. This happened to Church Stretton in 1593 when a fire started at the north end and rapidly spread throughout the town. The church, with the fire-break of the churchyard, was undamaged. The only other property in the central area of the town which escaped serious damage was the property now known as the *Buck's Head Inn*, possibly because it was built mostly of stone.

The damage to buildings and livelihoods was so great that, by an order of the Queen's Council in the Marches of Wales issued from Ludlow Castle, a collection was made throughout the area in aid of those who had lost their houses and belongings. This resulted in 46 shillings and 10 pence being distributed.

The rebuilding was carried out mainly with timber and thatch, though it would have incorporated more use of brick and stone and better designed fireplaces. Many of the town's present properties, some of which now hide behind Georgian and Victorian frontages, including the *King's Arms*, Hardwick House, the *Lion Inn*, the Old Barn, Greengates and Tudor Cottage date from this period.

Civil War

Shropshire was a Royalist stronghold during the early years of the Civil War. Like most of the country Church Stretton's population would have suffered the hardships of billeting soldiers, forced service for some of the able-bodied men and the commandeering of crops, livestock and possessions. After Parliamentary forces took Shrewsbury in 1645 depredations increased as large forces of soldiers and horses moved frequently through the Stretton Gap *en route* between Shrewsbury and Ludlow castles.

Tithes

Every parishoner in Church Stretton who bred animals or raised crops was bound to pay a tenth of the yield to the church. As Stretton was a royal manor the King tended to use his patronage to reward officers in royal service with the benefice of Church Stretton; they in turn regarded the parish simply as a source of income. The Rectors were therefore absentees who pocketed the greater share of the income of the living and employed a curate to perform their duties. Thus in the 1770s the (absentee) Rector, Cambridge Professor John Mainwaring, leased the tithes for £180 and had income from the glebe land of £45 but needed to pay only £40 for a curate.

There was inevitable ill feeling created by the collection of the tithes but it was not until 1836 that reform occurred in the form of conversion of the tithe to a charge based on the prevailing price of grain. This was much easier to collect. In 1851 Rector Robert Pemberton received £505 in lieu of tithes, a substantial sum which, with the income from the glebe, made the parish a very desirable living.

Church Stretton, a Small Rural Town

Until the middle of the 19th century Church Stretton was still primarily a small rural market and agricultural town with most of the basic agricultural and domestic trades such as wheelwrights, blacksmiths, carpenters, glaziers, coopers, masons, tinmen, tailors, shoemakers, bakers and butchers, etc. represented in the town. Malting was an established industry by 1587 and there were fulling mills by the late 17th century. Textile and leather trades in the town included weaving, tailoring, tanning, shoemaking and gloving. It was a self sufficient community little affected by outside events. The town consisted of the Bristol Road (High Street) and Brook Street (Burway Road), with outlying settlements at World's End, Ashbrook, Hazler, Carding Mill and Watling Street. In the 1841 census the population was 634, comprising 276 males, 355 females and three travelling chimney sweeps who had slept in a barn the previous night. The number of houses was 129.

After the arrival of the railway in 1852 Church Stretton began to develop, albeit slowly, as a holiday resort. Visitors came to enjoy the scenery and the peace and quiet, taking up all the accommodation available in July and August. The first special provision for them quickly followed the arrival of the railway when *The Crown Inn* replaced *The Talbot Inn* as the main inn of the town; the coaching trade was in decline and *The Crown Inn* was nearer to the railway station. Ralph Benson, having bought *The Talbot Inn* and *The Crown Inn*, sold *The Talbot Inn* and in 1865 built the first part of *The Hotel* at the other end of the town, nearer the railway station.

Burgage Plots Today

Behind many of the shops along the High Street in Church Stretton, particularly on the east side, is a narrow strip of land with an assortment of old buildings and outhouses on it. Some are extensions tacked on behind the main houses, others, former barns and stables, have been converted to modern uses. Most of the plots originally had a path at the side for access, but many of these spaces have been filled by further building.

Most of the shops on the High Street today have similar sized frontages because, although the buildings have changed, they stand on the original plots marked out several hundred years ago. From the back these buildings do not appear to be of any great architectural interest but it is not so much the buildings as the shape of these burgage plots and their arrangement in relation to the market place that is interesting.

A lane ran along the back of these plots to give rear access, known simply as the back lane. For those on the west side of the High Street it was indeed called Back Lane until it was given the more formal name of Church Street, first recorded as such in the 1841 census. The back lane on the east side has disappeared under development.

Good examples of burgage plots are still to be seen behind Berry's, Salts and Clee Hill Electrics.

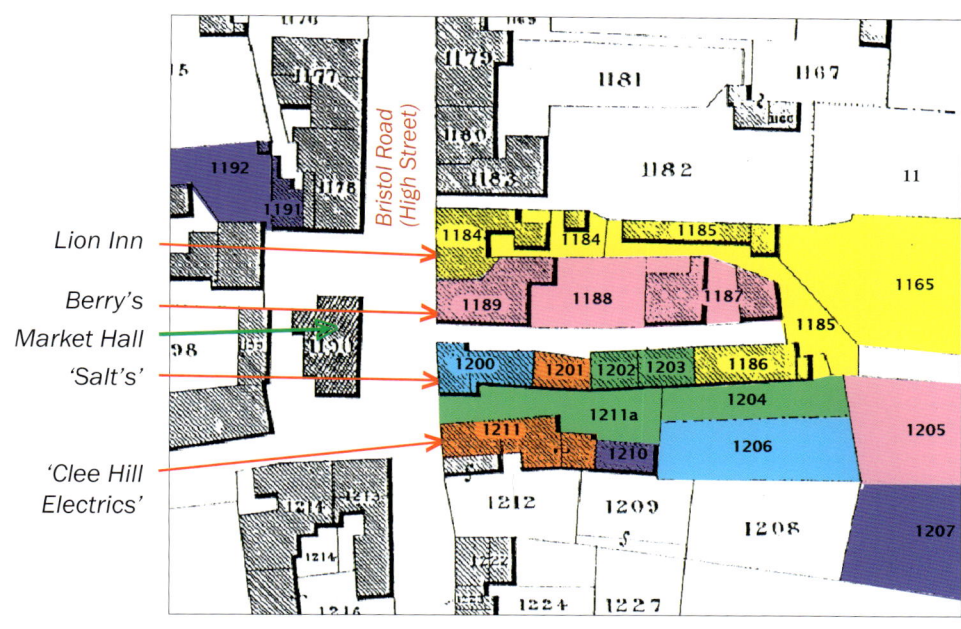

Lion Inn
Berry's Market Hall
'Salt's'
'Clee Hill Electrics'

Part of the 1838 tithe apportionment map showing the buildings and plot numbers. The colours show the different occupiers.

🟨 *The Lion Inn burgage plot was owned and occupied by Jonathan Mills. The front plot (1184) was the Inn and (1185) was stables and yard. He also occupied stables (1186) at the end of 'Salt's' burgage plot. The remaining plots were yards and a garden (1165).*

🟪 *Berry's burgage plot was all owned and occupied by William Wilding. The front plot (1189) was the house as we know it today, with out-buildings (1187) at the rear. He also owned a garden (1205).*

🟦 *The 'Salt's' burgage plot was owned by John Robinson but had four different occupiers. The front plot was the home of Thomas Glover and he owned the garden (1206).*
The fourth plot 🟩 *(1203) was the home of Thomas Gough with his workshop next door (1202). He also occupied the court and garden to the side (1204 and 1211a).*

🟧 *The 'Clee Hill Electrics' burgage plot was also owned by John Robinson. The front plot (1211) was his shop and warehouse shared with Richard Home, and his house (1201) was across the court behind that of Thomas Glover (1200). At the end* 🟪 *(1210) was a smithy occupied by Richard Childe who also occupied the house (1191) in the market square and the adjacent garden (1192). He also occupied the garden (1207).*

Left picture:
Berry's (on the left) and Salt's (on the right) are good examples of buildings on burgage plots. Behind Salt's four further buildings were built on the long plot.

Right picture:
View looking back up Salt's burgage plot towards the High Street. The cottage at this end (plot 1186) was stables in 1838.

The Parish Church of St Laurence

A pencil sketch by William Vickers of the church in 1841 before the pyramidal roof had been added. The view is from the churchyard gate at the Churchway/Church Street corner. [SA]

The first documentary evidence for a church in Church Stretton is the reference in the Domesday Book (1086) to the presence of both a church and a priest in Stratun. Christianity had existed in Mercia for several centuries and so a Saxon church could have been well established here with a building almost certainly made of wood.

The Norman Church

After exerting their civil authority by building castles the Norman's next priority was to emphasise their ecclesiastical authority by building imposing cathedrals, abbeys and larger churches. Stretton would have been low on their priorities, but the church was almost certainly built between 1100 and 1130 at a time when the Welsh border was relatively quiet and there was a growing population and prosperity in the region. By then local masons had mastered the new technology and style of Norman architecture. The stone in the church is local Hoar Edge Grit and Chatwall sandstone. The design would probably have been a simple two-cell building with a small nave and chancel, very similar to the one at Heath in Corvedale which dates from the same period (below).

The main entrance was by the south door with its typical Norman round arch. Another, narrower, door on the north side is more elaborate and was traditionally used for funeral processions. It was often called the 'devil's door' because of the tradition of keeping it open during baptisms to allow the devil to escape. Medieval worship involved processions

8

around the church and the door would have been used for that purpose also.

The south door

Above the north door is a sheela-na-gig (below), a female figure carved in stone, usually considered to be a pagan fertility symbol. This one was probably inserted into the original Norman wall by the builders who had retained some belief in the old pagan practices, for popular religion was deeply coloured by superstitions. There were hundreds of these carvings on churches and castles throughout Europe. Though they were not meant to be obcene, most were spoiled during the Reformation and by Victorian restorers.

The Early Thirteenth Century Extension

The beginning of the 13th century saw a steady increase in the population of the country and a growing prosperity arising largely from an increasing demand for sheep products - wool, milk and skins. Stretton benefited from this increased prosperity which was manifested in the town being laid out more formally along the High Street and by the decision of King John in 1214 to hold a weekly market and annual fair in Stretton.

A major extension to the church at this time involved the building of a new chancel and

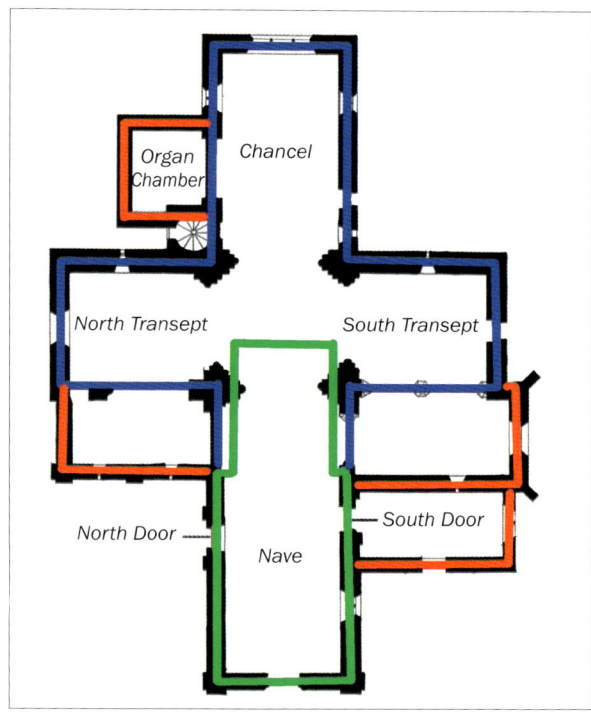

Stages of building
■ *Norman*
■ *13th Century extension*
■ *Victorian additions*

transepts to form a 'cruciform' church with a tower above the crossing.

The use of pointed arches above doors and windows together with those built to support the tower heralded the new Early English style of building. However, the church would have been very dark inside, having only very narrow splayed lancet windows.

A century later all but two of the lancet windows (one illustrated here) were enlarged to the window size seen today.

In time the tower was enlarged by a magnificent upper storey with the new Perpendicular style windows which are

9

cusped and pointed under square heads. The tower is characterised also by rich ornamentation, fine gargoyles and slender buttresses.

Interior

From an early date the internal stone walls were plastered over and covered with religious paintings, the Lord's Prayer, the Creed and psalms. On the wall on either side of the west window were large representations of a skeleton and of Father Time. At the Reformation these paintings were whitewashed over, images destroyed and the royal coat-of-arms displayed. The great wooden screen (the rood screen) which blocked off the chancel was removed so that the congregation could see the altar. The north door was closed in 1818.

However, the Victorians had different ideas of how a church should look. The walls were cleared of plaster and a major reordering of the interior took place during 1867 - 68. Side aisles were added to both transepts and an organ chamber built on to the north-east corner. The old box pews were removed as well as the gallery from the west end.

The lords of the manor have always been absentee lords and so no great family graced the church with fine tombs and memorials. Any small ones that had existed were removed during the Victorian restoration.

Inside the bell tower, there are instructions to the bellringers made in 1773:

> If that to ring you do come here
> You must ring well with hand and ear
> And if a bell you overthrow
> 4d to pay before you go
> And if you ring with spur or hat
> 6d you must pay for that
> Or if in this place you swear or curse
> 12d to pay - pull out your purse.

The tragic death of the three Goulder brothers in *The Hotel* fire on the night of the 2-3 April 1968 (see page 37) is commemorated by a stunning memorial (illustrated) above the crossing called 'The Symbol of St Laurence' by sculptor John Skelton which has won much praise. It takes the form of an iron grille with copper flames, clearly representing the nature of the death of the church's patron saint, recalling too how the boys died and symbolizing also the tongues of fire at the first Pentecost.

The Chancel Screen

Screens were an important part of the late medieval parish church and were used to separate the laity in the nave from the clergy taking the mass in the chancel; they were meant to enhance people's appreciation of the 'holy mystery' of the mass. The original rood screen was demolished at the Reformation but a new simpler one designed by G F Bodley was built to commemorate Queen Victoria's Diamond Jubilee of 1897. It was removed in 1983 to form part of the Emmaus Chapel being built into the north aisle, but the chapel itself was removed in 2010 as part of a further reordering of the interior of the church.

The Catholic and Protestant Church

Until the Protestant Reformation of the 16th century the English Church was Catholic, ruled from Rome. In all churches, including St. Laurence's, the Mass was celebrated in Latin. In 1534 the Act of Supremacy made Henry VIII Head of the Church in England and an English Bible soon had to be placed in every church. In the reign of his son, Edward VI, an English Prayer Book was introduced.

That was suppressed in the reign of the Catholic Queen Mary (1553-58) but under her half-sister and successor, Queen Elizabeth, the English Prayer Book returned and the Protestant Church of England was established, though practice changed only late in the century at St Laurence's, where old ways died hard.

Why was the Church Dedicated to St Laurence?

St Laurence was a deacon in Rome when, in the year 258, the Pope and seven deacons including Laurence were martyred. Tradition says that he was slowly roasted on a gridiron; whether or not this is true, he is always depicted with a gridiron. There is a stone effigy of St Laurence on the SE corner of the tower, complete with gridiron in his left hand (below).

The Churchyard

The churchyard (God's Acre), previously bounded by a fence, was enclosed by a stone wall in 1798. On several dressed stones there is a carved number and initials; one such reads 'W C H 1798' and refers to W C Hart Esq. Each member of the parish contributed to the cost of erection and maintenance of the wall and the numbers refer to the subscribers.

A headstone in memory of the village barber refers to Francis Hick whose friends concocted the epitaph (1802)

> Here lies the barber Hick,
> Who cut and shaved and was so quick.
> And now has gone to his long whum [*home*],
> He killed himself with drinking rum.

The grave of Ann, wife of Thomas Cook, is referred to as the Thursday grave (1814). The inscription may still be read:

> On a Thursday she was born,
> On a Thursday made a bride,
> On a Thursday her leg was broke
> And on a Thursday died.

In 1827 a stone coffin (below) was found under the south transept with a lid and an alabaster slab bearing an illegible inscription. It appears to have been taken to the hermitage in Rectory Wood and brought back when the Rectory and its lands were sold a century later. One theory is that it is the coffin of the founder of the Lady Chapel set up in the south transept in the early middle ages.

The churchyard was closed for burials in 1868. The additional burial ground on part of Talbot Meadow in Cunnery Road was consecrated in 1869, but itself became full and the new burial ground at Greenhills was opened in 1942.

The book by Douglas Grounds, *A History of the Church of St Laurence, Church Stretton* provides a wealth of further information about the church and the town.

The Old Rectory

The Old Rectory, from a watercolour by John Homes Smith, 1824. [SA]

For much of the early history of Church Stretton, the lord of the manor was the King. He was also patron of the living and thus had the right to nominate the incumbent. With the King as patron the living could not be appropriated by any monastery so it did not lose its tithes and income. As a result it was for many years one of the richest livings in Shropshire with income from both tithes and a large amount of glebe land together valued at £565 in 1851.

According to an inventory of glebe lands of 1699 Henry Clayton (Rector 1671 - 1725) lived in the same house as William Harries did whilst Rector (1579 - c.1621). This comprised 'a decent hall, two parlours, two butteries, five chambers, a kitchen, a boulting-house and a malt chamber, a stable and an ox-house all under one roof'. It stood on the site of the present Old Rectory for it is described as being between Sir George Norton's land (which lay to the south), Coneyborough (Rectory Wood) to the west, the Burway (to the north) and the yard of Prill Cottage (to the east). On the south side was a large kitchen garden. The Rector was also a farmer as the list of outbuildings included cow houses and the glebe land consisted of a number of fields and closes. There was also a five-bay barn which could have been the old tithe barn which still stood in 1830.

In the 17th and 18th centuries the Rectors of Church Stretton were men of wealth and property. One such was John Mainwaring, Rector from 1749 to 1807. He was a Fellow of St. John's College, Cambridge and later Professor of Divinity, a lucrative appointment. Most of his life was spent in Cambridge so for many years he did not live in the parish but left it in the charge of a Curate who was paid a small salary. However he spent the vacations in Stretton and came to live here on his retirement in 1797, where he officiated until his death in 1807.

Mainwaring rebuilt the Rectory used by Clayton and Harries soon after his appointment to Church Stretton in 1749. About 1775, he began to improve the glebe land including the planting of Rectory Wood.

The next Rector, T B Coleman (1807-18), remodelled the Rectory by moving the entrance, now flanked by Doric columns, to the west end (illustrated below) so that all the rooms on the south face overlook the Rectory Field and have views of Ragleth Hill. He also laid a drive across Rectory Field to the church, emerging opposite the church through imposing gates by the lodge.

His sucessor, R N Pemberton, was Rector from 1818 to 1848. In 1834, he built a high boundary wall largely from bricks from the old Hall to provide seclusion from the town of the Rectory, part of the glebe and his private estate, these properties comprising virtually all the land between the town and the Long Mynd.

Rectory Wood covers 16 acres of mixed woodland. It and the adjoining Rectory Field are in the ownership of the Shropshire Council, both being managed as part of its leisure facilities. The Wood was opened to the public in 1967 and a ¾ mile long nature trail through it was officially opened by Sir Jack Longland on 30th May 1970.

The magnificent entrance to the Rectory built by the Rector, T B Coleman, about 1810.

Rectory Wood

Rectory Wood is part of a historic park associated with the adjacent former Rectory. The well preserved remains comprise woodland walks, a stream and artificial pool and sites of buildings, which include a pumping house and an ice house.

The Rector from 1749 to 1807, Professor John Mainwaring, had amongst his many friends Lancelot (Capability) Brown who visited him at the Rectory in 1775. Soon afterwards Mainwaring began to improve the glebe including Rectory Wood and it seems possible that at least informal guidance was provided by Brown. It is not certain which improvements are of that period and which were the responsibility of later 19th century Rectors. It seems likely, however, that it was in the earlier period that the brook down Town Brook Hollow along the northern boundary of the wood was modified and a pool formed. It was probably also then that formal walks were laid out around the steeply sloping wooded hills, from which views out to the hills beyond could be enjoyed.

Rectory Wood was entered from the west side of the Rectory grounds adjoining the walled kitchen garden (now under modern housing) via an elaborate stone gateway with a Gothic arch which is no longer in existence. A rockery may form part of the entry complex. From there the path leads to the pool which is dark and still and shaded by yew trees. A stone lip or weir controls the water height. On the north side of the pool is a ruined stone and brick building with Gothic windows which was built in the early 1760s as a folly or hermitage and is shown on a 1767 plan. Later, it was converted to a pumping house which supplied Church Stretton with water from 1865 when the reservoir higher up Town Brook Hollow was built until its replacement by that in New Pool Hollow in 1901/2.

There was an ice house on the south side of the pool which has survived in reasonable condition. Icehouses started to become features in the formal gardens of country houses from the early 17th century and by the mid 19th century most country houses would have at least one for cooling wine and preserving perishable food. This one was dug into the hillside and lined with 18th century bricks. The roof would have been covered with earth and turf so that the ice was packed into a compact space, well insulated to slow the melting process. The ice would have come from the adjacent pool. Sadly the roof has fallen in.

The path continues along the north side of the stream to the west edge of the wood where there is a slight platform on which, in 1834, was a summer house with, then, views down the stream to the yew-ringed pool and folly and across to the hills opposite. Incorporated into the floor of the structure is a mosaic of pebbles with the letters 'I' or 'J' and 'M' in a rectangular border picked out in white pebbles suggesting that the summer house was built by John Mainwaring as part of his development of the garden.

50 years later the woodland on the estate was extensive and had become mature. A watercolour (1824) by J H Smith (page 12) shows a possible temple building, no longer extant, set on the edge of mature woodland and the extent of this woodland is shown on the 1834 plan. Only fragments survive of two of the four footbridges across the stream and the ice house has almost completely disappeared, as have a number of other buildings shown on the 1834 plan and the 1824 painting.

The wood planted by Mainwaring about 1775 was felled by Pemberton and the coppiced trees replaced by trees for timber. Whilst the archaeological remains that do survive are not of great significance in themselves, they are important collectively as surviving elements of an important Shropshire park. [*Ref: Hannaford*]

Both Rectory Wood and the adjoining Rectory Field are now owned by the Shropshire Council and are managed as public open spaces.

The ruins of the folly or hermitage which was later used as a pumping house.

The Hall

The lords of the manor of Stretton-en-le-Dale were all absentee landlords until the Rector, Rev'd Thomas B Coleman, became Lord of the Manor in 1808. Prior to this the manor had been held for most of the time initally by the Crown, then the FitzAlan family, then from about 1580 by the Thynne family, now the Marquises of Bath. Day to day management of the manor was left to resident stewards who were important people rewarded by their lord for their loyalty. The stewards resided in the Hall, a large property (arrowed) standing in what is now known as Rectory Field.

There is mention by John Leland of a large residence in his *Itinerary* which describes his travels around England in 1538 as follows:

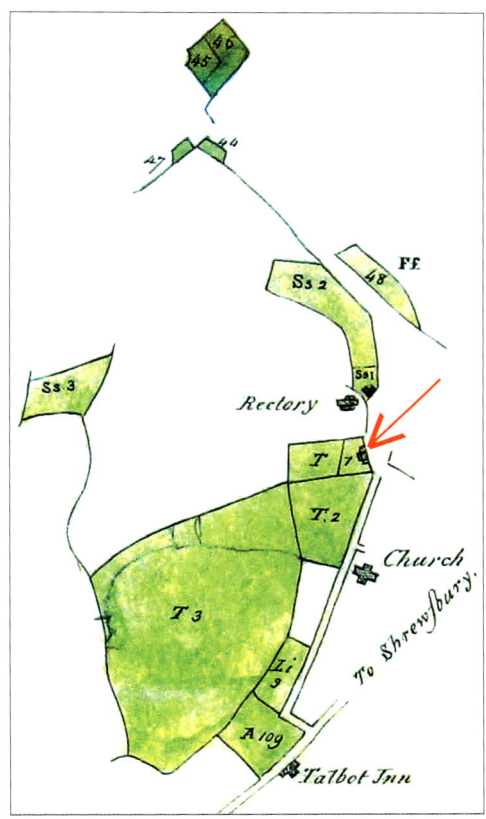

This map is from an indenture dated 1833 relating to the sale of the land (coloured green) by Anne Coleman, widow of the Rector Thomas B Coleman, to Robert Pemberton the succeeding Rector. In the description, areas T1 and T2 are together described as 'now called Orchard Meadow and formerly called Hall Garden Yard (T1) and Orchard (T2)'. Presumably remains of the Hall, indicated by the arrow, could still be seen in 1833. [SA]

I left the Egge [Wenlock Edge] and the Longe Forest, 2 great wodds havynge roe deer, on the right hande coming to Stretton. Thens I rode a 3 miles by well woddyd ground to Streton, a prati [pretty] uplandishe townelet, where by the churche one Brooke a lawyer hathe a praty howse, and here rennythe a broke (the same, as one told me, that goeth by Stretford).

This townelett is the chefist buildinge that is in Streton Dale. Streton Dale is inclosyd with grete hills, well woodyd in some places. It is in length but a 3 miles, and in it be 3 Strettons, Little Streton, Great Streton and Old Streton. This Stretton Dale longgith to the Erle of Arundle.

From Streton to Libot Woode a thorough faire 3 miles, by hilly and woody ground.

'By the church' suggests that the 'praty howse' was the Hall. At the time Francis Brooke, an attorney and deputy steward of the manor, was living there. Later in 1585 Francis Brooke's eldest son Edward who was living at the Hall and may well have also been the steward married Frances Leighton and they moved to the nearby Bank House which had been owned by the Leighton family for many generations [*Ref: Hardwick*].

Around 1600 Bonham Norton, a prominent landowner and building developer in Church Stretton, purchased the Hall and the surrounding park. The park was extensive, reaching uphill as far as the Long Mynd common and including a warren and the Over Field, one of the town's open fields. He rebuilt the Hall and took up residence there, it being described as 'a large timbered mansion'.

The 1662 Hearth Tax returns show that it was then owned by Sir George Norton, grandson of Bonham Norton, but occupied by a Mr Thomas Powell. It was the largest building in Church Stretton with eleven hearths. In 1714 Sir George Norton sold the Hall and the park. Eventually after a series of owners it was bought by Thomas B Coleman, Rector and the new Lord of the Manor, who pulled it down probably not long before his death in 1818. There is no longer any evidence on the ground for the Hall.

Park House, Cub Lane (Churchway)

Park House opposite the Hall may have originated as a parker's or warrener's cottage, the residence of the Hall's park keeper. The Hall's stables seem to have been near by, as well as an old barn where strolling players 'fretted and strutted', mountebanks performed and stage plays took place. It is believed that the tithe barn stood here facing the churchyard.

The first reference to The Park (Park House) appears in a manor court record of 1735 when William Lutwyche of Lutwyche Hall acquired a large amount of property in Church Stretton which included 'several pieces or parcels of land, meadow and pasture with the appurtenances called and known by the several names of the Park, the Cunnery, Suters Close, Ox Leasowe, the Little Elmith, the Great Elmith, etc.'

An internal beam has been dated to 1692 which suggests a date for the construction of the house.

In 1861, by which time it was known as Park House, it had become a girls' boarding school, with Susannah Shingles the Principal, after the closure of the Misses Corfield's school at Ragleth House. Miss Shingles had thirteen pupils ranging in age from eight to seventeen. The prospectus says that 'pupils are carefully taught with mild but firm discipline and have all the comforts of home with unlimited diet'. She was still running the school twenty years later.

By 1885 the house was occupied by A E Demetre de Stourdza Zrinyi who was born about 1836 in Moldavia and became an officer with the Austrian army. Tradition has it that he was exiled from Austria for taking part in a duel and came to England where he eventually become naturalised. In 1866 he married Fanny Pitt at Atcham and came to live in Church Stretton. He was eventually pardoned but refused to return to his native land without his wife.

He and his son, Arthur Edward, together played an important part in the life of Church Stretton. By 1905 Arthur was living at Park House and had carved out quite an empire for himself; he was an accountant, Assistant Overseer of the Poor, Collector of Rates and Taxes, Superintendent Registrar of Births, Deaths and Marriages, Clerk to the Parish Councils of All and Little Stretton, Agent to the Royal Fire and Life and Norwich and London

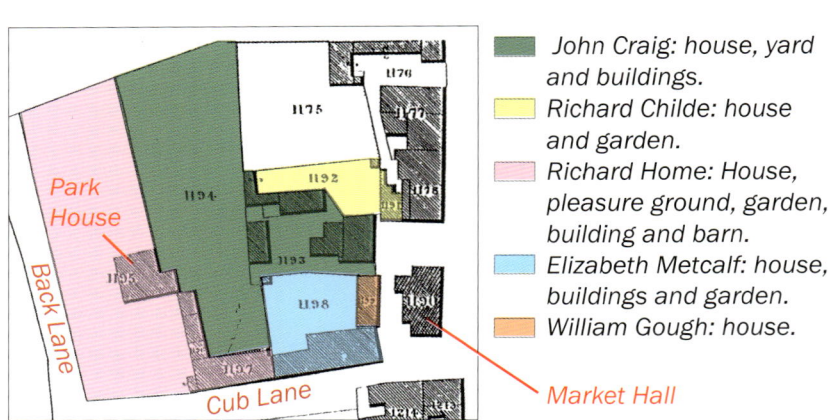

Occupiers of the property behind the Market Hall stretching back to Back Lane (Church Street). Based on the 1838 tithe map.

Accident Assurance Companies and Secretary to the Church Stretton Gas Company.

After he died in 1930, his wife and daughter carried on a succesful welfare clinic at Park House for a number of years.

In Churchway are the remains of part of the stables (above) of the Hall which have been restored and now used as offices.

Advertisement for Miss Shingles school for young ladies.

Park Cottage

On the land adjacent to Park House once owned by Richard Childe (see map opposite) a house called Park Cottage was built about 1880 attached to Park House. Some extensions were built linking it to the old stables and a barn. Park Cottage was demolished in 2006 to allow a small development of houses on the site.

Park House and Park Cottage. [David Bilbey]

The Bank House, Longhills Road

The Bank House in 1861. A sketch by Stanley Leighton. [SA]

This is believed to be the site of the residence of the Cambray family one of whose heiresses (Maud) married John Leighton. For a number of generations the Leightons resided here. In 1585 Edward Brooke, the eldest son of Francis Brooke, married Frances Leighton. They left the Hall where he lived and moved to The Bank House, a large timber framed building having six hearths. The Bank House remained in the Brooke family for several generations and was eventually sold to the Rector Robert Pemberton in 1835. Indeed, Pemberton had lived there for two years from when he was appointed to be Rector until his marriage in 1820, whereupon he moved to the Old Rectory.

Some time in the eighteenth century the Brookes built the imposing brick residence shown in the picture above, near to the old house, probably on the lawns in front.

Both buildings were pulled down by Charles Orlando Childe Pemberton (heir of the former Rector) about 1880 and replaced by the present house (below) which was built in 1892. This was one of the first large neo-timber frame houses in the town, It is a superb example of late Victorian craftsmanship and design, built with Ruabon brick.

Frederic Leighton, The Lord Leighton of Stretton

Frederic Leighton was a direct descendant of the Leightons who long ago lived in The Bank House. He was a noted painter and was President of the Royal Academy from 1878 until his death in 1896. He was elevated to the peerage and, remembering his family roots in Church Stretton, took the title of Baron Leighton of Stretton in the County of Shropshire which was gazetted on 24th January 1896. Unfortunately he died the following day and so holds the record for the shortest lived title of any peer. As he was unmarried the title became extinct. A memorial window in St Laurence's Church was given by Stanley Leighton, M.P. for Oswestry, a distant relative.

Bank House Lodge

In the extensive grounds of The Bank House three cottages were built at the same time in Ruabon brick for gardeners and grooms. One, Bank House Lodge (right) for the groom and later the chauffeur, lies just below The Bank House in Longhills Road. The other two face Shrewsbury Road.

Longhills, Shrewsbury Road

This tasteful and picturesque cottage just to the north of The Bank House was built in 1833 by the Rector, Robert Pemberton, on the site of an earlier house on land which he owned. He built it to house his second curate. The first to occupy it was William Harries in 1835, followed by James Gambier and others. It was purchased in the 1890s by Robert E McCartney, a maltster who inherited the malting business of his father Robert McCartney. Subsequent generations of the McCartney family continued to live there until the 1940s.

Mynd Court, Longhills Road

The architect Emil Quäck designed Mynd Court which was built about 1905. In 1922 the Parochial Church Council felt that the former Rectory was too expensive to maintain and decided to purchase Mynd Court as the residence of the new Rector Henry Dixon. It was described as 'whilst not being too large, it maintained somewhat the dignity of the position of the Rector of Church Stretton'. Dixon let the Old Rectory to tenants until it was sold in 1934. Mynd Court continued as the Rectory until 1981 when it was sold and Norfolk Lodge in Carding Mill Valley Road was purchased for use as the Rectory.

Rev'd Robert Norgrave Pemberton, Rector and Landowner

Robert Norgrave Pemberton was born in Shrewsbury on 7 August 1791. His father was a lawyer in Shrewsbury and the owner of extensive property in the county. He graduated from Christ Church College, Oxford with a B.A. in 1814 and an M.A. in 1816, in which year he was ordained.

In December 1818 following the death of the Rector, Thomas Bernard Coleman, Pemberton was instituted as Rector of Church Stretton, the advowson (the right to appoint a priest to the living) having been purchased for £11,000 by his uncle Thomas Pemberton, a barrister-at-law. He held this post until his death in 1848. On 11 November 1820 he married Caroline Pechell of Berkhamstead, Hertfordshire. The couple had no children.

Because of the tithe income and inheritances from his father and uncle he became a very wealthy man. This enabled him to acquire a considerable amount of land and property in Church Stretton. These included The Bank House in Longhills and Ashford House in the High Street, which he extended.

Pemberton also built The Priory opposite the church in Church Street in 1832. Eventually, by extensive purchases of land and property in the parish, he owned nearly all the land from the Rectory south to World's End where he built a new lodge to mark the end of a carriage drive. He also owned land along Shrewsbury Road and along the east side of Watling Street.

The tithe apportionment map of 1838 showed that Pemberton owned a total of 369 acres in Church Stretton plus the glebe of 68 acres. He also owned 15 acres in Little Stretton and 142 acres in Minton.

Millichope Hall, where Pemberton lived whilst Rector of Church Stretton.

In 1832 Pemberton inherited the Millichope estate in Corvedale from his childless uncle Thomas Pemberton. Here he built the present Millichope Hall between 1835 and 1840 at a cost of £30,000. He went to live at Millchope in 1841. His annual income from his estates was eventually about £5,000, a very substantial sum for the time. In effect, by becoming a large landowner Pemberton became a country gentleman who was also a clergyman.

He made extensive alterations to St Laurence's Church, including the installation of the east window in 1819, built a gallery over the doorway at the rear of the church, rebuilt the wall of the south transept, added the reredos of carved Jacobean panels behind the altar, erected a new vestry, provided a new entrance at the west end and introduced coke fired heating. His public benefactions included a substantial financial contribution towards the cost of the new market hall and support for the school in Burway Road.

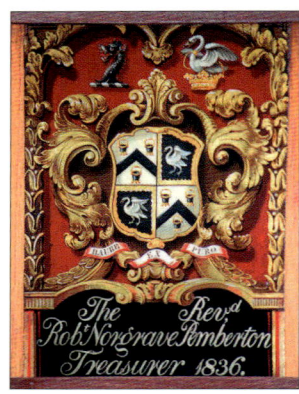

Pemberton's coat of arms depicted at the Salop Infirmary.

During the 1820s and 30s, Pemberton made further improvements to the Rectory including, probably, building a service wing to the east and north of the staircase block and raising the height of the central room. He built the brick wall which extends along the east side of Rectory Field, possibly reusing some of the bricks from the Old Hall which Coleman had demolished.

His standing in the county as a wealthy country gentleman and major landowner was confirmed by his being appointed Treasurer of the Salop Infirmary in 1836.

Pemberton died on 7 October 1848 at Millichope, aged 58. After his death the furniture and other items at the Rectory were valued at over £2,000; the furniture, china, plate and glass at Millichope at nearly £5,000 and the wines in his cellar at over £1,000.

The Town Brook

This watercolour (painted in 1852 by an unknown artist) is a view of Burway House (with a bell tower), Park House and the Church from where the war memorial is now located. An interesting feature is the open Town Brook before it was culverted. [St Laurence PCC]

The abundant clean water of the Town Brook was one reason for the location of the Saxon settlement, Stratun, possibly in the vicinity of the present old Rectory. In later years the water was used by the animal skin yards and malting businesses which grew up along its bank in Brook Street (now Burway Road). There was a bridge opposite Burway House and the stream could be dammed to form a pool for sheep washing.

Opposite the *Crown Inn* (later *The Hotel*) there was a pond fed by the brook and used for washing horses's legs.

The brook continued down the middle of Lake Lane (now Sandford Avenue) until it reached the marshy flood plain near the railway station. It then slowly wended its way southwards to join the Quinny Brook which flowed into the Onny river.

Town Brook was conduited in the mid 1850s. The tunnel was about 2ft 6ins to 3ft wide and made of blue engineering brickwork. The brook enters a tunnel near the entrance to Rectory Gardens and emerges between Central Avenue and the railway line; the exit can be seen from Coffin Lane. It was common practice for boys to crawl up the tunnel as a dare!

The naming of Lake Lane has been a bit of an enigma. The use of the word 'lake' is unusual in Shropshire where meres and ponds abound. It derives from the Old English word *lacu*, meaning watercourse or stream, a word widely used in the Midlands and adjoining parts of Wales [*Ref: Morgan*].

To improve the reliability of the water supply for the town a small reservoir was built in 1865 in Town Brook Hollow (originally called Oakham Dingle) just west of Rectory Wood. Water was then piped to the community. This arrangement continued until 1901-2 when the growth in population outstripped the supply of water and a new reservoir was built in New Pool Hollow in the Carding Mill Valley.

Burway House, Burway Road

This watercolour of Burway House, complete with bell tower, was painted by Thomas Farmer Dukes about 1830. [SA]

This building was erected as the village school in 1779, possibly on the site of an earlier school building. The land was held in trust for the school by the Rector and nine others and the income of £27 per annum from land at Lower Wood was used to help defray the schoolmaster's salary of £40 p.a. He lived in the house free of rent. In addition to his normal teaching duties, he taught in the Sunday school.

In 1792 the school had only 19 pupils. By 1840 numbers had increased to about 70. Most attended free of charge because of the poverty of their parents. Only eleven pupils had to pay fees of between two and seven shillings a quarter.

The school moved to a new purpose built building in Church Street at the beginning of 1861 (see page 118).

Burway House then became a private house for a time. Then for some years in the early 20th century it was again a school, a privately funded one called The Collegiate School run by Geoffrey Dixon. It later became a dentist's surgery and has since been converted into flats.

A 1905 advertisement for the private Collegiate School in Burway House.

Pryll Cottage, Burway Road

Left:
Watercolour by an artist known only by the initials E A R. About 1900.   [Reg Heiron]

Below:
A postcard of 1908.

Bottom:
Pryll Cottage from the rear.

The 1838 tithe map shows that Pryll Cottage was in the Rectory kitchen garden and owned by the Rector, Robert Norgrave Pemberton. The part of the cottage bordering the road is the oldest part, probably dating from the early 17th century. It is referred to in various manorial records from 1740, when, on one occasion, the property included outhouses, barns, stables, gardens and backsides, suggesting a larger establishment than the cottage that exists today. The 1871 census refers to a gardener and a butler living in cottages adjacent to the Rectory, one of which may well have been Pryll. The 1881 census shows John Grosvenor, a gardener, living at Pryll.

The name Prill is an old Marches dialect word meaning 'a stream of clear running water' and refers to the Town Brook running by the cottage.

For a short period around 1905 the cottage was a public house called *The Besom Inn*.

Fairs

The horse and pony fair at the foot of Longhills road in 1905. Note the sheep pens on the left against the wall.

From the late 12th century the right to hold a fair was granted by a royal charter or command. This would specify the day or days on which the fair could be held. Fairs were usually established for the buying and selling of cattle, sheep and horses at the appropriate time of the year. Fairs were not restricted to these commodities; all types of commerce took place and pedlars travelled the country with their wares. They were places for the exchange of news and gossip and for the hiring of labour.

Over the years, Church Stretton had been granted several fairs. By 1888 these had grown to six fairs which were held on:
  1) the second Thursday in January
  2) the third Thursday in March (for cattle and sheep)
  3) the 14th of May (the statute and hiring fair, the so-called Mop Fair). At this fair, prospective servant girls brought with them a new mop which they held to indicate that they were available to be hired. The new mistress would give the chosen girl a shilling for the mop thus hiring her for one year until the next Mop Fair, a tradition carried through to the 1930s. This fair was important for the sale of cows and calves. There was also a funfair with swingboats, gallopers, sideshows, acrobats and shooting galleries - one of the main events of the town's social life.
  4) the 3rd of July (the wool fair)
  5) the 25th of September (the sheep and pony fair)
  6) the last Thursday in November. This was the last fair of the year and became known as the 'dead man's fair' because over the years a number of people had lost their lives going home over the Long Mynd due to bad weather.

Horse breeding and rearing was an important part of the economy of Shropshire's uplands from the Middle Ages. Later on many ponies were bought for use in

Sheep sale in Lion Meadow.

the mines. In the 20th century, partly as the demand for pit ponies fell, the number of horse fairs held in the country declined.

As the Market Square grew smaller with the encroachment of buildings, the various livestock fairs had to find locations elsewhere in the town.

The sheep and pony fair was moved to a triangular piece of ground at the junction of Burway and Longhills Roads but would often extend down to Shrewsbury Road. Wooden pens were erected against the perimeter walls and along the lower Burway Road for the large numbers of sheep which were sold at this fair.

When increasing traffic levels made this arrangement inconvenient the sheep fair was held on the Lion Meadow in Easthope Road until about 1982 when King's Court was built (1984).

Crowds gather for the horse and pony fair in Burway Road which reached as far as Shrewsbury Road.

Spring Terrace: the Skin Yards and Malthouses, Burway Road

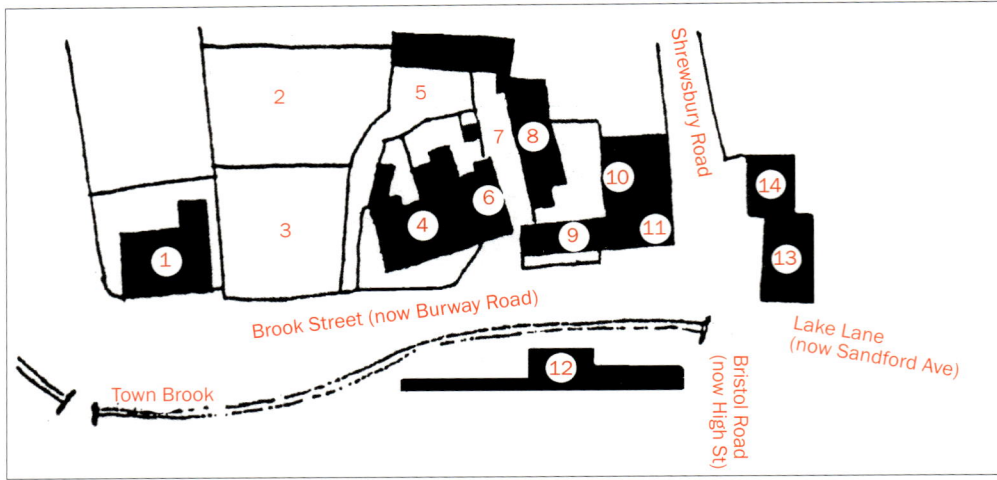

The north side of Brook Street (now Burway Road), based on the 1838 tithe map.

1	Burway House	8	The Beddoes' out buildings
2	John Lucas' garden	9	Brook Cottage, the Beddoes' house
3	The Beddoes' garden	10	Malthouse
4	Spring Cottage, John Lucas' house	11	The Post Office
5	John Lucas' yard and buildings	12	Malthouses
6	Malthouse (now Hollybush Café)	13	Copper's Malthouse
7	The Beddoes' skin yard	14	Crown Inn

The group of three cottages on the north side of Brook Street (now called Burway Road) was called Spring Terrace for many years in the 1800s. They comprise Spring Cottage, the property now called Hollybush Café and Brook Cottage. They were at one time all associated with the trades of malting and skinning.

The Skin Yards

From as early as 1788 the Beddoes family owned and resided in Spring Terrace at Brook Cottage and Spring Cottage with Thomas Beddoes, a skinner, living in Spring Cottage. From then until the end of the 19th century the Beddoes family occupied the premises and operated as skinners or fellmongers. In the 1838 tithe award, the area at the rear of Brook Cottage was described as a skin yard (see map, no. 7) and over the next hundred years or so there are numerous references to skin pits in the Beddoes' garden (see map, no. 3).

The hides were bought from the butcher or farmer. The process of preparing skins for tanning was a lengthy and rather smelly one, taking from three to nine months, after which they were then ready for the actual tanning process.

So the skinner had to be one of the more affluent tradesmen to be able to have his capital tied up for such a long period. His rôle was to use all that the butcher left; the hide and fleece were processed, wool was pulled and sorted, hair was removed from the hides to be used in the upholstery trade, while the fat and gristle was boiled down to make tallow.

The trade required a good supply of water and one wonders whether the Town Brook, which was an open stream in those days, was used, although it is possible that the name Spring Terrace refers to another, now forgotten source of water. In any case the stream running down Lake Lane must have been polluted by the effluent while the stench of the skinyard and lime pits must have affected the area; perhaps the prevailing south westerly winds dispersed it for much of the time. On the other hand living in early 19th century England involved quite a different attitude to smells from that which we have today.

The Malthouses

In addition to the skin yards in 1838 there were five malthouses near the Town Brook. The malting process required a large amount of water and it seems possible that the industry developed here in order to take advantage of the supply provided by the stream and perhaps local springs.

One malthouse, on the site of the Hollybush Café (see map, no. 6) adjacent to Spring Cottage, was owned by the Beddoes and let to John Evans, a butcher and maltster. Later, David Hyslop occupied these premises. Another malthouse at the corner of Shrewsbury Road (see map, no. 10) was let to John Broome, a farmer who had left the town by 1841. William Barnett, a maltster employed by Edward Lewis, probably occupied and worked at this malthouse later. This property was subsequently divided into the Lewis's building and ironmongery business and George Windsor's Post Office.

Copper's malthouse (see map, no. 13) was occupied at one time by the Beltons who lived in the adjacent farmhouse on the Shrewsbury Road (later pulled down to make way for *The Hotel* extensions). John Lewis, a maltster, glazier and painter who employed William Galliers as a maltster, seems to have occupied the property. Two malthouses on the south side of the road (see map, no. 12) were both used by John Craig a young maltster from Scotland. He lived at 3, The Square, but had left the town by 1851.

These maltings seemed to cater just for the local trade, supplying the numerous local inns which all brewed their own ale and beer.

Around 1840 George and Robert McCartney arrived with their sister Isabella from Kirkcudbright, near Dumfries, Scotland, as travelling tea dealers. By 1856 Robert McCartney was described as a maltster, hop and tea dealer. He married in 1866 and lived at no. 3, The Square. He employed two maltmakers but there is no indication as to which premises he used. By 1881 Robert McCartney, now described as a maltster and seedsman, was still living in the Square but no other maltsters are listed in the Church Stretton area. The scale of his business had put the other small maltsters out of business.

Robert McCartney died in 1892 and his son, also called Robert, continued the business under the name Robert McCartney and Sons. About 1904 the son Robert erected a purpose-built malthouse with a retail shop in Sandford Avenue which continued in operation until about 1940. During World War II the building served for a time as an industrial training centre for St Dunstan's. The building is now the Antiques Market and on the second floor the perforated ceramic floor tiles of the kiln room are still clearly visible. [See also page 157].

The malthouses were supplied by hops grown locally and supported a thriving cottage industry of spinning and making hop sacks.

McCartney's malthouse at the corner of Sandford Avenue and Easthope Road is the only former malthouse remaining in the town. At the front there was a retail outlet selling Allsopp's ales.

Note the tall doors on the side of the building and the remains of the lifting hoist below the gable. These were used for bringing in the sacks of barley and hops.

Brook Cottage, 4 Burway Road

At the time of the tithe award in 1838 and the 1841 census the row of cottages on the north side of Burway Road was called Spring Terrace.

Brook Cottage, now known as Brook House, has the date 1733 carved in stone above the door, but this could refer to the date of alterations rather than the original building. In 1838 it was occupied by Mary Beddoes and in 1841 by Elizabeth Beddoes. These women were skinners who had a skinyard and outbuildings at the rear. The family remained there for several decades, being described as fell-mongers in 1861 but in 1871 as farmers of 50 acres. Spring Cottage also belonged to them at that time.

One of the interesting remnants of the era before public fire services is the fire mark under the eaves. This shows that the building was once insured against fire with The Salop Fire Office. This company was formed in 1780 and became part of Sun Alliance Insurance Ltd in 1959. During this early period it was the practice of fire offices to mark insured premises by affixing their badge and as a result fire marks can be seen on many older buildings.

The company advertised that it had *'a sufficient supply of fire engines, buckets, ladders, fire-hooks etc'.* which were kept in constant readiness, examined and oiled monthly, and when necessary repaired. One hundred pounds value in houses, goods, merchandise, could be insured for the trifling sum of two shillings per annum; if hazardous, only three shillings, or if doubly hazardous, five shillings.

The Church Stretton Posting Establishment, Burway Road

The Posting Establishment in Burway Road, 1908.

In 1867 David Hyslop, a Scot from Mainsriddle near Dumfries and friend of the McCartneys, bought a small posting business from a Mr Robinson. It was initially concerned with the provision of saddle horses, hunters, ponies and dog-carts for hire as well as a range of horse-drawn carriages such as Broughams (suitable for weddings and funerals), Landaus, Victorias (with rubber tyres) and Brakes. A list of recommended rides, complete with timing and a tariff, was published in the local guidebooks. By 1908 the business was called The Church Stretton Posting Establishment Ltd and was managed by Frank Blower. He describes his coachmen as 'most careful and experienced drivers and are provided with private livery'.

However, with the coming of the car the emphasis gradually changed. The first mention of the motor car appeared in a 1916 advertisement when there were 'open and closed motors' for hire and 'motor runs' were mentioned.

The name Central Garage first appeared in the advertisements in 1920 when in addition to having motors for hire and chauffeured motor runs, tyres, inner tubes, petrol, oils and greases were stocked and overhauls and repairs undertaken. By 1928 the business had changed to one concerned solely with motor vehicles.

The business became a substantial one employing many staff and was for many years the main motor vehicle repairs facility in the town. It remained in Burway Road until the 1980s when it moved to the Crossways Industrial Estate near the A49.

David Hyslop demolished a stable, coach house and four small cottages on the south side of Burway Road and replaced them with a terrace of four houses (below). He occupied Beaconsfield, the house on the far right in the photo below. After his death in 1907 this was occupied by the then Manager, Frank Blower. These houses were demolished in 1962 to make way for a petrol forecourt and car showroom now the Crown Carpets shop.

In the 1880s the Posting Establishment housed the town's horse-drawn fire engine.

Spring Cottage, 8 Burway Road

Spring Cottage has a roof which is hipped at the western end and gabled at the other and in plan it is out of line with its neighbours. Bilbey has suggested that it may be on a building line of a much earlier road; it lines up with an ancient path across the Robinson field and the Old Cardington Road and, in the other direction, with the site of the old Hall and the dry valley across Rectory Field up to the top of Cunnery Road. The house has obviously been altered and extended but parts are very old and the arrangements of doors and rooms does suggest the plan of a hall with a cross passage.

A manor court document of 1757 records that 'Thomas Russell, a maltster, surrendered (i.e. gave up his tenure) a messuage or tenement formerly called Stephens, then called the *Swan Inn* and now known as the *Swan and Malt Shovel*, together with malthouse, barns, stables, buildings and folds'.

Later, it was occupied by John Corfield who married Mary Beddoes. In the 1830s their daughters ran a girls' school from the house before moving to Ragleth House where they set up a boarding school. Spring Cottage was owned by the Beddoes family for much of the 19th century together with the large garden between the cottage and Burway House. In the stone wall of the garden the initials JB are carved with the date 1871. This probably refers to John Beddoes who owned the gardens which are recorded in numerous documents as the site of skin pits. See the plan on page 26.

By 1871 it was let to David Hyslop, a Scottish born posting horse master, who seems to have started his business there before he extended into premises across the road which became the Church Stretton Posting Establishment. Mary, his wife, bought Spring Cottage in 1902 and it has remained with the family since then. When the house changed hands during the late 18th and 19th centuries, the property always included a malthouse on the site of what is now the Hollybush Café (see page 26, map, no. 6).

David Hyslop (1836 - 1907). [Oonagh O'Neill]

The café got its name in the 1930s when Molly Stanton and her partner, Daisy Lowther, worked a farm at Bryn, near Bishop's Castle, from where they delivered their own soft fruits, vegetables and cream to shops in the area. They supplied milk from the farm in the old malthouse and named it after Hollybush Farm where they lived, driving into Church Stretton each day in a large Austin car. They later opened the café.

David Hyslop's son, Charles James Hyslop, ran a coal business from Spring Cottage and had a coal wharf at the railway station (see page 167).

Burway Road showing Spring Cottage and Brook House (about 1900). [Oonagh O'Neill]

Below: Burway Road (1910). The corner shop was owned by Thomas Lewis, stationer and builder. The Jubilee fountain can be seen in its new position at the corner with Church Street. [Oonagh O'Neill]

George Windsor and the Old Post Office, 1 Shrewsbury Road

The corner property opposite The Hotel housed Lewis's shop and George Windsor's post office. [David Bilbey]

In 1841 the properties at the corner of Brook Street and the Ludlow-Shrewsbury Turnpike (as they were then called) comprised two small cottages occupied by John and Mary Middleton and William Davies, with John Broom's malthouse at the rear. There must have been considerable alterations by the time the Heighways moved in to establish the Post Office here in about 1870. It is now called 1 Shrewsbury Road.

Prior to this date the Post Office had been at 19 High Street (now Salt's) occupying the part which eventually housed the Shrewsbury Old Bank. From 1850 to 1870 it was run by Margaret Broome and then by Richard Home. At some stage the property had been divided so that the corner shop was occupied by Thomas Lewis (builder and stationer) with the Post Office adjacent in Shrewsbury Road (illustrated above).

George Windsor and his wife Sarah came to Church Stretton from Hampshire between 1866 and 1868. He was for a time a medical and surgical assistant to Dr Richard Wilding and initially lived in one of the cottages behind Ashlett House. They had three children. This Sarah died in 1874 and he then married Sarah Heighway who was the Church Stretton postmistress. George Windsor

> **GEORGE R. WINDSOR,**
> BOOKSELLER, STATIONER, AND NEWS AGENT,
> FANCY REPOSITORY,
> POST, TELEGRAPH, AND STAMP OFFICE,
> CHURCH STRETTON.
> ―
> *TO VISITORS.*
> A Complete List of Apartments kept, and every Information given.
> ENGLISH AND FOREIGN TOYS.
> ―
> GUIDES.
> Visitors to Church Stretton are strongly recommended to obtain a Guide. The price is 6d. It gives (besides a history of the locality, etc.) the most pleasant Walks and Objects of Interest.
> Botanical and Geological Guides same price, or 1s. the Three.
> ―
> EXCELLENT PHOTOGRAPHS OF THE SCENERY.
> ―
> THE LONDON AND BIRMINGHAM PAPERS
> Arrive about 11 a.m. Newspapers, Books, Periodicals, and Magazines punctually supplied. Agent for Messrs. W. H. Smith and Son.
> ―
> TOBACCO. PATENT MEDICINES. PRETTY PRESENTS.
> ESTABLISHED 1869.

George Windsor's advertisement in the Church Stretton Times, September 1881.

Church Stretton Times, AND VISITORS' LIST.

No. 1.   SATURDAY, SEPTEMBER 17, 1881.   Price Two Pence.

Advertisements.

THE CHURCH STRETTON AERATED WATER COMPANY

Take this opportunity of thanking the inhabitants of Church Stretton, and of the County of Salop generally, for the liberal support which has been accorded to them during the season.

They wish at the same time to express their determination to manu-

Advertisements.

TEMPERANCE REFRESHMENT ROOMS, CHURCH STRETTON.

TEA AND COFFEE AT ALL HOURS,
Cyclists specially attended to.

MRS. JAMES—PROPRIETRESS.

Part of the first issue of Church Stretton Times and Visitors' List, 17 Sept. 1881.

took over the Post Office and became Postmaster until the mid 1890s when the family left Church Stretton on his appointment to Head Postmaster at Lymington. Harold Gunn then took over the Post Office. In advertisements George Windsor described his business as 'bookseller, stationer, news agent, fancy repository, tobacco, patent medicines and pretty presents'.

George Windsor was an influential person in the town. He had a great love of Church Stretton and realised very early the potential economic value of visitors to the area and tried in a number of ways to publicise the attractions of the town throughout the country. He described Church Stretton as

> 'One of the most delightful spots in the West of England with hills as high, scenery as beautiful, air as bracing, water as pure and accommodation as good as shall be found at the most hackneyed of summer resorts, with this advantage over them all, that Stretton has the virtue, the charm of being almost unknown.'

He wrote and produced a guidebook to Church Stretton called *A Handbook to the Capabilities, Attractions, Beauties and Scenery of Church Stretton* in 1885. In this he stated that the Post Office was open from 7 am until 9 pm, that he kept a list of furnished apartments and that the Post Office was also an enquiry office for visitors. He dispatched copies of this handbook free of charge to the railway companies for display in their waiting rooms to promote the beautiful area in which he lived.

He also produced *The Church Stretton Times and Visitors' List*. The first issue of 4 pages appeared on Saturday 17 September 1881, priced at 2d. He intended to produce it each year during July, August and September, the 'Stretton season'. It contained advertisements for local shops, hotels, businesses, etc. and a list of visitors and where they were staying. The second (and last) issue appeared on 24 September 1881 with an 'au revoir until next summer' but no more issues appeared. Three years later Windsor wrote a novel called *Laura Heathjohn* set in Stretton and on the Long Mynd.

In addition to being Postmaster, Stationer and Newsagent he was honorary secretary to the Sandford Avenue committee formed by the Rev'd Holland Sandford (see page 146), inspector's secretary to the Gas Works, secretary and treasurer to the Volunteer Fire Brigade, secretary to the Stretton Cottagers' Gardening Society and local correspondent for the *Shrewsbury Chronicle*.

The Old Post Office Stores, 2 Shrewsbury Road

A 1907 postcard showing the shop entrance facing the Hotel. [Eddie Conning]

After the Post Office moved to its new premises in Sandford Avenue about 1906 the old shop was taken over by William Henry Lewis where he developed his grocery business. After his death in 1926 at the age of 51 his wife, Elizabeth, continued running it until the early 1940s. The photo in the advertisement below shows how it was extended to include the whole corner with Burway Road.

A 1937 advertisement.

Lewis's shop in 1907 with a man, presumably William Lewis, sweeping snow from the pavement near the Burway Road entrance.

The Hotel

After the arrival of the railway in Church Stretton in 1852 the town began to develop as a holiday resort. Visitors would arrive to enjoy the scenery and the peace and quiet, taking up all the accommodation available, especially in July and August. The first special hotel provision for them quickly followed in 1865.

The first recorded buildings on this site were *The Crown Inn* and, on the corner with Lake Lane (now Sandford Avenue) a malthouse built by a Mr Copper and his son 'W'. A stone from the malthouse, dated 1587, was later incorporated into the wall of *The Hotel* when it was built and is still *in situ* (below).

The inscription reads
'ERECTED BY I COPPER & W
HIS SONNE
ANO DNI 1587'

When the railway arrived, the stage and mail coaching traffic quickly declined, forcing *The Talbot Inn,* at the south end of the High Street where the coaching horses were changed, to close. Because it was much nearer to the railway station at the east end of Station Road, *The Crown Inn* grew in importance and became the main inn of the town.

The Hotel was built in 1865 on the corner site of Copper's malthouse adjacent to *The Crown Inn,* effectively as a major extension to the original inn. It is not clear how much of the old *Crown Inn* was incorporated into *The Hotel*, but the capitals of the entrance pillars and the portico to the inn have been rebuilt in the form of a crown.

The Hotel was built in a Victorian Gothic style with much elaborate stone and external wrought iron works. This first portion cost £6,000, including furnishings.

[David Bilbey]

Being on the corner of Shrewsbury Road and Station Road (now Sandford Avenue) it formed a prominent feature for visitors approaching the town from the railway station. Behind the hotel were stables and a paddock kept by George Robinson who supplied post horses, ponies and carriages for the use of visitors.

By 1899 the number of visitors to Church Stretton had increased and an extension was needed. This was built along Sandford Avenue and cost £5,000.

Both parts were entered by the short flight of steps to a foyer leading to a drawing room, dining room,

The Hotel prior to the extension along Sandford Avenue in 1899.

35

two sitting rooms with balconies, and lounges overlooking the large walled garden. Steps down to the garden (which had an ornamental fountain) also provided access to lawn tennis courts, croquet and bowling greens.

On the floor below there were handsomely appointed smoking and billiards rooms with doors onto the garden, as well as a bar. On the two upper floors there were twenty four guest bedrooms with 'several' bathrooms and WCs and two further sitting rooms.

In 1906 the hotel was enlarged again. This time it was extended along the Shrewsbury Road onto the site of a former farmhouse, Bell's Messuage, owned by Richard Edwards. This third section contained two double fronted shops and three guest bedrooms on the ground floor and nine bedrooms on each of the other two floors, served by two bath rooms!

By this time more visitors were arriving by car so eventually a motor garage was built with petrol pumps, an inspection pit, washing facilities and three lock up garages, run by a Mr J F Wiggins.

The Hotel was described in guidebooks as 'very commodious, being well lighted and ventilated and the rooms expensively furnished and kept beautifully neat and clean. The household arrangements were regular and business-like, the wines, spirits and bill of fare good and the tariff moderate'.

The Hotel was the centre of the town's social life, the place for business meetings and the venue for formal dinners. The poet A E Housman stayed at the hotel for nearly a month in 1899 among his 'blue remembered hills'.

The Hotel was badly damaged by fire on the night of 2-3 April 1968. The central portion was gutted

The Hotel foyer.

Examples of the elaborate stone and iron work.

The lounge and, below, the gardens.

and five people died in the fire. These included the three young sons (Korwin, Alastair and Jonathan) of Mr and Mrs G Goulder who were staying overnight prior to moving into their house Windyways in Shrewsbury Road the following day. Two of the staff, Mary Wilkinson and Olive Guest, also died in the fire. Their bodies were found in a pantry where they had taken refuge. Though the damaged portion of the building was rebuilt the hotel never re-opened as such. The part of the building damaged by the fire, though repaired, now has a flat roof and is a pub called *Old Coppers Malt House*. The rest of the building has been converted to flats, offices and shops. A hint of the original beauty of the interior may still be seen in the Sandford Art Gallery which is housed in one of the lounges overlooking the High Street.

The Hotel before the extension down Sandford Avenue in 1899. The house on the right is Beaconsfield.

THE ✢ HOTEL, ✢ CHURCH ✢ STRETTON
SHROPSHIRE

THIS first-class Family Hotel is supplied with every accommodation for the comfort of Visitors. It has lately been re-decorated and re-furnished, and new Rooms have been added. It is situate within a few minutes walk of the Railway Station, and in easy distance of the excellent and popular Golf Links.

EVERY ACCOMMODATION FOR CYCLISTS, INCLUDING A CYCLE STORE HOUSE.

TENNIS LAWN.   BILLIARD ROOM.
TABLE D'HÔTE AT 7 O'CLOCK.

The Hotel Porter meets all the principal trains and conveys Visitors' Luggage free of charge.   Special Week-end Tickets are issued from all principal Stations

For full particulars and boarding terms, apply to THE MANAGERESS.   Proprietors: The Church Stretton Hotel Company.

"Illustrated ―――on News" of 23rd September, 1893, says: "The large and well-planned Garden lies at the back of the House: the whole place indeed is a true haven of rest to the weary in brain and body."

An advertisement of about 1905.

The Hotel gardens, looking east

Midland Red buses terminating in Church Stretton stopped in Burway Road near The Hotel.

Motor Car Rally, 1908

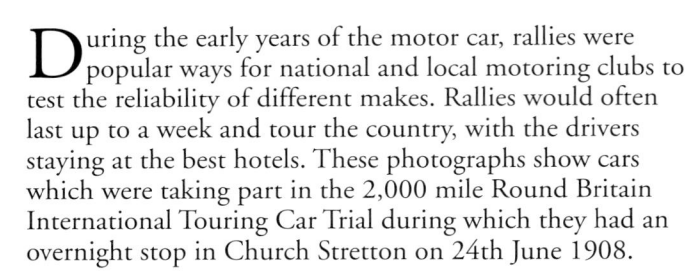

During the early years of the motor car, rallies were popular ways for national and local motoring clubs to test the reliability of different makes. Rallies would often last up to a week and tour the country, with the drivers staying at the best hotels. These photographs show cars which were taking part in the 2,000 mile Round Britain International Touring Car Trial during which they had an overnight stop in Church Stretton on 24th June 1908.

George Preece's House, corner of High Street and Sandford Avenue

This photograph shows George Preece's house after a light fall of snow.

This attractive Georgian house, at the corner of High Street and Sandford Avenue, on to which it faced, was built around 1700. In 1838 William Wilding, a surgeon, rented it together with the garden and a paddock at the rear. His surgery was in the small room to the left. The house was next occupied by Edward Glover, a saddler, then by John Faulkner, a carpenter and wheelwright and the ex landlord of the *Crown Inn*. George Preece, a gardener, was the next resident. He was commissioned by the Rev'd Holland Sandford in 1884 to plant the 153 lime trees in what was to become Sandford Avenue (see page 146). The family also occupied the adjoining small cottage in High Street, seen to the right in the photograph. The garden extended some way down Sandford Avenue and a small part of the boundary stone wall still exists next to the Bank.

Preece's family occupied the house until it was pulled down to make way for Lloyd's Bank, opened in 1923. The bank had moved from 50 High Street where it had been located since about 1909, having taken over the Capital and Counties Bank Ltd in 1918.

The Jubilee Fountain

To commemorate Queen Victoria's Golden Jubilee in 1887 a drinking fountain was erected in a small planted area at the junction of High Street and Burway Road, where the HSBC Bank now stands.

The site was owned and made available by Ralph Beaumont Benson of Lutwyche Hall, who was then the Lord of the Manor. The fountain was unveiled by his wife, Mrs Caroline Essex Benson, on 21 June 1887.

View looking south down the High Street before the Midland Bank was built on the site of the fountain.

The town celebrated the Jubilee by holding 'amusing sports in the Crown meadow including races, catching a greased sheep and dancing around a pole'. As a conclusion there was dancing on the lawn of the Rectory and at night a torchlight procession up the Burway to the Pole and a large bonfire. The children were entertained the next day by the Rector.

In November 1906 the fountain was moved to a new position at the junction of Church Street, Burway Road and Longhills Road at the request of Mr Benson who wanted to redevelop the original site. The Midland Bank, now HSBC, was eventually built on that site about 1920.

The fountain remained in its new position until April 1963 when the then Church Stretton Urban District Council decided that it was an obstacle and a danger to traffic and should be removed; it had, indeed, been hit and damaged by a large vehicle some time before.

The lower portion of the fountain was broken up but the upper portion of the structure and the metal plaque containing the inscription have survived and are in the ownership of the Church Stretton Town Council.

The later site of the fountain in Burway Road opposite Burway House (1913).

Above: Looking up Brook Street with the fountain removed from it's position on the left corner (1911).

Left: Caroline Essex Benson who unveiled the fountain.

Above right: The damaged fountain with top askew.

Right: The Midland Bank, built on the original site of the fountain.

Below left: looking down Brook St towards the Hotel.

Below right: the metal plaque on the fountain.

43

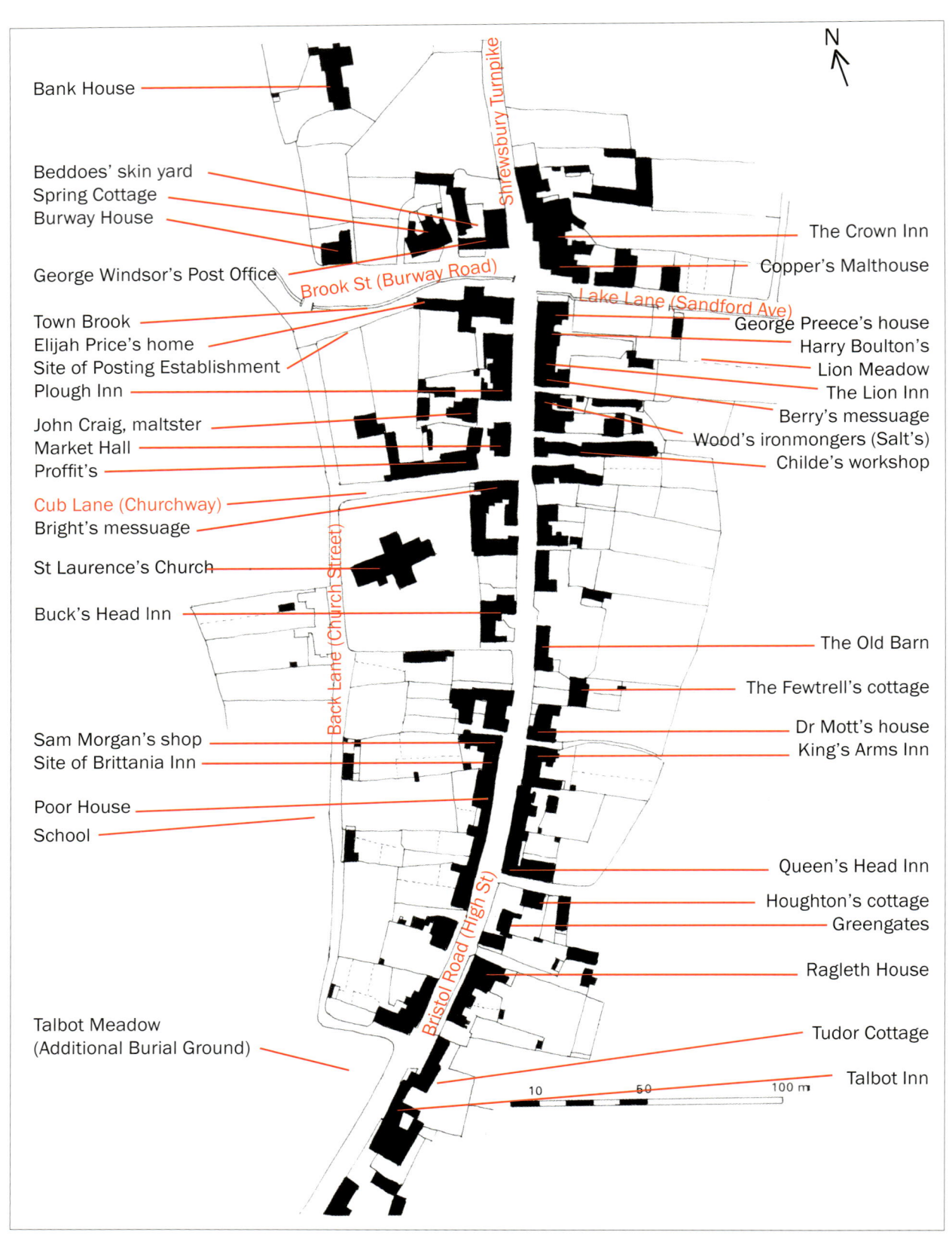

The Town buildings in 1838, based on the tithe apportionment map. The names of some of the buildings or occupants are in many cases of a later date and are marked because they are mentioned in the text later.

The High Street, formerly Bristol Road

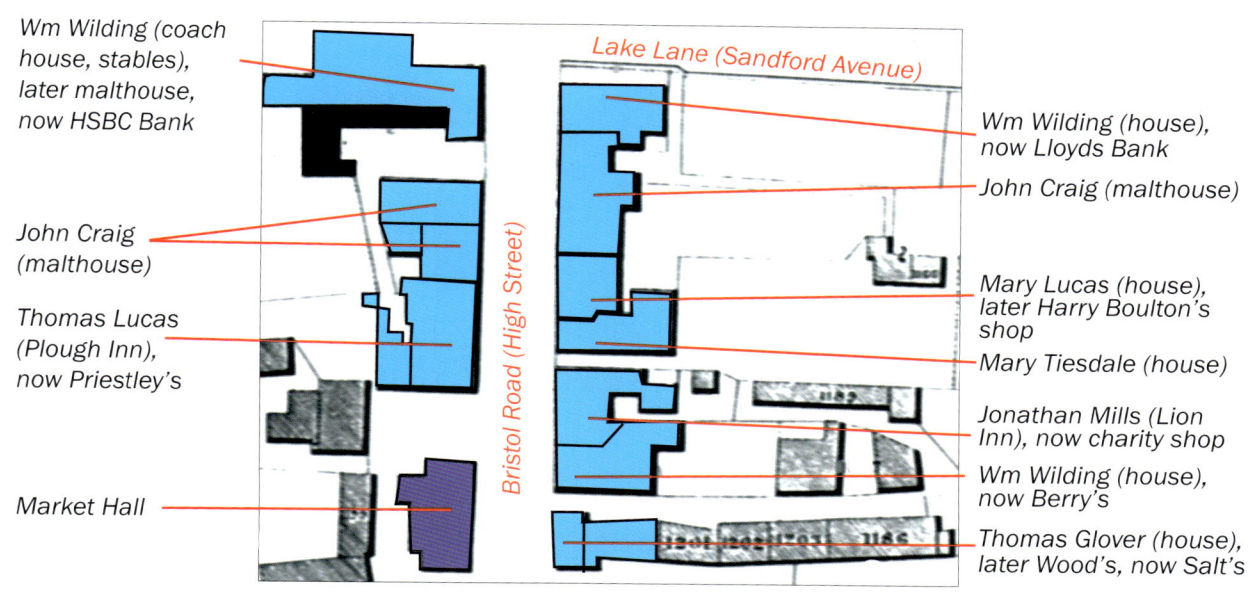

Map labels (left side):
- Wm Wilding (coach house, stables), later malthouse, now HSBC Bank
- John Craig (malthouse)
- Thomas Lucas (Plough Inn), now Priestley's
- Market Hall
- Bristol Road (High Street)

Map labels (right side):
- Lake Lane (Sandford Avenue)
- Wm Wilding (house), now Lloyds Bank
- John Craig (malthouse)
- Mary Lucas (house), later Harry Boulton's shop
- Mary Tiesdale (house)
- Jonathan Mills (Lion Inn), now charity shop
- Wm Wilding (house), now Berry's
- Thomas Glover (house), later Wood's, now Salt's

Detail of the north end of the High Street showing the properties and occupiers in 1838.

The Bristol Road, as the present High Street was called until the 1880s, was on the main trunk route linking the West Country with the North of England and Scotland. For many years before the opening of the Severn Bridge there was a ferry crossing the river Severn at Aust. This ferry was an important link in the Chester to Bristol road which passed through Church Stretton and along which coaches and wagons ran. The Ludlow to Shrewsbury section was made into a turnpike in 1756 with a Trust set up to keep the road in good repair. To raise revenue it was permitted to erect a gate, or turnpike, across the road and levy a toll on travellers who wished to use that stretch of the road. The two local gates were in Little Stretton and near Leebotwood.

Because the town had a weekly market and six fair days each year it was the natural trading centre for those living in the local villages. They found it easier to get to Church Stretton than to Shrewsbury, Ludlow, Much Wenlock or Bishop's Castle. This hinterland covered a large area extending to Longville, Stokesay, Leebotwood and even to the west side of the Long Mynd.

Most of the basic trades and crafts were present in the town in the 1840s, usually operating from workshops down the burgage plots. There were also tailors, shoemakers and butchers operating from their homes or farmsteads. However there were few shops, just a linen draper, two ironmongers and two general shopkeepers. A number of malthouses supplied the local inns which then brewed their own ale. The weekly market and regular fairs provided an opportunity for buying goods which the local shops did not provide. Church Stretton was basically a self sufficient community.

George Robinson, Butcher, 3 High Street

This sketch by David Bilbey shows how the group of houses and shops on the east side of High Street looked before Lloyd's Bank was built in 1922/3.

George Preece	George Robinson	John Lucas	Thomas Andrews
Lloyd's Bank	Richardson's Butcher	Boulton's Poulterer	

Occupiers in 1885.

Occupiers in 1970s.

When Lloyd's Bank was built in 1922/3 two substantial and attractive Georgian houses on the site were demolished. On the corner was George Preece's house (see also page 41). The next house along the High Street was occupied in part by Edward Glover, a saddler, with the other used as a malthouse worked by John Craig.

George Robinson occupied the farm next to *The Crown Inn* in Shrewsbury Road. This consisted of two cow houses, two stables, a barn, a fold and a stack yard adjacent to the farmhouse and a slaughterhouse on the other side of *The Crown Inn* down Lake Lane. He farmed land which extended towards the present Lutwyche Road and Beaumont Road. He is first recorded in local directories as a farmer and cattle dealer in 1856 and from 1861 also as a butcher. There was an out farm and slaughterhouse, called Robinson's Buildings, built about 1856-61 on the site of the Crown Cottages, Lutwyche Road. The slaughterhouse by *The Crown Inn* closed in 1861 and this left George Robinson having the only slaughterhouse in the town (see page 126).

George Robinson died in 1889 leaving his wife and two sons to run the farm and slaughterhouse. In 1921 one of the sons, Charles Edward, opened a butcher's shop in High Street until his death in 1926 whereupon his wife ran it for two further years until she sold it to Frederick Baldwin.

Above: As it was in 1997.
Below: An advertisement of 1908.

Harry Boulton, Fishmonger and Poulterer, 7- 11 High Street

Photo taken about 1937 with Harry Boulton and his staff.

Harry Boulton's business moved to the High Street about 1922 having been at the rear of the present Sandford Hardware in Sandford Avenue from about 1909. In later years he ran it with his two sons Bob and Harry. Like similar establishments he would have drawn his supplies from local farmers. Scenes like the above photograph were commonplace outside game and poultry dealers' premises, particularly at Christmas time. Note how much care was taken with the display, starting at the top with small bunches of misletoe, then lines of game birds and chickens to lines of turkeys and other birds at the bottom. The rods on which the produce was hung were *in situ* until quite recently. Modern health regulations mean that such displays will never be seen again.

Left: Harry Boulton standing in front of his shop in the 1940s.

47

The Lion Inn, 13-15 High Street

The Lion Inn is the pair of white buildings on the right adjacent to The Central Boarding House & Family Hotel. The large inn sign hangs well out over the pavement between the two entrance doors. From a 1922 postcard.

This building was originally a pair of cottages built by Edward Berry before 1660 on an area of land which became known as Berry's Messuage (meaning a dwelling house with outbuildings and land). It included the area on which the property now called Berry's (no. 17) was later built.

A licence had been held since before 1700. The inn was originally called *The King's Arms Inn*, then *The Red Lion* and finally the *Lion Inn*. It had stabling at the rear for twelve horses. The inn was run by the Mills family from about 1721 until 1864. Jonathan Mills also owned a yard and stabling to the rear of Salt's plot.

There was an area of land behind *The Lion Inn* extending east to the present Easthope Road which became known as the Lion Meadow, later Deakin's Field and more recently Sheep Sales Field. There was once a large cherry orchard on it. After this was uprooted the area was used for sheep sales in the 20th century after increasing traffic levels drove the animal sales off the streets. These sales ended about 1982 and King's Court was built on the site in 1984.

Shops have replaced the Lion Inn (1982).

Berry's, 17 High Street

This early 18th century town house was built on part of Berry's Messuage, which included the adjacent *Lion Inn*. It is a well proportioned and elegant Queen Anne house built about 1710 on a very narrow plot used, until then, to provide access from the High Street to the rear of the Lion Inn.

This probably explains why the door is on the side in Barn Lane and why the house is wider at the front than at the rear. The splendid entrance doorway has a fine cornice and consoles and a fanlight typical of the Georgian period to light the entrance hall. The windows were almost certainly altered later in the century when they were set back into the reveal and the original heavy wooden glazing bars were replaced by more fashionable lighter ones.

The interior is as interesting as the exterior. The imposing entrance leads into a panelled hall from which rises a fine staircase. Both door frames and doors on the landing are equally splendid as are the two principal rooms on the first floor which are panelled, possibly using woodwork saved from an earlier house.

The earliest record of Berry's is on the Rent Roll of 1731 when it was owned by a Mr Botvyle but was lived in by Edward Philips, a baker. It was known then by the 'sign of the *Green Dragon*', though there is no evidence of it being an inn. A series of surgeons then owned Berry's - in 1743 Richard Langslow, in 1789 Richard Bray, in 1828 his son Thomas and in 1837 William Wilding (who bought it for £600). On his death in 1845 his son Richard, also a surgeon, inherited the house and practice. He twice extended the house by adding a three storey wing at the rear and then another extension. Richard died in 1883 and one of his sons, William, inherited the practice whilst another son, Henry, inherited the property.

In 1898 Henry Wilding sold the house to Henry Rawlings for £1,000 and it became *The Central Boarding House and Family Hotel* with his wife Frances Rawlings as the proprietor. This existed until the 1930s. For some time during this period their daughter ran a small private school in one of the wings.

The Central Boarding House and Family Hotel, 1905. The photo shows Mr and Mrs Rawlings (left) and staff which include Mr and Mrs Tom Lewis (at the corner).

This unusual firemark (above) of the Royal Exchange Assurance Company showed that the building had fire insurance.

The fine doorway to Berry's. [Paul Miller]

49

The West Side of High Street, The Plough Inn

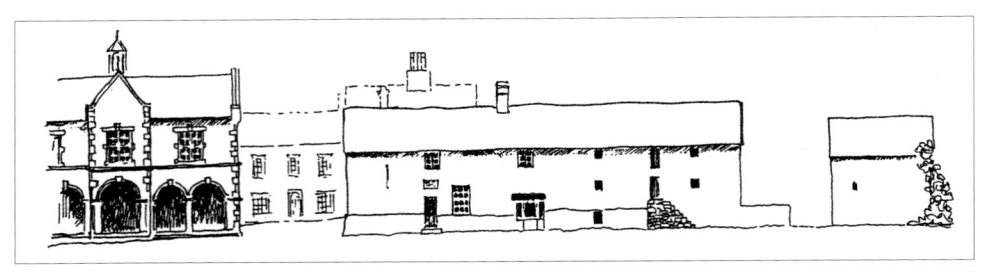

This sketch by David Bilbey shows how the group of properties on the west side of the High Street looked before the Midland Bank was built about 1920.

Town Hall	John Craig	Plough Inn (Thomas Lewis)	Malthouse, yard, stables and coach house (John Craig)			*Occupiers in 1841.*
Town Hall	Robert McCartney	Plough Inn (George Marsh)	Malthouse, yard, stables and coach house			*Occupiers in 1885.*
The Square	Burton's	Priestley's	P Gee	Archway	Estate Agent	HSBC Bank	*2011.*

In the mid 19th century the little garden on the corner of Burway Road and High Street, which was to become the site of the Jubilee Fountain, was adjacent to the gable end of the stable, coach house and entrance to the *Plough Inn* yard. The building with stone steps leading to the upper floor was a malthouse in 1838 and probably retained that function until the end of the century.

It is thought that this line of buildings, including outhouses, was probably an encroachment on to the original wide main street, with a back lane behind running from the Market Square to Brook Street (Burway Road) to provide access to the rear. A house (no. 2, The Square) was later built on this back lane, so blocking up the south end.

The malthouse was run by John Craig who had come from Dumfries with Robert McCartney about 1840. He lived at 3, The Square but stayed in Church Stretton for only a few years, as by 1851 Robert McCartney occupied the house with his brother, cousin and nephew, all tea dealers, and his sister.

Looking south down the High Street about 1910. The steps to the malthouse of the Plough Inn are on the right. The Jubilee Fountain has been moved to Burway Road and there is now a large advertisement for the Central Posting Establishment in its place. [Eddie Conning]

On the corner of the High Street and The Square was the *Plough Inn* (now Priestley's) which had not yet received the facelift which happened between 1904 and 1910 or the more recent one when the timber framing on its south elevation was exposed and a gable added at the front. Even more recently it has lost most of its brick chimney stack.

The 1838 tithe award lists *The Plough Inn* as owned by John Robinson, who also owned *The Raven* on the opposite corner of the Market Square. In the 1840s the landlord was Thomas Lewis but by 1851 he had been succeeded by George Phipps who died in 1868. George's widow Anne was still there in 1881. It was then taken over by George Marsh.

Looking north up the High Street. The Plough Inn is the building on the left with the women standing outside. The market hall is in the left foreground.

THE PLOUGH INN, CHURCH STRETTON,
Proprietor:—Mr. GEORGE MARSH.

THE Plough is an old established and most comfortable Inn. Large or Small Parties catered for. Excursionists most liberally dealt with.

Wines, Spirits, Ales, &c., of the Best; Single Bottles at Wholesale Prices. Cigars of the Finest Brands.

Agent for Messrs. THOMAS SOUTHAM & SONS, Splendid Ales, Stout, Spirits, &c., Delivered Free.

Left: Advertisement in Windsor's Handbook, 1885.

Below: The Plough Inn site, 2002.

The County of Salop Return of Licensed Premises, 1901 stated that a full licence had been held for about 205 years, that it was owned by the lord of the manor (Ralph Beaumont Benson) and had indifferent stabling for eight horses. The buildings were noted as being clean and in good repair.

The inn was in business until 1948 when the licence was transferred to the *Sandford Hotel* in Watling Street South. The malthouse and coach house were demolished in the early 1920s to make way for the Midland Bank (now HSBC) and the adjoining building. The support for the inn sign is still in position.

Markets and Market Halls

The Market Hall built by Bonham Norton in 1617. An 1832 engraving.

The decision to hold a weekly market on Wednesdays and a yearly fair on the date of the Feast of the Assumption (15th August) was made by King John (who owned the manor of Stretton-en-le-Dale) in an instruction to the Sheriff dated 26 June 1214. As Stretton was part of the King's demesne land no formal charter was necessary, so the Sheriff was instructed to announce throughout the county the holding of the market.

By 1253 the market day had been changed from Wednesday to Tuesday with, in addition, a four-day fair on the eve and day of the Feast of the Holy Cross and the following two days (2nd - 5th May). This became known as the May Fair.

In 1336 Edward III passed the lordship of the manor to Richard FitzAlan, 3rd Earl of Arundel, as a reward for good service. A year later the Earl was granted a Charter giving him the right to hold the market on a Thursday and an annual three-day fair at the Feast of the Exaltation of the Holy Cross (13, 14 and 15th September). The Thursday market continues to this day.

There was a dramatic fall in the population as a result of the plague (black death) which swept through the Welsh Marches in the summer of 1349 and recurred in 1360 - 69, in which over a third of the populace perished. The inevitable disruption to communities caused social and economic upheaval as land was left untended, wages rose and prices fell. An important effect was the demise of small markets and it seems that by the end of the sixteenth century the weekly market in Church Stretton had fallen into disuse.

However by 1616 the town was recovering from the effects of the disastrous fire of 1593. Bonham Norton, a wealthy printer/publisher and a freeman of the Stationers' Company in London, was by this time the leading landowner in Church Stretton. He was granted permission to hold a market to assist him with the improvement of the town, the relief of the poor and the building or rebuilding of inns and lodging houses, together with a court of pie-powder (from *pied poudre* meaning 'dusty feet') to resolve grievances with pedlars who travelled from fair to fair. In 1617 Norton built the timber framed market

The market hall looking north along High Street. The Plough Inn is the next building on the left.

hall, illustrated opposite. Sir Henry Townshend, who had family links with the town, generously contributed 25 trees 'to help build a market house, school house and court house in Stretton'. The building thus served many purposes. The market became notable for the trade in corn and provisions.

The market hall built by Norton was demolished in 1839 and replaced by a building of red brick with stone facings on stone pillars. This cost £1,000 which was raised by public subscription.

It had an open ground floor which was used for the sale of foodstuffs, meat, fish and poultry. Haberdashery, clothing and earthenware were sold from boards and trestles under the arches and open-air pitches outside.

This building was called the Town Hall. The upper storey was reached by stone steps at the rear. It consisted of a large hall with two large fireplaces and a dais where magistrates sat, whilst below was seating for the public. The hall housed the town officers and a subscription library and was also used as a polling station. It could accommodate up to 250 people and was also used for concerts, balls and public meetings.

The Town Hall was demolished in July 1963 because it was deemed unsafe. The weekly Thursday market is still held in the space where the building once stood.

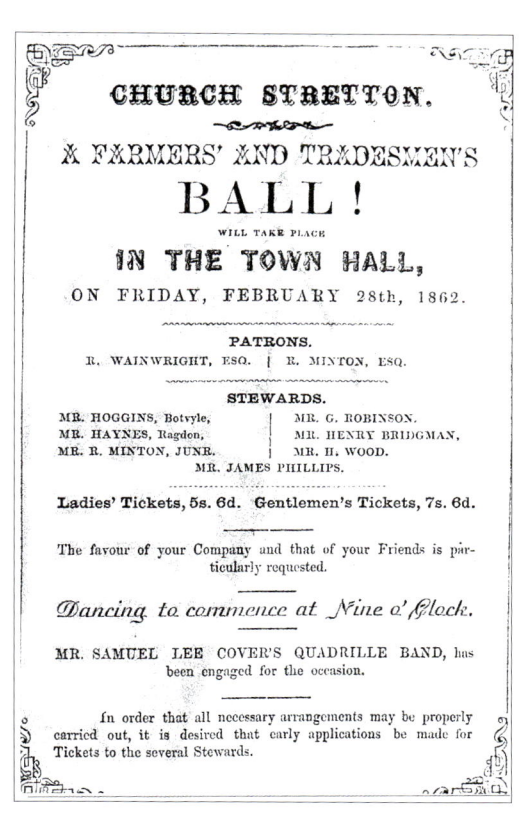

Poster advertising the Farmers' and Tradesmen's Ball in the Town Hall, 1862.

The Town Hall

The Town hall was demolished in July 1963. It had been considered by many as an eyesore. The space opened up now forms The Square. It is now a focal point of the town used for open air markets and civic celebrations.

The above photograph is from about 1906, whilst that on the right is from the early 1920s.

Bonham Norton

In addition to the lord of the manor, another person to own significant amounts of land in Church Stretton was Bonham Norton.

The Nortons were a Shropshire family. Bonham Norton was the only son of William Norton (1527-1593), a bookseller. William was a member of an Onibury family and owned property in Onibury, Ludford, Ludlow, Stottesdon and Cleobury Mortimer. William Norton was one of the original Freemen of the Stationers' Company and was granted a licence to print in 1561. He became Master of the Stationers' Company on three occasions. As such he was an important figure since printing and publishing was strictly controlled at that time.

Bonham Norton was born in 1565. He married into a notable local family, his wife being Jane, the daughter of Sir Thomas Owen of Condover, a judge in the Court of Common Pleas. Bonham Norton was at first apprenticed to his father, then became a bookseller in London in 1594, licensed to print several categories of book. He was admitted as a Freeman of the Stationers' Company in 1593 in place of his deceased father and was Master of the Stationers' Company in 1613, 1626 and 1629. He was also an Alderman of London.

His father, who died in 1593, left him a large fortune in real and personal estate. This was added to in 1612 when he inherited a further legacy from his cousin John Norton, also a Master of the Stationers' Company and a wealthy stationer.

Bonham Norton was a hard, calculating, ruthless and grasping man who was continually in the law courts seeking to get the best of his fellow stationers. In 1629, having accused a judge who had found against him of taking bribes, he was brought before the Court of Star Chamber and found guilty of contempt. He was given a heavy fine and imprisoned for a short time.

He was for a time friendly with Robert Barker, the King's Printer, who was made responsible for printing the King James' Bible of 1611. However this involved a very substantial financial and technical commitment as the work was massive and a considerable number of copies were required. So Barker sought partners in the venture. Among these was Bonham Norton, who advanced some of the money for printing the Authorised Version of the Bible in 1611 and may also have been responsible for part of the printing.

In 1611 Norton was appointed Sheriff of Shropshire and was given a coat of arms (*Or, two bars gules, a chief azure charged with an inescutcheon ermine*) possibly in recognition of his part in the production of the King James' Bible.

Bonham Norton and the Church Stretton Market

Following the fire in 1593 it is likely that Norton began to assemble a considerable estate in the Church Stretton area by means of a number of small purchases of property. A wealthy man from his inheritances and his publishing business, Norton was in a position to profit from the possible effect of the fire on local property values and from rebuilding work. Certainly by 1613 he owned a great deal of property in the manor including much of the land between the town and the Long Mynd.

Bonham Norton's effigy in Condover Church.

It is possible that by this time the weekly market (granted to the Earl of Arundel in 1337) had fallen into disuse, for on 14 June 1609 the Sheriff of Shropshire held an inquisition into the matter which concluded that the re-establishment of the market at Stretton would not, despite claims to the contrary from Bishop's Castle, be detrimental to existing markets in the area.

Bonham Norton was given the right to re-establish the market in a Charter dated 6 January 1616 from King James I. Presumably the then lord of the manor, Sir Thomas Thynne, waived his own claim to the market rights to enable this to happen. Bonham Norton then paid for the erection of a new timber-framed market hall in The Square. This lasted from 1617 until its demolition in 1839.

Besides his market hall, he also built a school, a court house and the Hall (for his own use), which stood on the west side of the back lane, now called Church St. (This was eventually demolished by the then Rector, Thomas Coleman, probably not long before his death in 1818). Bonham Norton died on 5 April 1635 and was buried at St. Faith's Church, London.

The Square

West side of The Square

The west side of The Square comprises three properties numbered 3, 4 and 5 whose frontages would have been along the original Bristol Road which was wide enough in medieval times to house the market. This would have stretched from Brook Street (now Burway Road) southwards to beyond the *Buck's Head Inn*.

The enigma is the house (no. 2) tucked into the corner. This is clearly a later addition into the narrow lane which resulted from an encroachment into the original market area by the building of the *Plough Inn*. It probably dates from the late 18th century. In 1838 it was owned, together with a large garden on its west side, by John Robinson and occupied by Richard Childe, a tinman (which means a worker in any metal). His workshop was at the end of the burgage plot behind what is now Clee Hill Electrics.

On the west side of The Square (left) are numbers 4 and 3. At the end is number 2 and to the right of it is the end of what was the Plough Inn, now Priestley's.

In 1871, no. 2 was a grocer's shop run by Catherine Lewis. Then Edward Phipps took it over and for a time it and the *Plough Inn* were interconnected. Later the shop became a bakery and confectionery business.

No. 3 is now Burton's (estate agents). In 1838 it was occupied by John Craig, a Scottish maltster who owned a maltings on the site of what is now McCartney's Estate Agency and rented the malthouse which subsequently became Richardsons (butchers), now van Doesburgs (delicatessen). Craig left the town in the 1840s and his house was later occupied by Robert McCartney, a travelling tea dealer from Dumfries, who carried on his tea business from a cottage behind Salt's. McCartney became a maltster and subsequently built the large maltings in Sandford Avenue (now the Antiques Centre).

John Hughes, another provision dealer, lived in no. 4. His epitaph in the churchyard reads *John Hughes of the Market Square in this town. Died 1894 aged 86*. The premises are now occupied by the estate agents Miller and Evans.

No. 5, now a restaurant, was a shop occupied by Thomas Proffit, a draper. He was from

This photo probably shows Thomas Proffit's son John with two of his children outside his shop in The Square. It would have been taken in the mid 1880s.

MRS. A. PROFFIT,
Grocer, Tea Dealer, Confectioner, &c.,
MARKET SQUARE, CHURCH STRETTON.

MRS. PROFFIT, in returning her thanks to those customers, who have Patronised her Establishment for the last Thirty-six Years, beg to assure them it is her wish and intention, in the future as in the past, to supply to all, really good genuine articles, at a fair price.

Visitors are respectfully solicited to call and give orders, or if preferred, will be waited upon.

CAKES, CONFECTIONERY, &c.,
MADE TO ORDER.
Home-made Bread, Buns, Tea-Cakes, Rolls, &c.
ORDERS BY POST RECEIVE SPECIAL ATTENTION.

Above: Advertisement from Windsor's 'Handbook', 1885.

Right: Advertisement from 'Church Stretton Illustrated', 1912.

Below: Mosaic tiles at the entrance to Thomas Proffit's shop.

Wavertree and came as assistant manager to John Robinson's drapery business in The Square. Thomas's wife Anne opened a confectionery business at no. 5 to which she later added groceries. After Thomas Proffit's engagement with John Robinson ended, he joined her and added drapery to her business. By 1871 the business had expanded and Thomas and his son John Edwin were described as drapers and grocers and employed two assistants. Thomas died in 1881, aged 61, leaving his widow to carry on the business. She took a half page advertisement in Windsor's *Handbook* (1885) describing herself as a grocer, tea dealer, confectioner etc.

J. E. PROFFIT
Family Grocer,
Provision Dealer,
Italian Warehouseman.

HOME-CURED HAMS
AND
WILTSHIRE BACON
A SPECIALITY
FRESH BUTTER AND EGGS, DAILY.

5 The Square, (behind the Market),
Church Stretton.

From about 1881 their son John had opened a draper's shop at no. 25 High Street. After his mother retired from running her grocery shop, he took it over and ran the two shops until he died in 1910. His advertisement (above) indicated by the use of the term 'Italian Warehouseman' that he was importing such specialities as pasta, olive oil, pickles and fruits from Italy.

The name Proffit is still recorded in mosaic tiles at the entrance to the shop in The Square which is now the Spice Corner Restaurant.

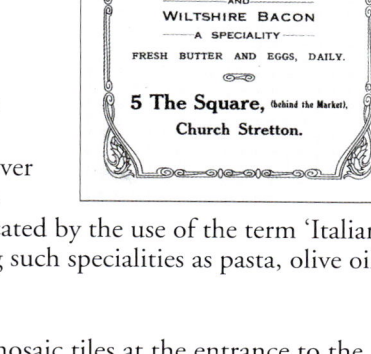

South side of The Square

On the south side of The Square lie what were once three properties joined up. On the corner with High Street was the *Raven Inn* and the remaining two houses became in the 1970s the shop called Eight The Square. These were all owned by John Robinson in 1838.

These houses were occupied by Richard Home, a draper, in 1841. Twenty years later James Robinson sold groceries, drapery and ironmongery as well as chandlering, making the candles on the premises. He must have enjoyed a good standard of living because he employed a house servant, two nurses to look after his children, two shop assistants and two apprentices, all living in.

W. J. ROBERTS,
DRAPERY ESTABLISHMENT,
MARKET SQUARE, CHURCH STRETTON,

DEPARTMENTS.
Carpets, Household Linens, Blankets, Flannels, Silks, Dresses, Velvets, Velveteens, Ulsters, Jackets, Mantles.
Millinery, Gloves, Hosiery, Trimmings, Hats, Woollens.
READY-MADES, GENTLEMEN'S, LADIES', & CHILDREN'S BOOTS, &c.
Knitting and Fancy Wools.
MANTLES and **DRESSMAKING**, with style, economy, and promptitude. Perfect fit ensured.
LONDON TAILORING, superior style, make, and material.
Agent for the Perth Dye Works, and Wanzer Sewing Machines.

In 1881 the shop was owned by W J Roberts, operating a similar drapery, mercery, millinery, tailoring and outfitting establishment whose advertisement in Windsor's *Handbook* of 1885 (above) lists many other activities including agencies for Perth Dye Works and Wanzer Sewing Machines.

Harman and Carey, The Square

Another draper, John Harman, later took over the shops on the south side of The Square and extended his range by selling boots and shoes. About 1906 he was joined in partnership by Leonard Carey and they expanded the business further with the sale of furnishings and by providing a funeral service. They extended the back of the property by building a warehouse between the churchyard and the *Raven Inn* yard. This building has since been turned into flats. Their painted sign high on the warehouse wall overlooking the *Raven Inn* yard is still just legible.

Right: An advertisement in Woolley's 'Church Stretton and District Guide', 1905.

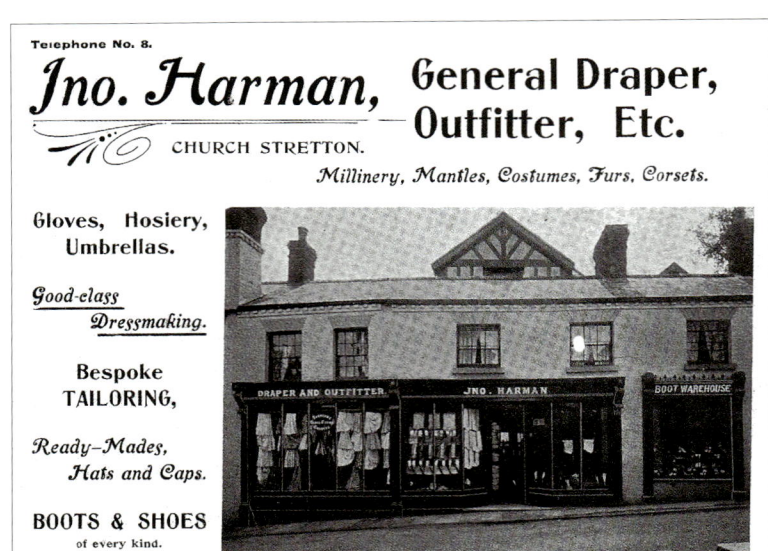

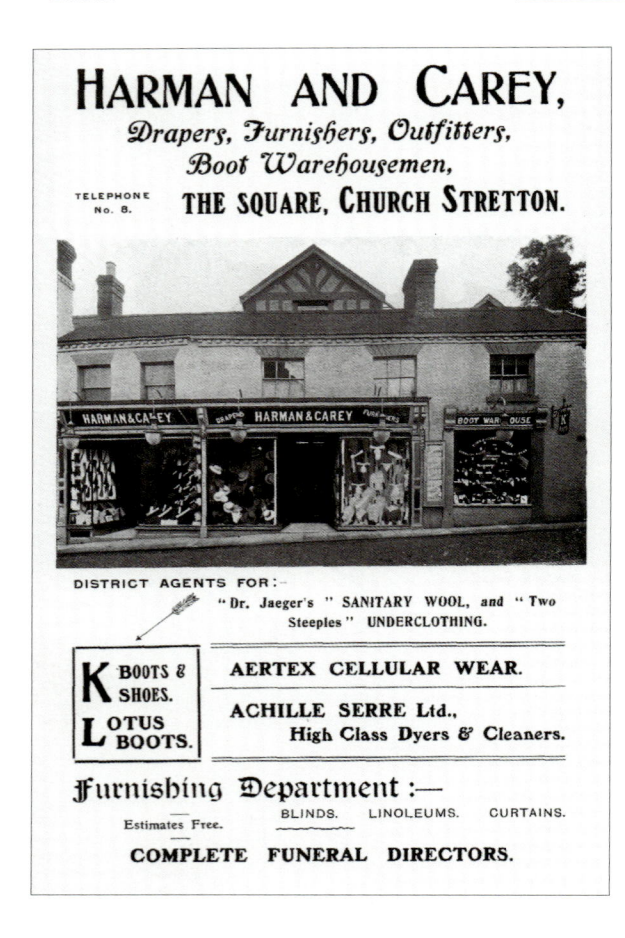

Left: An advertisement in 'Church Stretton Illustrated', 1908.

Above: the painted sign on the wall of the warehouse is still just legible:

> HARMAN & CAREY
> DRAPERS, FURNISHERS
> TAILORS, OUTFITTERS
> BOOT WAREHOUSEMEN

Eight The Square was a popular linen and drapery business (1971 - 83). Next door was Dartmouth Interiors and then Shropshire Piemen.

This view looking north up the High Street from the Town Hall was taken in 1931. Note that The Plough Inn was still operating, but that the Lion Inn had closed and was occupied by Arthur Pope who advertised as a 'Painter, Glazier, Plumber, Hot Water Fitter - Best Work - Moderate Charges'.

The Raven Inn

The Raven Inn about 1967.

The *Raven Inn* stood on the southern corner of The Square. It was built on a piece of land known as originally as The Lower Living, then as Bright's Messuage. This was probably a reference to the Bright family of Little Stretton who had a farm there with the same names. In the Rent Roll for 1664 a Thomas Bright paid 6s 10d for a messuage and tenement.

The Raven was an inn as early as 1733 when the Manor Court records describe how John and Jane Phillips surrendered into the hands of the Lord of the Manor:

> 'All that customary messuage, tenement and yard with backside leading from the buttery end to the workhouse door together with the stable and all other outbdgs. thereunto belonging called or known by the name of the Raven Inn, being part of a certain messuage known by the name of Bright's House.

According to the 1838 tithe assessment it was then owned by John Robinson (who also owned *The Plough*) and included the adjacent yard and stables as well as a yard and gardens opposite which is now the entrance drive to Queen's Court. David Evans was the landlord at the time and was still there in 1851, but by 1861 Sarah Marston was the licensee. *The Raven* had good stabling for eight horses and for a time the stage coach changed horses here.

For a time in the last century *The Raven* offered accommodation and advertised itself as a Commercial and Family Hotel. It remained a public house until the 1970s.

The stables, old toilets and yard of The Raven Inn.

Land around the Raven Inn

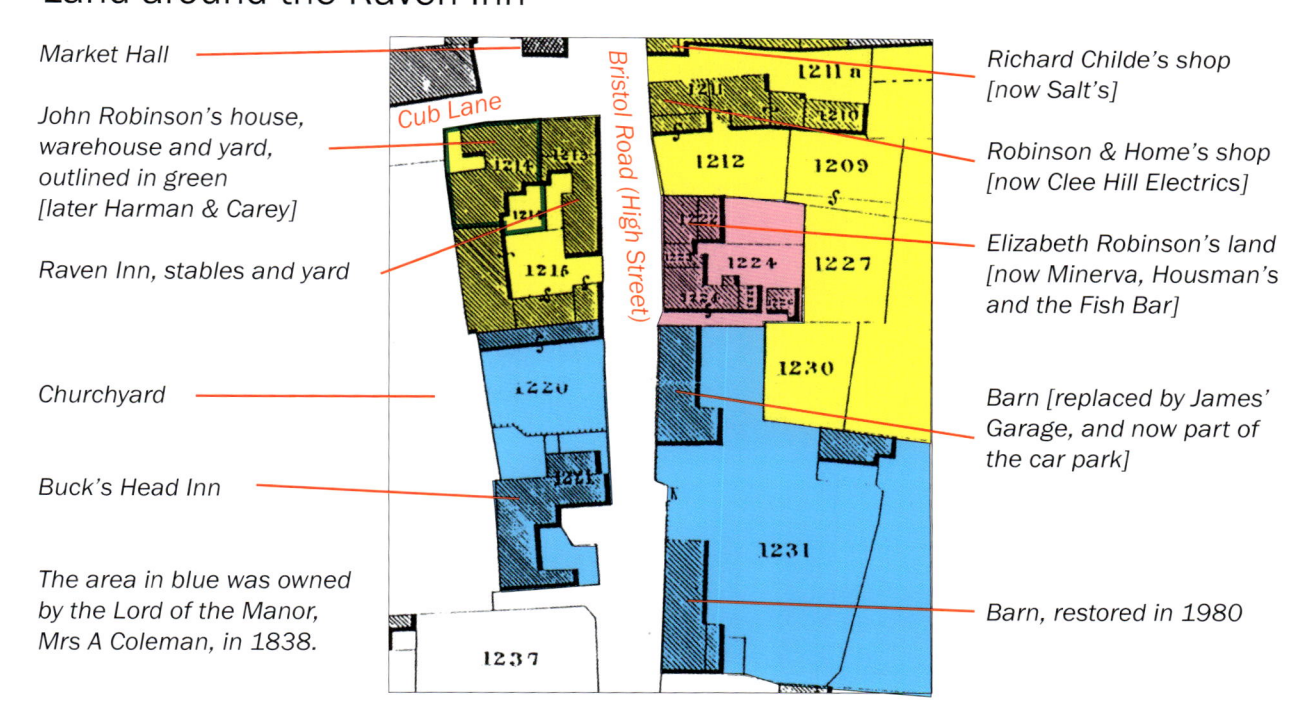

Market Hall

John Robinson's house, warehouse and yard, outlined in green [later Harman & Carey]

Raven Inn, stables and yard

Churchyard

Buck's Head Inn

The area in blue was owned by the Lord of the Manor, Mrs A Coleman, in 1838.

Richard Childe's shop [now Salt's]

Robinson & Home's shop [now Clee Hill Electrics]

Elizabeth Robinson's land [now Minerva, Housman's and the Fish Bar]

Barn [replaced by James' Garage, and now part of the car park]

Barn, restored in 1980

Plan of property around The Raven Inn based on the tithe Map of 1838.

In the 1840s John Robinson was a major landowner in Church Stretton, especially of property in High Street. He owned the areas coloured yellow above, together with the *Plough Inn* and many other plots and fields. Elizabeth Robinson, probably a cousin, owned the plots marked in pink above, the *King's Arms Inn* and some land at World's End.

61

Salt's, 19 High Street

The Salt's building before the new front was erected in 1901, showing the Shrewsbury Old Bank occupying the left part. Below, the new shop front.

The original building dates from the early 17th century. It was built as the town house of the Medlicott family who were substantial farmers in Wentnor.

In 1838 the front portion was let to Thomas Glover, a shopkeeper, whilst Thomas Gough, a stonemason, had the house and a workshop in buildings extending down the burgage plot (see page 7). Further back, at the extreme rear, Jonathan Mills of *The Lion Inn* owned a yard and stabling. Glover's shop was taken over by Henry Wood, an ironmonger, possibly in the late 1850s since the 1861 census lists him as an ironmonger in the building on the front of Salt's plot. He was still there in 1886 but two years later the business was owned by Henry Salt who had worked for Wood as an apprentice.

From about 1850 to 1870 part of the premises was used as the Post Office and then by the Shrewsbury Old Bank which opened only on Thurdays and Fair days from 12.00 to 3.30pm.

The present facade was built by Henry Salt in 1901 and is typical of ironmongers' shops of the period. The name Salt is still recorded in mosaic tiles in the entrance.

Gaius Smith, Grocer, 21 High Street

The elaborate frontage of Gaius Smith's grocery shop in the 1960s. Clee Hill Electrics now occupy the premises.

This property, like those occupied by Berry's and Salt's is a good example of a burgage plot (see page 6). The shop shown above was originally the town house where John Robinson lived about 1838.

It is possible that at one time the building was two establishments perhaps built at different times because the arrangement of the windows is not symmetrical and the brickwork is of two different patterns. There is also a distinct vertical line of bricks which could mark the division.

Behind the house was a warehouse and a smith's shop occupied in 1841 by Richard Childe and his son, tinmen (workers in metal). Later, John Pryce, a master blacksmith, had his home and workshop there. The trade continued until comparatively recently. The brick circle of a wheel-pit existed behind Salts until the King's Court flats were built, indicating that a wheelwright also worked in the vicinity.

In 1881 this was a grocer's shop belonging to George George who by 1885 had moved to *The Lion* as landlord. Henry Reddin took it over and his establishment was described as 'an excellent and commodious grocery and Italian warehouse and corn, flour, meal and hop merchant'. About 1905 the shop was occupied by Gaius Smith.

At some stage the rear part of the premises was occupied by a baker and the large ovens are still in existence. The middle photo shows the floor-level doors and the remains of the hoist for raising sacks of flour to an upper floor.

The ornate ironwork above the entrance doorway still exists and includes the initials of Gaius Smith.

Elizabeth Robinson's Home, 25 - 27 High Street

The substantial brick house (right) is part occupied by Minerva and part by Housman's. It was the home of Elizabeth Robinson which she built in 1841 according to the stone plaque high up on the north wall. At some stage after her death in 1857 it was divided into two shops.

John Proffit, Ladies' and Gents' Outfitters

The shop on the left was occupied from about 1881 by John Edwin Proffit (Ann Proffit's son) when he became 21. He had been apprenticed as a linen and woollen draper to his father Thomas who had the shop at 5, The Square. John advertised a tremendous range of goods for such a small shop, from linens and calicoes, velveteen and silks, millinery and corsets to collars and hosiery including 'the celebrated double knee ribbed black cashmere hose for children, clothing ready made and made to measure, and hats and haberdashery'.

There seems to be a link with the shop next door which until recently was the *Wine Vaults,* now *Housmans.* In the 1870s and 1880s Elizabeth Simpson, a wine and spirit merchant, lived there, while John Proffit's household included his brother-in-law Thomas Simpson who was a wine merchant's clerk.

John E Proffit died in 1910 and the business was taken over by his son Thomas whose advertisement in the *Church Stretton Illustrated* for 1912 is shown (left). He continued with this shop until the 1940s.

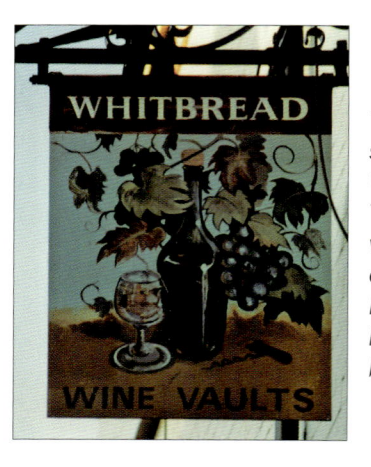

The hanging sign outside the Wine Vaults. The premises were taken over in 2009 by Housmans, and is now a wine bar.

29 - 31 High Street

No. 29 and 31 High Street were occupied by Charles Edwards, a pork butcher, and William Tarbuck and his son Percy, grocer, greengrocer and flower dealer. Photo about 1960. [Simon Madin]

This property is very old and largely timber framed although of a very inferior quality compared with the Old Barn. Elizabeth Robinson lived in it in 1838 before she built the large new house next door (Nos 25 - 27). At the rear were two poor quality cottages rented by John Smith, an agricultural labourer, and Thomas Childe the tinman. It is now occupied by the Church Stretton Fish Bar.

At the rear in recent years were the workshops of Fred Lewis and his brother, cabinet makers and undertakers (Fred was always known as 'Fred the dead'). Later, they were taken over by Dennis Price, builders and demolished when Queen's Court was built in 2002.

David Bilbey's sketch of how the property may have looked originally.

Below: Lewis Brothers workshop. [Ray Tipton]

The Buck's Head Inn, High Street

The Buck's Head Inn from a pencil sketch by Stanley Leighton, 1898. [SA]

After the church this building is the oldest in Church Stretton and one of the oldest box-frame structures in the county.

The original parts of the *Buck's Head Inn* consist almost certainly of a hall (at the rear, orientated north - south) and a cross wing (orientated east - west). The latter may date from the 13th century, since a crown-post in this part has been dated by dendrochronology to between 1286 and 1316.

According to Madge Moran it would appear that the crosswing has been extended at both ends. At the eastern (High Street) end the present gable end wall is set some 2 feet 6 inches forward from the original end truss. This wall dates from the late 16th or early 17th century. It is made of hand made bricks with diaper work in vitrified blue brick and has large stone quoins. A new chimney stack is contained within the interior space so is not visible from the outside. The original end wall had a jettied upper storey containing a central, possibly an oriel, window. [*Ref: Moran*]

At the western (churchyard) end a similar gable wall marks this end of the extension but here the new chimney stack is set out from the line of the wall. The stone work of the hall range (which is best seen from the churchyard) is mainly of Soudley banded sandstone.

The building was possibly at one time the farmhouse at the centre of the demesne farm of the lord of the manor. This would account for the barns and other farm outbuildings which once stood across the road. It was almost certainly where the half yearly manorial courts were held and where the administrative business of the manor was carried on.

Tradition has it that the building may have been originally the town house of a John Botefelde who thus became known as John o' th' Inn (later corrupted to Thynne) whose descendants later built Longleat in Wiltshire. The Thynne crest is a reindeer and the hall at Longleat is liberally furnished with buck's heads. This may well account for the name of

BUCK'S HEAD

Family, Commercial & Tourists'

HOTEL,

CHURCH STRETTON.

First Class Wines and Spirits.

NEW BOWLING GREEN.

BILLIARDS.

Horses and Carriages (open & closed)

FOR HIRE.

JOHN DABBS, Manager.

A 1905 advertisement for the Buck's Head promoting itself as a family, commercial and tourist hotel and providing a bowling green for guests.

the inn. The Thynne family were lords of the manor for over 200 years from about 1580 until 1803 when they sold it to Thomas Coleman of Leominster for £14,510. He was the father of Thomas Bernard Coleman who was Rector from 1807 - 1818 and lord of the manor from 1808-18.

After the Rector's death in 1818 the manor passed to his widow Mrs Anne Coleman. On her death in 1862 she left it to her grandson Edward B Coleman who in 1868 added the two storey porch on which is the letter 'C' for Coleman. He sold the manor to Ralph Beaumont Benson, presumably together with the *Buck's Head*, in 1888.

In the 1901 survey the inn is listed as having stabling for ten horses. The condition of the building is described as clean and in fair repair. In 2008 the premises were substantially refurbished and updated.

The rear of the Buck's Head is equally interesting with some fine stonework. The west end of the cross wing is clearly seen to the left. The Inn backs onto the churchyard, the gateway to which is on the right. Sketch by Stanley Leighton. [SA]

The Buck's Head Inn Yard and James' Garage

James' Garage in 1960.

Opposite the *Buck's Head Inn* on the other side of the road were two barns and a primitive toilet in the inn yard which was entered through a gateway. Like the inn, it was owned by the lord of the manor and leased to the Inn. The land also served as the manorial pound, used to impound animals which had strayed or were illegally pastured on the manor lands. Behind the yard stood an area of land which on the 1838 tithe map is described as a garden whilst in 1905 it was a bowling green for the use of guests at the *Buck's Head*.

The northern barn was part stuccoed and part weatherboard cladding and was probably used as stabling for the *Buck's Head Inn*. There was also a long shed-like building with a less steeply pitched roof than the barn but there is no indication of its use apart from the fact that it had an outside stairway.

This barn was demolished to allow the erection in 1922 of James' Garage, which had petrol pumps originally at the side and later at the front (see the 1960 photo above). The company later became Caradoc Motors and the property was eventually taken over by the Church Stretton Carpet and Furniture Centre.

For many years the area around was overgrown with trees and became derelict and an eyesore. The land was eventually cleared as part of the construction of the Lion Meadow road and associated works in the mid 1990s. The remnant of the garage and furniture store was demolished in 2002 as part of the Queen's Court development scheme.

The southern barn is a typical 17th century three bay timber frame building and was beautifully restored in 1980 (see page 70).

The men's toilets for the Buck's Head were in this building opposite the Inn next to the south barn and in use until the barn was restored in 1980. There was no running water in it! [Ray Tipton]

Left: The Stretton Carpet and Furniture Centre took over the building vacated by Caradoc Motors. Photo taken in 1982.

Below: Advertisement from 'Church Stretton: The Beauty spot of Shropshire'. About 1922.

The James Garages Ltd.
CHURCH STRETTON

Motor Touring Service.

First-class Cars and Motor Wagonettes are always available at Standard Charges, and Rates will be quoted for any journey. Special attention will be given to enquiries for visiting places of interest in the immediate neighbourhood.

Motor Wagonette Excursions

Will be arranged throughout the Season, and full particulars can be obtained at the Garage.

Complete Stocks of Tyres, Tubes and Accessories.
First Class Electrical Service.

TELEPHONE NO. 27. TELEGRAMS: JAMES' GARAGE, CHURCH-STRETTON.

The derelict site before Queen's Court was built. The buildings shown are on part of the burgage plot behind Clee Hill Electrics.

The Old Barn

The Old Barn was the southern of the two that stood in the Buck's Head yard and was used to house their horses and carts. It is a typical 17th century three bay timber frame building probably built soon after the great fire of 1593 which would have destroyed any earlier barns and/or houses on this site.

Access to the upper floor of the barn was by means of a ladder and there were tales of a man who lived at one end and made a living by collecting and selling bracken and bilberries from the Long Mynd. At the other end, hens roosted and flew around.

The Barn was beautifully restored in 1980 by David and Sylvia Witting. After completion of the restoration, they opened it as an antique shop. It is now occupied by the wholefood shop Entertaining Elephants.

Top: Before restoration the front of the barn had oak boarding covering a timber framed structure with brick infill. The stone building abutting the left of the old barn was the public convenience for the Buck's Head. Beyond it is the Church Stretton Carpet and Furniture Centre, originally James' Garage.

Above: The rear of the barn.

Left: After restoration.
[Photos: David Witting]

The south end of the High Street

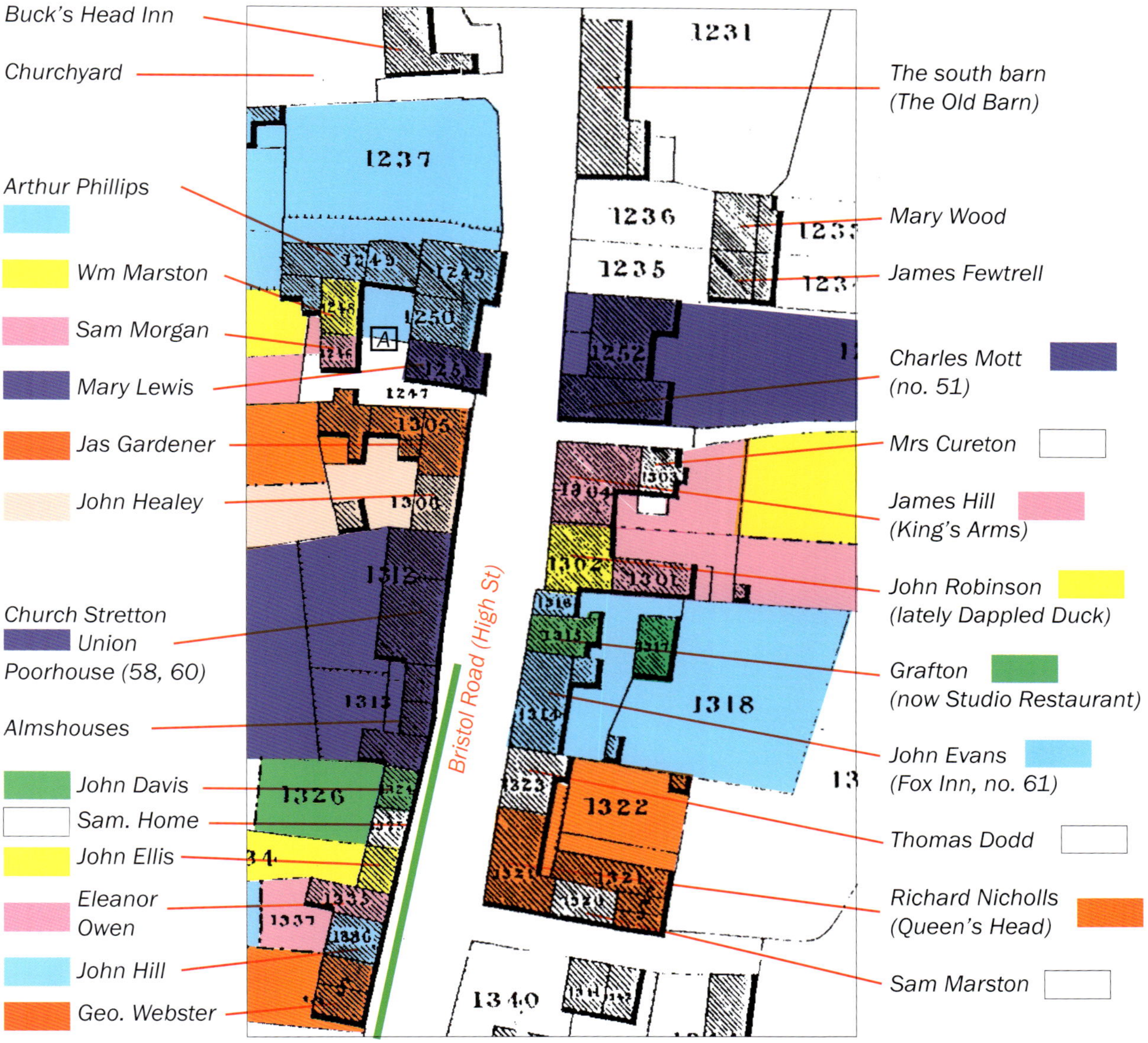

Buck's Head Inn
Churchyard
Arthur Phillips
Wm Marston
Sam Morgan
Mary Lewis
Jas Gardener
John Healey
Church Stretton Union Poorhouse (58, 60)
Almshouses
John Davis
Sam. Home
John Ellis
Eleanor Owen
John Hill
Geo. Webster
The south barn (The Old Barn)
Mary Wood
James Fewtrell
Charles Mott (no. 51)
Mrs Cureton
James Hill (King's Arms)
John Robinson (lately Dappled Duck)
Grafton (now Studio Restaurant)
John Evans (Fox Inn, no. 61)
Thomas Dodd
Richard Nicholls (Queen's Head)
Sam Marston
Bristol Road (High St)
1231
1237
1236
1235
1250
1247
1305
1306
1312
1313
1326
1304
1302
1301
1318
1322
1340
A

Properties and their occupiers in 1838 in the southern part of the High Street from the Old Barn and the Buck's Head Inn. The group of houses which were replaced by the Silvester Horne Institute (bottom left) is indicated by the green line in the street. This plan is based on the 1838 tithe map.
Ashlett Court is marked thus [A]

The south end of the High Street has changed considerably since 1838. A major change has occurred on the west side where late Victorian development has taken place from the *Buck's Head Inn* south to Ashlett House. The biggest change has occurred with the building of the Silvester Horne Institute (opened 1918) on the site of some cottages and almshouses.

The great fire of 1593 probably swept through all the cottages that would have lined this part of the High Street. Because of rebuilding many of the properties in this area have a timber frame structure now, in many cases, hidden by subsequent improvements.

45 - 47 High Street

Photo taken in the early part of the 20th century.

No. 47 is the large house at the back. No. 45 is the timber framed building on the left.

There seems no logical reason why no. 47 should lie behind the building line; perhaps there are foundations of earlier buildings under the front garden. It is an old building probably constructed in the eighteenth century. In 1841 it was two cottages, the left one occupied by Mary Wood (a baker), her two daughters and three lodgers, a cooper, a horsekeeper and a mason. James Fewtrell, a tailor, held the other cottage. His family carried on the same trade there until at least 1885. In the back garden there is a shed which had been used for the accommodation of someone suffering from TB.

Number 45 is the timber framed building shown on the far left of the photograph above and was built in the front garden of no. 47 in the second half of the 19th century. It has tall floor to ceiling south facing windows which would provide maximum light, suggesting it was probably designed as a weaving or knitting workshop. From about 1925 the front part was Harry Ruscoe's cycle shop, then Stan Edward's wireless shop, then Angela's and now Anthony's hairdressing salon.

In the 1980s another small shop (below) was built in the front garden abutting the adjacent building no. 49 (see opposite page) and hiding the right hand part of the old property at the rear.

The milepost showing 13 miles to Shrewsbury was erected for the benefit of coaches and carriers when the Bristol Road from Ludlow to Shrewsbury was made into a turnpike in 1756.

The front of no, 45 as it was in 1997.

72

49 and 51 High Street (sometimes called Insurance House)

Wall plate on which original roof rested

Upper floor added from here

Wall post

49 High St.

Number 49 and the adjacent property no. 51 (overleaf, sometimes known as Hannett's and Insurance House, respectively) were one establishment occupied by Dr Charles Mott from before 1838 (and probably even from 1819) until 1863 when he died. On the tithe award map of 1838 the whole property was described as a house, stables and court with a garden at the rear, the latter being a long narrow field adjacent to The Narrows, the pathway between no. 51 and the *King's Arms Inn*. Presumably no. 49 was the stabling and no. 51 the residence.

No. 49 (above) is a building which has been substantially restored and altered since the 19th century and is now divided into two. It is an interesting timber framed building, the design of which suggests that it was built early in the seventeenth century or even very soon after the great fire of 1593.

The front shows ten original wall posts, some of which have been cut to accommodate windows and a second door which has been inserted at a later date. The original sill upon which the wall posts rest lies below the present ground level because the road and frontage have been raised over the years. The continuous wall plate upon which the original roof would have rested shows that, when erected, the building was totally open inside to the roof. The absence of smoke blackening on the interior timbers shows that there was no open hearth, suggesting that the original building was not used for domestic purposes and may have been a stable or dairy.

At a later date, the roof was raised and an upper floor added. The spaces between the timber framing would had originally been filled with wattle and daub but this at various times has been replaced by brickwork. The timbers have been hacked to provide a key for stucco added at a later date to provide insulation; this was removed recently by the von Wedelstedts to expose the timber frame seen today.

There were interconnecting doors with the main house (no. 51) to the right but these were blocked up in 1962 and the properties separated.

Dr Charles Mott and other occupants of 51 High Street

Originally this house and the one to the left (no. 49, previous page) were one building with this being the domestic residence. It has been rebuilt and the first record of occupation is by Dr Charles Mott, a surgeon who moved to Church Stretton about 1819. It is unclear how the house was divided or where the stabling was; certainly on the maps drawn about that time no outbuildings are shown. Mott died in 1863.

By all accounts he was a very well-liked member of the community. His medical practice seems to have included many of the outlying areas of the parish. There is a tradition that the pack horse track from Carding Mill Valley over the Long Mynd is named after him because he is supposed to have used it to reach the homes of outlying patients; certainly it is commonly known as 'Dr Mott's Road' and was improved in his honour in 1850 by public subscription.

Mott was succeeded in this house by Dr John McClintock. At the time he was aged 34 and single, but in 1871 he married Hannah, daughter of Harriet Bakewell who owned The Grove in All Stretton which was a private lunatic asylum for ladies. In about 1878 he moved to manage and live there.

The next occupant was Samuel Harley Kough, a solicitor, who resided at no. 51 (by which time the house was called The Limes) until he died in 1911. Dr Horatio Barnett (photo), who was medical superintendent at the Stretton House Asylum (and a Major with the 1st Shropshire Artillery Volunteers) then took up residence and continued his general medical practice from here. Prior to this he had lived at Burway House.

Horatio Barnett has been described as short and rather stout, with a moustache and 'a bit sharp'. His wife Margaret Elizabeth Webb was a Commandant in the Voluntary Aid Detachment and Superintendent of the private hospital established at Essex House for convalescent soldiers during the First World War. She was a sister of Captain Matthew Webb, the first man to swim the English Channel.

The room in the left part of the property next door, now numbered 49b, was the Doctor's waiting room, while behind was his surgery. Dr Barnett had large gardens on both sides of The Narrows and grazing rights in the fields beyond. The stables for his horse and trap were in the garden area at the back of the house. Dr Barnett died in 1938 at the age of 76 whereupon the house was bought by the Misses Patterson.

On the death of the last of the Miss Pattersons in 1960, Harry Ruscoe bought nos. 49 and 51 and moved his bicycle business from no. 45. He died two years later whereupon Frank and Mary Hannett bought no. 49 while Mrs Ruscoe continued to live in no. 51.

Dr Horatio Barnett

For a year or so about 1964 the downstairs rooms of no. 51 housed the *Stretton Gazette* published by Henry D Woods. It has been described as quite a good local paper but the history of its final period is rather obscure; certainly after it closed the rooms are reported to have been filled with thousands of unsold copies of the paper.

The King's Arms, High Street

Above: The High Street in 1910, looking north.
Right: View down The Narrows (Coffin Lane) showing the fine close-studded timbers of the side wall

The King's Arms is of a timber framed construction which could date back to the rebuilding of the centre of the town after the fire of 1593. Originally built as a house it occupies three messuages, two at the front, one at the rear. It almost certainly was built having a hall (running parallel to The Narrows) and a crosswing, though these are now two separate premises, *The King's Arms* and a private house which, until recently, was a shop called the Dappled Duck occupying the southern part of the crosswing.

The presence of fine close-studded timbers visible on the north wall of the hall portion suggests a building of quality. Presumably similar timbers are covered by the stucco on the front.

The 1838 tithe award says it was owned by Elizabeth Robinson, the landlord being James Hill. In the 1851 census the landlord was William Teague and from 1861 to 1881 it was William Hayes. The 1901 Report on Licensed Premises described *The King's Arms* as having good stabling at the rear for eleven horses and the condition of buildings was described as clean and in fair repair. The stables can still be seen.

A Mrs Cureton lived in a small cottage which had been built abutting the back of *The King's Arms* with its door opening directly on to The Narrows. It has since been incorporated into the inn.

> **King's Arms Inn, Church Stretton.**
>
> **William Hayes**
>
> Thanks his patrons for past favours, and begs a continuance of same.
>
> BEST WINES, SPIRITS, AND FINE ALES.
> Good Stabling and Excellent Accommodation.
> The Manchester Unity of Odd Fellows' Club House. If you want Comfort—a home from home—call on HOST HAYES.

Above: An advertisement from the Church Stretton Times and Visitors List, 1881.

Left: How the King's Arms might have looked when it was built.
[David Bilbey]

57 High Street, The Dappled Duck

The front room of this property was originally a barn or stable attached to the crosswing of the *King's Arms*. When restoration work in 1985 involved removing the stucco from the upper storey of the front, interesting stonework was exposed which strongly suggested the property had been a barn or stable.

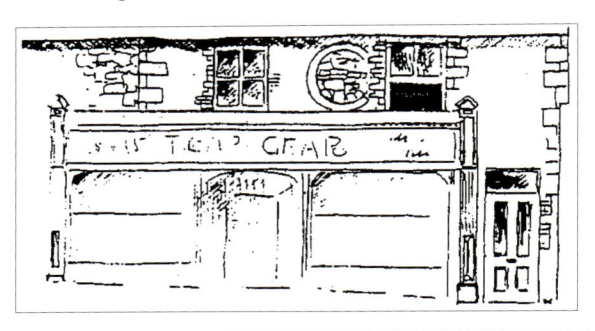

Top: The stonework at the front exposed during restoration in 1985.
Below: This property may have looked something like this when it was originally built as a barn or stable. [David Bilbey]

The dressed quoins that were exposed showed that this part of what had been thought of as the continuation of the crosswing of the inn was erected as a separate structure. In the centre of the upper part of the wall there is a circular opening framed in dressed stone which has been roughly filled with rubble stone. It is of a type common in barns or stabling. The frame of the opening had been cut from one piece of stone but a part had subsequently been broken away, possibly when the two upper windows were inserted. The new window openings had been knocked out and the corners squared with brick before the wall was covered again in stucco. Part of the quoins were revealed on the ground floor at the south end but these had been cut away when a door was inserted and brick had again been used to square up the opening. The bottom four or five courses are rubble stone, perhaps the remains of an earlier building. It seems probable that this building was originally a barn or stabling for the inn.

By 1838 the barn or stable had been converted to a house and shop accommodation occupied by John Robinson, a shoemaker. In 1885 Thomas Keenan, a tailor and clothier, lived and had his shop here.

57 High Street, Humphreys Family Butcher

[Eddie Conning]

About 1899 Henry, the son of Thomas Humphreys, a butcher, inherited his father's business which may have been at no. 55; he certainly was here in 1913. About this time Henry Humphreys took over the licence of the *King's Arms* in addition to continuing as a butcher. It was effectively one business because the cellar continues under the *King's Arms* and still has a brick plinth for beer barrels and a drip gulley and drain. The shop frontage had a central doorway and two large sash windows on either side with the remains of marble meat slabs which now form the window sills.

More recently it was a clothing shop called Top Gear, and latterly Dappled Duck. It is now purely residential, typical of many former shops which have become residences as this end of the High Street as it ceased to be part of the main shopping area of the town in favour of Sandford Avenue.

59 - 65 High Street

Between the Studio Restaurant and the present Masonic Hall, formerly *The Queen's Head Inn*, lies a pleasant terrace of houses (nos. 59 - 65) usually occupied in the mid 19th century by shopkeepers and tradesmen. In the 1841 census these included a shoemaker, ironmonger, butcher, excise officer and saddler. By the 1871 census these had changed to a tailor, poulterer, game dealer and a baker.

William Baldwin had owned all this 'customary cottage or mansion house' since his marriage to Margaret Edgerton in 1748. It was later divided into two properties, for by 1760, Samuel Mathews, a surgeon, was occupying the left hand part, now numbered 59 and 61.

The Studio Restaurant, No. 59 and to its right the former Fox Inn, no. 61 High St.

By 1769 Mathews had moved to live elsewhere but continued to own it. He rebuilt 59 and 61 and turned the new building into the *Fox Inn* with his brother-in-law as licensee. Ownership passed in 1786 to John Evason, a blacksmith, who continued as licencee. He died in 1801 and there is no evidence of it continuing as an inn after that. A recent owner named it Shepwardine after Mary Webb's pseudonym for Church Stretton in her novels.

The 59 - 61 house was divided again by 1838, for in the 1838 tithe award no. 61 was listed as a private house occupied by John Evans, a butcher, but owned by the Rector, the Rev'd R N Pemberton, whilst no. 59 was occupied by a Mr Grafton.

59 High Street, Studio Fiftynine

Left: Studio Fiftynine as a restaurant.   [Simon Madin]

Below: This earlier photograph shows part of the old coach house doors, used as a potter's studio next to the gift shop selling English, Swedish, Italian and French pottery as well as lamps and shades.

Number 59 was for a time after World War II a potter's studio and shop, together with a coach house, run by Cornelius William van der Veen and called *Studio Fiftynine*. It later became a restaurant run by the Bull family, with the coach house rebuilt as the dining area. They lived in the house next door, no. 57.

63 High Street

The land upon which no. 63 and the former *Queen's Head Inn* (no. 67) stand was at one time called Wilkes' Messuage. In 1838 it was owned by Richard Nichols (see the area coloured brown on the map on page 71). Part of it, number 63, was a house and shop occupied by Thomas Dodd, a boot and shoe maker.

Like its neighbour properties in the terrace, this building was rebuilt about 1820.

Later occupiers were Henry Bowcock, a saddler and Henry Bond, a watchmaker, who also regulated the Church clock and supplied clocks to the workhouse, *The Hotel*, the Poor House and *The Raven Inn*.

It is now the Ying Wah Chinese Take-away.

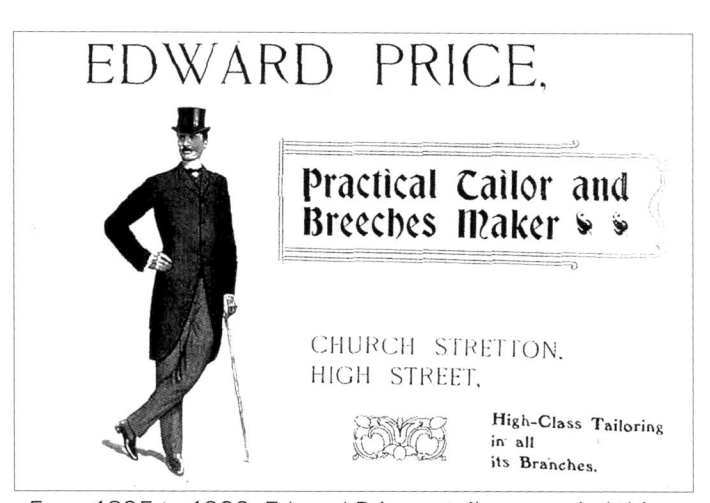

From 1895 to 1922, Edward Price, a tailor occupied this house. This advertisement is from a 1905 guide.

65 High Street, Queen's Head Inn

The building of which the *Queen's Head Inn* was part was built about 1820. In 1838 this corner block was owned by Richard Nicholls but included another house at the rear occupied by Samuel Marston. The land had originally been called Wilkes' Messuage.

The inn operated from about 1820 until just before the First World War when the last licensee was John Rogers. In 1840 Richard Nicholls was the innkeeper, but the status of the premises seems to have changed for by 1871 the landlady, Ann Andrews, described herself as a beer house keeper.

After the inn's closure it was converted into a shop called the Queen's Stores and occupied by, among others, George Ball, a grocer. Since 1975 it has been the Masonic Hall.

The lane to the side of the property is an old pathway to Prosser's yard field at the rear. On the south side of the lane, there was at one time a pair of timber frame wattle and daub cottages (illustrated below) covered in stucco and owned, in 1838, by Richard Nicholls of the *Queen's Head Inn*. One was the home of Richard Haughton, a cowleech, and the other was occupied by James Bellingham, a hairdresser. Richard Haughton's son succeeded him and called himself a beastleech. A person with that trade would have done simple medical work such as pulling teeth besides helping with the healing of animals. In her novel *Precious Bane*, set in the early 19th century, local author Mary Webb writes:

'in one corner of the market place the beastleech was pulling teeth at a penny each and had a crowd watching'.

Eventually the cottages were demolished and the land was sold in 1925 to Mary Deakin of Greengates, the house next door, and incorporated into its garden.

GEO. R. BALL

Queen's Stores

For High Class Groceries and Provisions

Cigarettes and Tobacco

Agent for Leading Makes of Confectionery

Fresh Fruits in Season, Frozen Foods

———

High Street, Church Stretton

A 1957 advertisement for the Queen's Stores.

[David Bilbey]

Greengates, 69 High Street

Greengates in 1998.

Behind the Georgian façade of this property lies a two-storey two-bay timber frame cottage built in the early years of the 17th century and known as Hayles's Messuage. It is likely that a cottage existed here before the great fire of 1593 for it is known that John Hayles sold the messuage to Bonham Norton some time after the fire which presumably destroyed the original cottage. After it was rebuilt it remained in the hands of the Norton family until it was sold, along with its associated land which extended down to Watling Street, to Thomas Waring in 1715.

The rear half still exists with its original timber framework but the front rooms were replaced by a double fronted brick structure in the mid 18th century. The name was changed to Greengates in 1829.

Sheep being driven up the High Street in front of Greengates for the sheep sales on Lion Meadow (then called Deakin's Field and lately Sheep Sales Field). These sales continued every September until about 1982.

A room downstairs has incorporated into one wall the only remaining panelling from the late sixteenth century box pews from St Laurence's Church.

46 - 52 High Street

Left: Victoria House in 2001. Right: Nos. 46 to 52 High Street

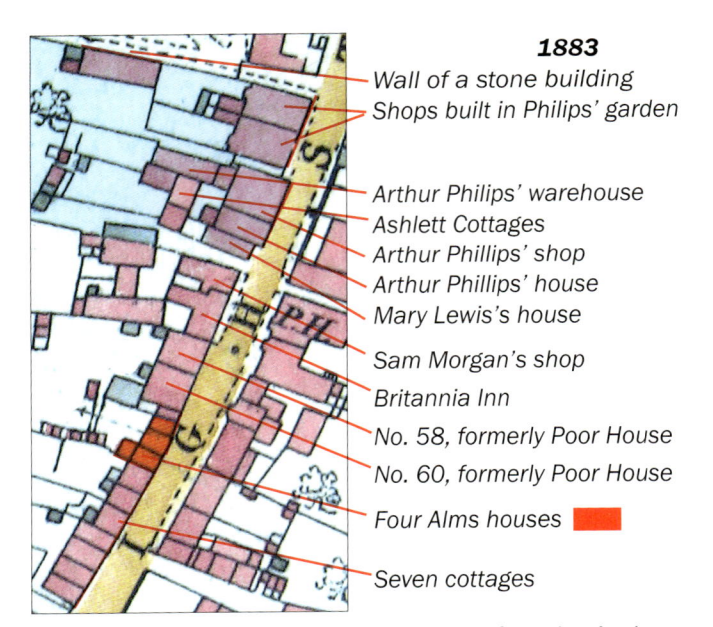

1883
- Wall of a stone building
- Shops built in Philips' garden

- Arthur Philips' warehouse
- Ashlett Cottages
- Arthur Phillips' shop
- Arthur Phillips' house
- Mary Lewis's house

- Sam Morgan's shop
- Britannia Inn
- No. 58, formerly Poor House
- No. 60, formerly Poor House

- Four Alms houses

- Seven cottages

2010
- Wall now part of churchyard wall
- Rebuilt as no. 46 - Corner offices
- Rebuilt as no. 48 - Victoria House

- Converted to one of the Ashlett Cottages
- Ashlett Cottages
- These three properties replaced by two: rebuilt as no. 50 (half of Jubilee Building) rebuilt as no.52 Ashlett House (other half)

- No. 54, Amber Room Hair Salon
- No. 56, private house
- No. 58, private house
- No. 60, Town Council Offices

- Institute Cottage

- Silvester Horne Institute

The 1883 OS map shows the buildings referred to in the text.

In 1773 a Thomas Phillips is recorded as holding Mund's House comprising a shop and a yard bounded by the Bristol Road (now High Street) on the east, by Back Lane (now Church Street) on the west and by the churchyard to the north. The 1838 tithe map shows that an Arthur Phillips, presumably a descendent, owned this area (marked in blue on the maps on pages 71 and above) as well as Mary Lewis' house, south to what is now Ashlett House, until recently occupied by Tipton's shop. A long stone outbuilding formed a boundary with the churchyard to the north. Although this building no longer survives its wall forms part of the churchyard wall and is clearly visible.

At that time (1838) the north east corner of this open piece of land, bordering the churchyard, was Arthur Phillips' garden. Next down High Street, adjacent to his garden and fronting the street, were three properties, the first two being his shop and house. Behind his shop was his warehouse. The third building was another house, occupied by

Mary Lewis, a launderess. These houses and shop were replaced by the Jubilee Buildings in 1897.

A semi-detached pair of houses/shops was built in the mid 19th century on Arthur Phillips' garden. These, in turn, were pulled down and replaced about 1887 by a semi detached pair of houses with shop fronts. The first to occupy these was Mrs Francis Mansell who provided visitor accommodation at the corner building (no. 46). At Victoria House (no. 48) Lucy Cook and her sister provided similar accommodation, sold stationery and books and established a library. Their business continued under the ownership of Sampson Wright and then of C E Norgate.

The premises were then used from about 1922 to 1937 by Dr John McClintock, a Scot from Dumfries, who had his surgery there. He kept his pony and trap at the rear with an entrance in Church Street. He lived at The Grove in All Stretton where he also ran the Private Mental Hospital for Ladies.

Lucy Cook's advertisement in Wilding's Directory of 1903.

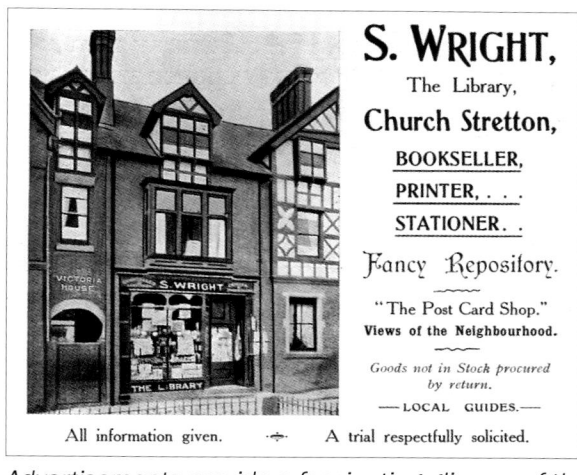

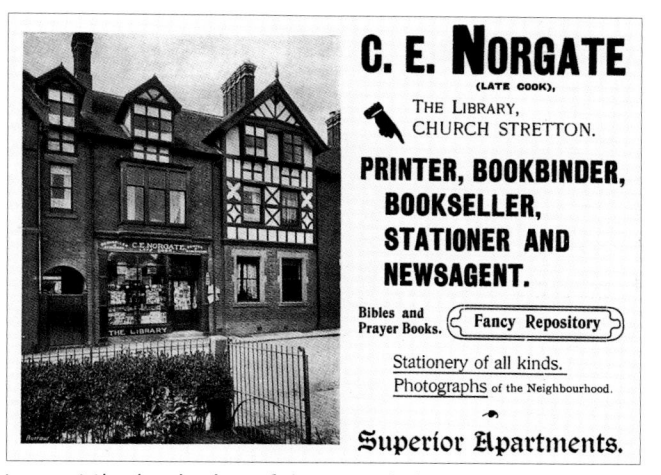

Advertisements provide a fascinating glimpse of the town at the beginning of the twentieth century.
Left: 1908, Right: 1915.

The photographs of Victoria House above show how originally there was no mock-Tudor woodwork on the part of the building housing the shop in contrast to the residential part on the right. Compare this with the added mock-Tudor woodwork now (opposite page).

Jubilee Buildings, 50 - 52 High Street

A 1912 advertisement for the Church Stretton High School for Boys which was housed in Ashlett House. Charles Tipton is at the foot of the ladder where the house next door is being painted.

Arthur Phillips' house and shop and Mary Lewis's house were pulled down in the early 1890s. The upper part of these can be seen in the photograph on page 89. They were replaced by a semi detached pair of houses built by Henry Salt in dark red Ruabon brick (above). Number 50, built in 1895, is now occupied by Middletons and Ashlett House, no. 52, built in 1897, has returned to private accommodation. Ashlett House seems to have been designed as a boarding house which Mrs Salt ran.

From about 1909, no. 50 housed the Capital and Counties Bank which later was taken over by Lloyds Bank and moved to the new purpose-built premises at the top of Sandford Avenue in 1923.

From 1909 to about 1916 Ashlett House was a boy's boarding school run by the Rev'd Charles Bryant. Judging from the photograph above, the number of pupils was small; only eight are standing on the steps.

From 1955 Ashlett House was the home of Belton Tipton and his family. From here Belton ran his decorating and wallpapering business. His wife managed the shop which gradually expanded into hardware and ironmongery. From 1972 until 2002 this was continued by their son Ray.

Belton Tipton kept his paints and equipment in a shed in the garden of the Buck's Head Inn.

The elaborate front door of Ashlett House shows the initials HS, for its builder Henry Salt and the date 1897.

The plaque reflects the excitement in the nation caused by the Diamond Jubilee of the accession of Queen Victoria.

Ashlett Cottages

Behind Arthur Phillips' house and shop and Mary Lewis's house there is a small courtyard bounded at the north end by Phillips' warehouse and on the west by two small cottages (see photograph). In 1838 they were occupied by William Marston, a tailor (in whose tiny cottage lived his wife, three children, a journeyman tailor, an apprentice and a shoemaker) and Samuel Morgan, a shopkeeper. The passage leading to this courtyard is along the side of Ashlett House. Phillips' warehouse has since been converted into residential accommodation.

The Poor House, 58 - 60 High Street and the Almshouses

The buildings in this terrace are, from left to right, numbers 60, 58, 56 (the site of the Britannia Inn), and 54 (site of Sam Morgans' shop).

Until 1917 a row of fifteen houses and cottages stood between Ashford House and the passage beside Ashlett House (better known until recently as Tipton's DIY shop). Seven were then pulled down to make way for the Silvester Horne Institute. Four almshouses which were immediately south of no. 60 High Street were sold in 1921 to be replaced by Institute Cottage, the caretaker's house.

The Almshouses

The four almshouses, built in 1829 by John Robinson, each had one room varying in size from 13ft by 12ft down to 13ft 6ins by 7ft 6ins. They shared one earth closet in the back yard. The almshouses were in use until 1920, being pulled down the following year. The lower part of the side wall of no. 60 still shows the roof line of the adjacent almshouse.

Typical residents, listed in the 1881 census, were Anne Smith (85 years), Mary Reynolds (77 years), Elizabeth Williams (76 years), Elizabeth Marston, a charwoman and her sister.

The Parish Poor

In medieval times the duty of relieving the poor was nominally the responsibility of the lord of the manor but in practice it fell increasingly on the church.

After 1535 responsibility for the maintenance of those poor who could not look after themselves was given to the parish. An Act of 1601 authorised the appointment of Overseers of the Poor and allowed the building of a house of correction and a poorhouse for the incapacitated poor. In 1697 the Settlement Act encouraged parishes to send the poor back to their home parish for relief.

In 1684 a two acre meadow in Little Stretton called The Pools was given to Thomas Hawkes under trust so that rents and profits could be used to relieve and succour poor people of the Parish. In his will of 1703 he left £30 for the purchase of Walter's House (now 58 - 60 High St) for the accommodation of poor people. This was bought in 1708 and any rental income was used to finance the distribution of bread for the poor.

The 1834 Poor Law Amendment Act grouped parishes together into Poor Law Unions, each centred on a market town. From that date relief to a poor person was available

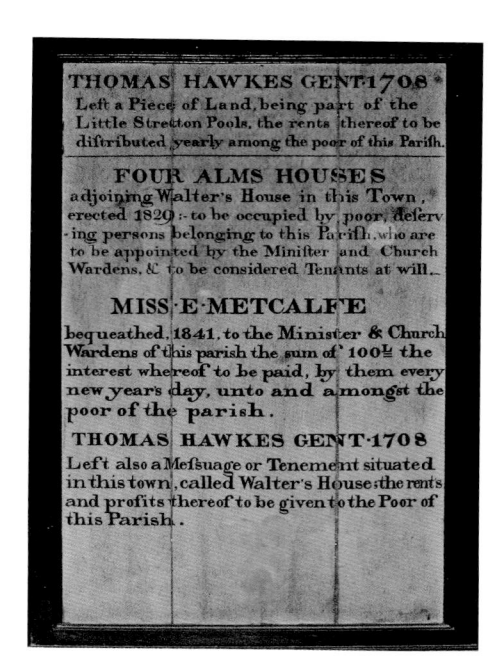

This benefaction board in St Laurence's Church Vestry is one of three listing benefactors to the Parish. This board shows the legacies of Thomas Hawkes whose gifts allowed the purchase of the Poorhouse. The public display of such benefaction boards was intended to safeguard the generous gifts of local philanthropists from misappropriation.

only by entering a poorhouse or workhouse, both of which were designed to be as unpleasant as possible; there were to be no shirkers seeking an easy existence at the ratepayers' expense. Church Stretton was the centre of a Union of fifteen local parishes. After the passing of the 1834 Act the Guardians of the Poor built a new workhouse in Shrewsbury Road which was opened in 1838.

The Parish lock-up with two cells, built in the 1820s, was a building at the back of the alms houses. After a new lock-up was built at the Police Station in Shrewsbury Road in 1846/7 the old building was then used to house the Parish bier.

Walter's House (now 58 and 60) belonged to the parishioners of Church Stretton. In 1840 the Parish Vestry meeting considered selling it but decided to divide the property into two dwellings and rent them out.

Modifications being carried out in 1960 to Jack and Barbara Taylor's antiques shop (no. 60) previously owned by Constance Davies The workmen are Eric Lucas, Alan Edwards and Mick Morris.

An advertisement in the Church Stretton Times, 1881. John Charlton's business operated from 60 High St.

60 High Street

In the early 1880s John Charlton had a book and stationery shop called The Library here. Subsequent occupiers were Thomas Humphreys, a butcher who slaughtered his animals in the yard behind. Constance Davies shoe repair shop (above), Quintessence, Mary Long's café and Stretton Galleries also operated from no. 60.

The building now houses the offices of the Church Stretton Town Council.

54 - 60 High Street

After nos 60 and 58 were separated, no. 58 became a shop and remained so until it was turned into a private residence in 1995. This 1987 photograph shows the pair of properties as two shops, the left as Stretton Galleries and the right Christopher Morris's estate agency.

Temperance Refreshment Rooms, Church Stretton.
TEA AND COFFEE AT ALL HOURS,
Cyclists specially attended to.
MRS. JAMES — PROPRIETRESS.

By 1881 Ann James had opened her Temperance Refreshment Rooms at no. 58. Her advertisement that year shows that cycling was becoming a recreational pastime in a time of solid tyred pennyfarthing machines. In 1891 it was called the *Temperance Hotel*.

The corner shop, no. 54, below, has had many owners since Sam Morgan and his large family moved from his cramped cottage in Ashlett Court to here about 1840.

Another occupant, Thomas Holt, a baker and confectioner, had moved to The Square by 1885.

No. 54, The Curio Shop in 1985. This later became Crocker's and is now the Amber Room Hair Salon.

The Britannia Inn, 56 High Street

The sale of the contents of the Britannia Inn in 1893. In the photograph the auctioneer is Mr Edwards, the clerk with the bag is Jimmy Mundy, the lady in the bonnet in the centre is Mrs Fewtrell. On the left of the auctioneer is Nancy Wragg and the child with the daffodil is Maud Roberts.

The *Britannia Inn* was one of a terrace of cottages which still stand on the west side of the High Street. It was converted into an inn by Richard Everall by 1851. Then the landlord was his son John Everall who remained there until the 1870s, followed by Mary Everall until she died in 1883. The inn closed in 1893 whilst Andrew Evans was the landlord and the contents were sold by a public auction in the street on 23rd March 1893.

In the background of the photo can still be seen Arthur Phillips' house and shop and Mary Lewis's house before the Jubilee Building (including Ashlett House) had been built to replace them, whilst Victoria House and the premises to the north had already been built on Arthur Phillips' garden.

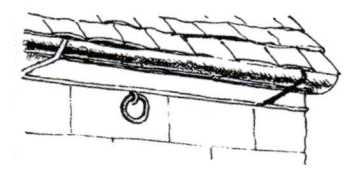

The fear of fire haunted every town, especially after long dry summers when the thatch would be tinder dry and water in short supply. Great hooks attached to long poles were used by fire fighters to drag burning thatch away from the roof. When in use they were attached to ropes looped through rings on the walls under the eaves to steady the poles. There are five rings set on the wall under the eaves of the *Britannia Inn* and the next door house no. 54 which may well have been used in this way.

Rings for ropes to steady fire hooks from under the eaves of the Britannia Inn.

Silvester Horne Institute

The Silvester Horne Institute was built on the site of seven cottages to honour the memory of Charles Silvester Horne.

Born in 1865 Silvester Horne was a Congregational Minister who achieved national renown as a preacher. He was Minister at Allen Street Church, Kensington, then at Whitefield's Tabernacle from 1903 until his retirement in 1913 because of ill health. He then came to live at The White House in Sandford Avenue, which he had built for himself. It is now the site of White House Gardens.

He was also interested in politics and was elected as a Liberal MP for Ipswich in the January and December general elections of 1910.

In January 1914, despite medical misgivings, he went to America and Canada to fulfil speaking engagements, accompanied by his wife Katherine. After lecturing at Yale University he went to Niagara by train and then to Toronto by boat to address a further meeting. As the boat was entering Toronto harbour on 2nd May 1914 Horne, who was standing on deck, collapsed and died of a heart attack. He was only 49. His body was brought back to Church Stretton and, after a service at the Congregational Church in the High Street on 15th May 1914, was buried in the Cunnery Road Cemetery.

The Institute was built by the Congregational Church Union in his memory to serve as a religious, social and educational centre for the people of Church Stretton. It cost £2,530 which was raised by a national appeal and was opened on Tuesday 3rd September 1918.

The building is now run by the Church Stretton Town Council which are its trustees.

Charles Silvester Horne.

Ashford House, 74 High Street

*Left:
Ashford House.*

*Below:
A 1905 advertisement offering holiday accommodation.*

*Bottom:
A view of the back of the house showing the garden in 1912.*

Ashford House was built in 1775 on an area of waste land known as Well's Messuage which extended from Bristol Road (High Street) to Back Lane (now Church Street). The site was owned by William Phillips but he sold it to Edward Phillips, an apothecary of Acton Burnell, who agreed to build a house. A detailed specification was drawn up with Robert Roberts, a master builder of Church Stretton, who agreed a sum of £200 for it's construction. The property passed to Phillips' niece Frances Baker and eventually to the Rector, Rev'd Robert Norgrave Pemberton, in 1818.

The house was extended about 1824 and occupied by the Rev'd Preston Nunn, curate of Church Stretton for 53 years from 1824 to 1877.

Around 1905 the then owner Maria Howell was offering holiday accommodation with board, if required. It even advertised that hot or cold baths could be taken! The attractive grounds contained croquet and tennis courts.

Later, in 1912, Ashford House was being advertised as a nursing home for medical, surgical and convalescent patients. This was run by Miss Emily Nicholls until 1928.

Ashford House, Church Stretton.

Superior Furnished Apartments in Suites,
BOARD IF REQUIRED
Croquet and Tennis Courts in Private Gardens.
BATH (HOT AND COLD).
Near Golf Links.   Highly Recommended.
COOKING AND ATTENDANCE EXCELLENT.
Five Minutes from Railway Station and Two Minutes from G.P.O.
Sunny Aspect.   In Own Grounds.   Every Home Comfort.

Enquiries please Address to :— MRS. HOWELL'S (late Bason).

Cunnery Road corner

These two cottages in Cunnery Road at the corner with High Street are largely unchanged today. The photograph was taken in 1906. Joseph Jones' stonemason's yard is in the background.

From at least the early 19th century there were eight cottages forming a continuous row between Ashford House in the High Street round the corner into Cunnery Road. They still exist, though several in High Street have been joined together. In 1838 the occupants included Rachel Lee, aged 93, of independent means, John Robinson, a carpenter, William Humphreys, a mason, who lived with his mother and two lodgers and John Cureton, a butcher, the owner of much of the property.

The yard at the corner with Back Lane (Church Street) above was occupied in 1838 by John Robinson for his timber business. Later a monumental and general mason, Joseph Jones, occupied this yard which was conveniently situated opposite the cemetery gates. He made the font for St Michael's Church, All Stretton.

Jones' advertisement from Wilding's 1906 Directory of Shropshire.

This view looking northwards up the High Street in the early 1900s shows the cottages opposite the Congregational Church, and, on the right, Diamond Cottage and Ragleth House.

This group of cottages (right), nos 76 - 84 High Street, has changed little since the late nineteenth century. The nearest cottage (the corner one painted white) is the oldest. It was formerly two separate cottages built in the early 1600s and now called Thursdays Corner. The other three were built in the mid to late nineteenth century on the site of four cottages identified on the 1838 tithe map.

Brockhurst, 71 High Street

Renamed Somerhey about 1990 this house (left) was rebuilt on the site of an earlier property in the early 1890s by the noted Shrewsbury architect A E Lloyd Oswell for Mrs Anne Proffit who had retired from her grocery and confectionery shop in The Square (see page 57) and lived here until she died in 1902.

The next owner was Anne Proffit's widowed daughter Elizabeth Kenion who lived here until she died in 1930.

The house has been extended on several occasions since it was built.

Ragleth House, 73 High Street

This fine Georgian house, built about 1790, was originally set in its own grounds. These extended eastwards almost to the line of the present railway. The house has subsequently been altered and extended and the roof raised to provide further accommodation.
It has a fine front door but it is unlikely that the bay windows were part of the original structure. It has the honour of being mentioned favourably by Pevsner in 1958. It is possible that the stone base could be part of an earlier house.

For a time it was the home of George Corfield, a draper and grocer, and his wife Mary, formerly Mary Beddoes. They had seven daughters and five sons. Their son George owned Brooks Mill in the Carding Mill Valley from 1824 - 36.

About 1838 five of the daughters, Anne, Martha, Elizabeth, Susannah and Jane, established in Ragleth House a boarding school called *The Misses Corfield's Ladies' Academy* (they had previously lived and had their school at Spring Cottage in Burway Road). In 1841 the boarding school had 32 pupils aged between 7 and 14 but it had only 8 in the 1851 census. It is hard to imagine the cramped dormitory arrangements for this number of girls. The school closed about 1852 and in the 1861 census the sisters were described as 'retired governesses'. Four of these sisters remained as spinsters and lived to be a great age. Anne died at the age of 84, Martha aged 88 and blind, Elizabeth 68 and Jane 82.

For many years Ragleth House was the home of one of the Church Stretton medical practices. From about 1895 until he died in 1931 Captain George Higginson, an army doctor, lived and practiced here. He was followed by Dr Horace Gooch until he died in 1951 whereupon the practice was continued by his wife Winifred.

Throughout this period surgeries were held in the small stone building at the rear of the house (right). One room was the waiting room with benches around the walls, the other was the surgery.

The rear of Ragleth House (left) presents its best face with particularly attractive arched windows on the first floor.

The Coach House

Within the original curtilage was a large coach house belonging to Ragleth House (below) which has since been converted into residential accommodation. For a period before the Roman Catholic Church was built in 1929, it was used for services.

The Old Coach House.

95

The Congregational Church (now URC), High Street

The Congregational Church was built on the site of two cottages. Another cottage called Diamond Villa, to the right (above), was bought in 1947 and pulled down to provide space for a car park and a new church hall opened in 1957.

In 1858 people connected with Congregational churches in Shrewsbury, Ludlow and Dorrington decided to hold services in Church Stretton. At first these were held outdoors under the Market Hall. This was impractical in the winter so at the end of that year they used a room on the upper floor of a building which had once been a carpenter's shop, approached only by a narrow step ladder. It held between 70 and 80 people but many could not stand upright. The use of this room continued for several years.

On 14th February 1860 a Congregational Church in Church Stretton was formally formed under the auspices of the Castle Gates, Shrewsbury, church. Eventually the present site was bought for £295, the money being donated by Thomas Barnes, M.P.

There were at the time three cottages and a barn between Ragleth House and Tudor Cottage where Ann Gibbon lived. Two of these were pulled down to provide a site for the Church. The architect, Joseph Bratton of Birkenhead, produced the plans free of charge. He designed a west front which is a good example of the Gothic revival style. The building cost £1000, raised by voluntary contributions.

The Church was opened on 29th May 1866. The first permanent minister was Rev'd J McKiddie of Harmer Hill who held office until October 1870. He was followed from 31 March 1872 by Rev'd John Hamer from Bishop's Castle but by this time membership had declined to only eight and the church had considerable debts which took a long time to clear. Electric lighting was installed in the church in 1917.

The third cottage, Diamond Villa (or Cottage), formerly called Kinnoul Villa, adjacent to the Church, was pulled down to provide an entrance to the new church hall which was built in 1957. Refurbishment of the hall was carried out in 2007 to provide an entrance for physically handicapped people. Recently the original main door at the front of the church was made into a window and a new entrance opened on the south side again with access for the physically handicapped.

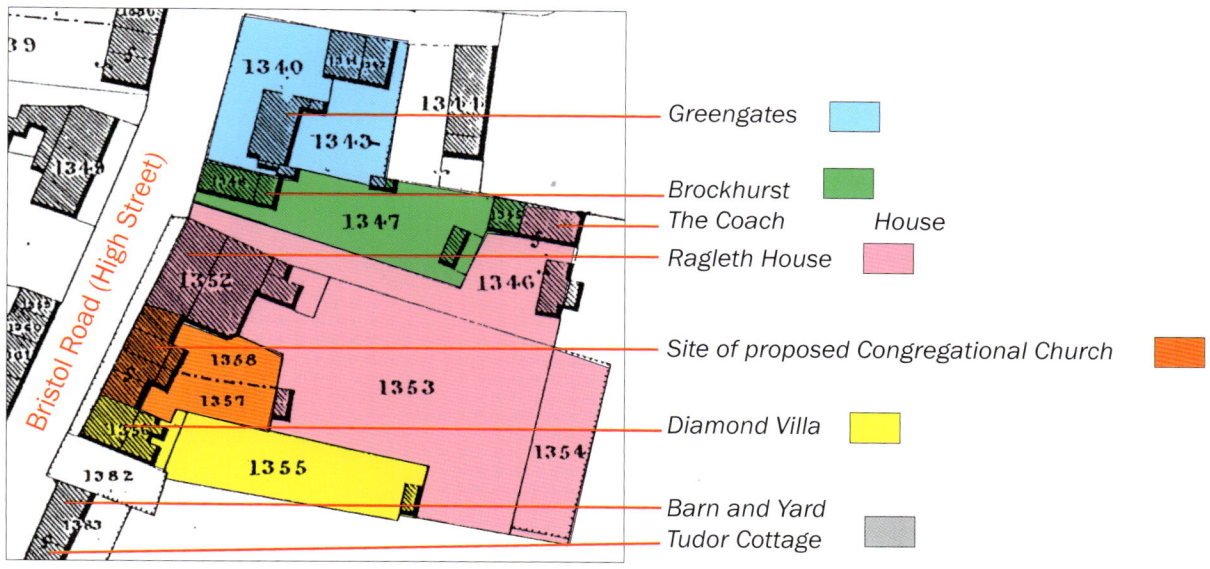

Part of the 1838 tithe map of the southern end of Bristol Road (High Street)

Greengates
Brockhurst
The Coach House
Ragleth House
Site of proposed Congregational Church
Diamond Villa
Barn and Yard
Tudor Cottage

View looking north up High Street in 1905. In the foreground is Tudor Cottage.

Tudor Cottage, 81 High Street

This 1881 watercolour of Tudor Cottage is by Worthington G Smith. [SA].   Below: As it is today.

Tudor Cottage is typical of the building style of the l6th or early 17th century. It was probably built soon after the great fire of 1593. The picture above shows part of the barn adjoining the left of the building which is also shown on the 1838 tithe map (page 97) but has since been removed. To the right the next door house has encroached upon land at the front and was occupied by William Jackson, a hostler working at the adjacent *Talbot Inn*.

It is not clear if Tudor House was built as one house and later divided or if it was built as two houses which were later joined. In 1838 the tithe map shows the building as two separate residences with John Pugh occupying the northern part and Ann Gibbon the southern. However after about 1850 residents occupied the whole property. Until the 1940s it was simply referred to as the 'Black and White Cottage'.

The timbers of the north wall reveal that the roof has been raised at some time. It is possible that this lower roof line is the remains of an even earlier building and that the south wing was a later addition. The front of the house is a particularly good example of the close studding and decorative framing typical of buildings of high status at the time. The rear of the house is simpler, with the timbers in square framing typically used for less visible parts. It is the best exposed half-timbered building in the town.

The rear of Tudor Cottage.

Originally the south wing extended further to the rear. This was probably removed in 1779, a date which appears on the end of what was originally an internal truss but which became the outer wall when one or two bays were dismantled. All that remains of this cross wing is at the front of the house.

On the front part of the cross wing is a hewn jetty, examples of which are relatively rare. The origin of the jettied construction of timber framed buildings is uncertain. The jetty or overhang is a feature of the 15th, l6th and early 17th centuries which may have evolved to provide extra space on upper floors, to provide protection from the rain for the lower floors or simply as a status symbol. In this building the lower part of the corner posts have been cut away to enable a jettied construction. Each post has a simple carved decoration. If an owner was willing to go to such lengths and pay for a carpenter to expend so much effort to produce this effect, then the idea of this kind of jetty as a status symbol is more likely in this case.

For a period around the 1910s Tudor Cottage was owned by the Stretton House Ltd. asylum though it is unlikely that any inmates lived there. It was probably used for staff accommodation and was sold in 1947 when the asylum closed.

The jettied construction at the front.

The Talbot Inn

Front view of the Talbot Inn complex. The main part of the inn is labelled (A), (B) is the tap room, larder and dairy, (C) is the new house. (D) is Tudor Cottage and is not part of the Inn. [David Bilbey]

The *Talbot Inn* was originally built as a farmhouse, though from at least 1724, when the innkeeper was Thomas Phillips, it was a hostelry. In 1758 it was recorded in the Manor Court roll that 'Thomas Blakeway and his wife Mary sold the house, together with a malthouse, garden, bowling green, stables and land which was formerly called Lower House that was then used as an inn called *The Talbot*'.

The old inn was rebuilt about the year 1820 as a large inn (A in sketch above) with the front of brick, the back of stone and with a slate roof. It had an entrance hall, four parlours, a bar, kitchen, brewhouse, washhouse, two pantries, two beer cellars, a wine cellar, a spirit cellar, coal house, poultry pens and yards with a pump of excellent spring water. On the first floor were a drawing room, six bedrooms and a store room. On the second floor were seven rooms, store rooms and closets.

Outside was extensive stabling with a five-stalled stable, two four-stalled stables, a large open stable for eight horses, a posting stable for eight horses and another for three horses. There were two double lock-up coach houses, one open coach house that could house four post-chaise, a barn with two large bays and one pig's cot. There was a newly fitted malthouse and a large granary.

On the north side of the property there was an excellent newly built tap room with a room above and also a new larder and dairy (B). Next to this was a newly erected timber framed house (C) with a pump, a yard and garden. This had replaced a cottage which fronted the road, occupied by William Jackson, a hostler, presumably to the inn. Each of these buildings was interconnected and attached to the *Talbot Inn* itself. Together with a ten acre field with timber, the value of the whole was assessed in 1826 as £3,630.

Until 1824 the *Crown Inn* had been the main posting house in Church Stretton run by John Broom and his wife. They retired and their son-in-law William Haverkam took over the posting business. About the same time Broom bought *The Talbot* and William Haverkam became innkeeper and postmaster.

In the mid 1830s the daily Royal Mail coach from Liverpool to Bristol stopped at the *Talbot Inn* in each direction as well as another coach running between Hereford and Shrewsbury.

By 1838 it had become the superior hostelry of the town and the principal coaching inn. It was where the coaches travelling between Shrewsbury, Ludlow and Hereford stopped to change horses and allow the passengers to take refreshment. It stood approximately mid-way between Shrewsbury and Ludlow, 15 miles from each, the sort of distance a team of horses could travel without rest.

In 1838 the *Talbot Inn* was owned by Ralph Benson though William Haverkam remained as the landlord. The 1841 census records Haverkam as employing a waiter, a boots, a chambermaid, a cook and a male servant. By contrast, the other inns in the town employed only one servant each.

Ralph Benson also owned *The Crown Inn* in Shrewsbury Road. During the 1840s the coaching trade generally went into decline with the advent of the railways. With the Shrewsbury to Hereford Railway due to open in 1852, only part of the *Talbot Inn* continued to function as an inn. By 1853 the coach trade had ceased and Benson closed and sold *The Talbot*. He later developed *The Hotel* on the *Crown Inn* site, closer to the railway station. The Post Office, too, moved nearer the centre of the town.

Part of the rear of the Talbot Inn. Tudor Cottage is the house on the right.

The *Talbot Inn* was soon to have a different use after Dr Samuel Glover Bakewell bought it in 1853. He converted the main house and its extensive ancillary buildings into the Stretton House Private Asylum for Gentlemen.

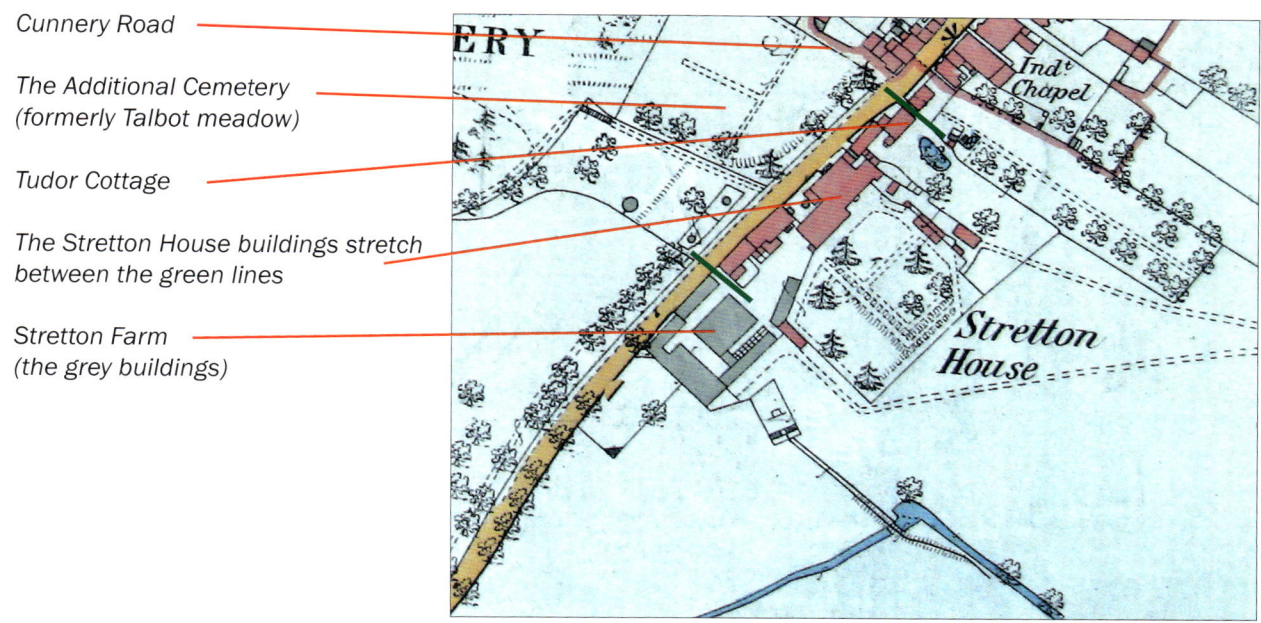

Cunnery Road

The Additional Cemetery (formerly Talbot meadow)

Tudor Cottage

The Stretton House buildings stretch between the green lines

Stretton Farm (the grey buildings)

Part of the 1883 25 inch OS map showing the Talbot Inn and other buildings being used by the Stretton House Asylum (see next page).

Stretton House, the Private Asylum for Gentlemen

Front view of Stretton House. Tudor Cottage is the building on the left and is not part of the asylum.
[David Bilbey]

Private asylums in England and Wales were first established in the seventeenth century and their numbers reached a peak in the nineteenth century. The asylum in Church Stretton was started in 1853 by Dr Samuel Glover Bakewell who was an enlightened practitioner in a profession which had, over the years, gained a very bad name and sometimes been referred to as 'the trade in lunacy'.

He adapted the former *Talbot Inn,* a place where coaches had stopped to change horses, a function which had ceased due to the coming of the railway to the town, and renamed it Stretton House. The asylum building, at the south end of the town, was described in brochures as an old fashioned, rambling and comfortable house used for 'the private care and treatment of upper and middle class gentlemen suffering from mental and nervous diseases'.

First class patients were provided with special accommodation and had their own servants and carriages. No mention was made of any provision for other classes of patients. There was a resident medical officer together with a number of nurses and attendants.

Initially, the asylum catered for sixteen patients but numbers steadily increased so that by 1868 there were 28 patients with ages ranging from 22 to 71.

After Bakewell's death in 1865, the lease was sold to William Hyslop who ran it until he died on 15th Dec 1883. The business seems to have prospered and he, too, enlarged the buildings to accommodate 30 more patients. Pleasant gardens were laid out and the adjacent Stretton Farm was acquired. Hyslop was widely known as a horse breeder and for the quality of his sheep and for a time he supplied mutton to the Queen. He kept a flock of 210 sheep, 16 cows and

Rear view

The garden and (bottom) the conservatory.

60 horses on his 60 acre farm. The farm stretched eastward towards Ragleth Hill and south to Brockhurst on both sides of the road and provided employment and therapy for the patients. The asylum was supplied from its garden and the farm.

Treatment included constant and congenial employment in the house, on the farm, in the gardens or in the workshops. Patients were encouraged to exercise in the spacious grounds. These included flower gardens, a summer house, an aviary, terraces, croquet and bowling greens, two tennis courts and a cricket field. Patients could also play golf, ride the horses and use the carriages. Indoor facilities included billiards, music and theatricals in the Barn Theatre building.

Lt. Col. William Campbell Hyslop.

On Sunday evenings Hyslop acted as spiritual shepherd to his human flock. On his death in 1883 the asylum was run by his son Lt. Col. William Campbell Hyslop (pictured previous page) until his death on the 7th April 1915.

In the 1890s Stretton House housed the town's fire engine, owned by The Alliance Insurance Company.

In 1924 new wards were built which increased the number of places to 100 but with the advent of the National Health Service in 1948 the Asylum closed. The building was then divided into flats but the house was demolished in 1976.

The site of Stretton House itself is now occupied by a small development of bungalows (1 - 7 Ludlow Road) and in the 1980s the Stretton Farm Road estate was built on the gardens and the farm.

An aerial view of the asylum.

Stretton Farm viewed from Woodcote, where Lt. Col. Campbell Hyslop lived. The Woodcote tennis courts can seen in the foreground. Ludlow Road separates the two properties.

The Barn Theatre

Although travelling comedians and strolling players periodically performed in the town, no permanent theatre existed until the Barn Theatre opened about 1905 in an outbuilding of the asylum, a former barn on the adjacent Stretton Farm. A theatre group called the Barn Owls was formed managed by the asylum's resident Medical Officer Dr Horatio Barnett. It was taken over by Church Stretton Entertainments Ltd. but this was liquidated in 1914 and the theatre closed as such around 1920. The barn was used for other purposes such as dances and the first films to be shown in the town.

Prior to this the barn had been used from about 1880 as a Working Men's Club and after the end of the First World War it became the local headquarters of the newly formed British Legion. It was also used in association with the common lodging house at World's End to give a night's shelter for any unemployed ex-servicemen who passed through the town.

In 1919, 1921 and 1922 films were shown in the Silvester Horne Institute whose management committee was concerned to prevent the building of a cinema and so retain influence over the choice of films shown in the town. After 1922 the Parish Hall was used for the showing of films and in 1937 the Regal Cinema opened in Sandford Avenue.

The Barn was taken down in 1933 after the new British Legion Club opened in Essex Road.

The cover of the programme for performances in May 1907.

The Barn Theatre.

Woodcote, Cunnery Road

Lt Colonel William Campbell Hyslop built and moved into Woodcote, a new house designed by Barry Parker and Raymond Unwin, in 1896. Pevsner describes it as a specially good house of the best period of Church Stretton. The house was regarded as a complete scheme of colouring and design in the Arts and Crafts style. It boasted central heating and hot and cold water in three bedrooms. The architects, who also designed the garden and furniture, were also responsible for the pair of staff houses opposite the drive entrance in Cunnery Road. They later draw up the master plan for Letchworth Garden City and Hampstead Garden Suburb.

The house was originally thatched.

The house has been considerably altered, for example with the removal of the first floor conservatory and other changes to the interior.

Some of the rooms with their original furnishings.

The architects also designed the pair of staff houses in Cunnery Road (left).

Cunnery Road and beyond

From Rectory Field a dry valley leads up to a small area of flat land between the *Longmynd Hotel* and Tiger Hall. This area together with the top of Rectory Field was called Upper and Lower Cunnery or Coneyborough. Cunnery is one of the many variants of the name for a rabbit warren. This area was part of the Rector's glebe land; artificial warrens were built here to encourage rabbits to live and breed in a place convenient for their capture and use in the Rectory kitchen.

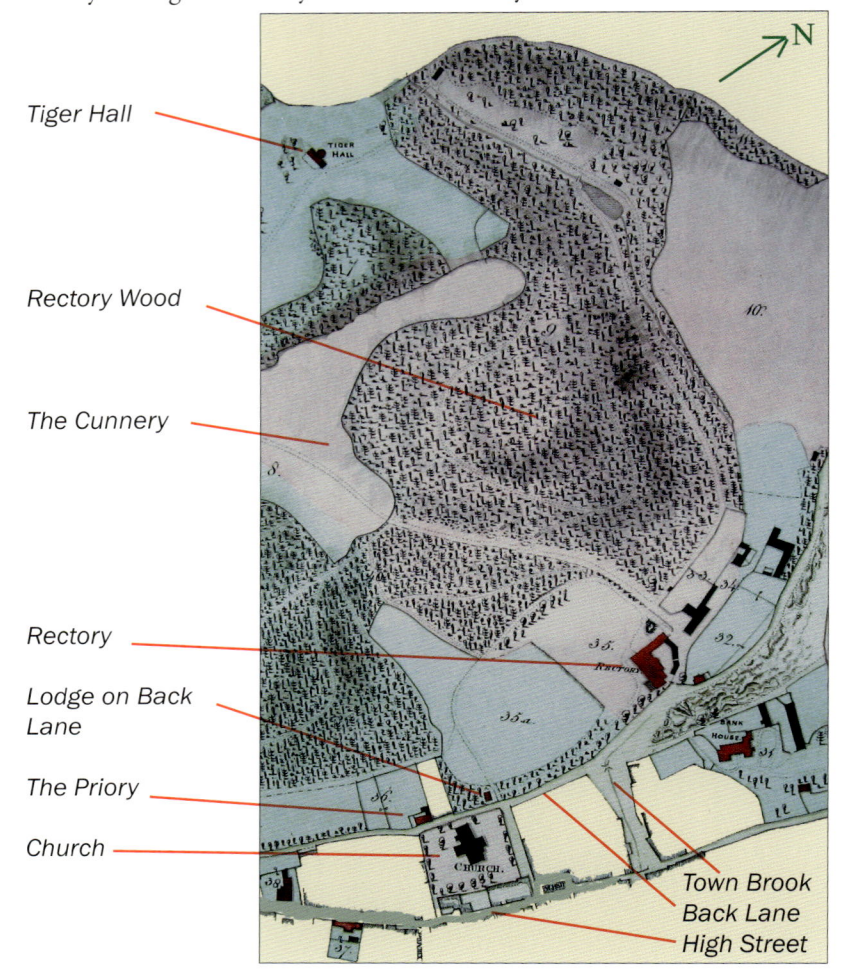

Robert Norgrave Pemberton, Rector from 1818 to 1848, had by 1833 bought from the Lord of the Manor, Mrs A Coleman, a considerable amount of land on the side of the Long Mynd between the town, World's End and beyond. Lodges were built on Ludlow Road (just beyond World's End) and by the Church.

Early maps show two driveways through the Cunnery and through Allen's Coppice which early Rectors had made. Cunnery Road was extended along these tracks about 1900 to allow access to the *Hydropathic Hotel* (later the *Longmynd Hotel*) built in 1901 and Tiger Hall.

1834 Map showing part of Pemberton's glebe (pink) and estate (green).

The Lodge on Ludlow Road

Pemberton built a carriage drive from the Rectory over the Cunnery through his new plantations down to the Ludlow Road just beyond World's End where he built a Lodge (right), presumably for his workers at the southern end of his estate.

This Lodge appears on Pemberton's estate map of 1834 as does that built opposite the Church at the entrance to Rectory Field.

Tiger Hall

The first record of Tiger Hall (named as such) is to be found on the map of Pemberton's glebe and estates made in 1834. In 1851 Thomas Lewis, a 61 year old agricultural labourer, lived there (ten years previously he had lived in a nearby cottage called The Hollys). Lewis was still at Tiger Hall in 1861 but by 1871 the new occupants were William and Sarah Davies together with their children. It was unoccupied in 1881 and was pulled down around the turn of the century. The present Tiger Hall was built about 1903. Quite why it is called Tiger Hall is a mystery.

The name Tiger Hall usually refers to the complex of three interlinking buildings of differing styles. The 1903 house, built in traditional style, kept the name Tiger Hall, whilst the large flat roofed edifice to the north (now divided into flats) is called Victoria Court. Between is a small red painted castellated building which was once the ballroom and is now a self contained house called Vermont.

The old derelict Tiger Hall about 1900. The tower was probably a folly and may have been built by the Rev'd John Mainwaring (Rector 1749 - 1807) who laid out Rectory Wood and was known to be an eccentric.

These buildings (left) are part of the Tiger Hall complex. The building on the right is Victoria Court. The pink castellated building called Vermont, was once the ballroom to the main house.

The house on the left is currently called Tiger Hall although that was once the name for the whole complex.

The Longmynd Hotel

The hotel was originally built with a tiled gabled roof.

This was built as *The Hydropathic Hotel* at a cost of £20,000 and opened on the 27th July 1901. It stands in its own grounds of about 9 acres. It was originally built in half timbered style with a fine large pitched roof containing two rows of dormer windows probably to fit into the landscape of the late Victorian housing developments. It was furnished by Heal's of London and offered tennis, billiards, croquet and golf. *The Hydro* made an auspicious start with 35 guests travelling in a special coach attached to the 2.40 pm train from Paddington.

In October 1901 a farcical position arose when the owner applied for a provisional licence. The police objected, saying that there were already ten inns within a ten minutes walk, despite the manager painting a heart rending picture of his plight if he had to send down to the town whenever a visitor required a drink with his meal.

An ambitious scheme to develop the town as a spa with water from a saline spring five miles away at Wentnor on the other side of the Long Mynd, piped to a pump room near an enlarged *Hotel,* came to nothing. As a result the *Hydropathic Hotel* was soon renamed *Longmynd Hotel!*

In the early 1920s the hotel was altered to the existing design by the removal of the pitched roof and dormer windows and their replacement with a flat roof.

In late 1940 St Dunstan's was moved from near Brighton to Church Stretton. The *Longmynd Hotel* was taken over and used for accommodation and Tiger Hall was used as a hospital for service personnel and civilians blinded during the war. (see page 190).

An advertisement from Church Stretton Illustrated, 1905.

The entrance to the Longmynd Hotel in 1954.

The rear terrace in 1920s.

111

World's End and the Gas Works

This view of World's End is taken from the slopes of Brockhurst before Woodcote was built in 1896. The two terraces of cottages still stand. The gas works is on the right hand side at the bend of the road, the view showing the gas holder with the retort house behind it. The manager's house is beyond the gas holder. The buildings beyond the corner belong to Stretton Asylum and its farm.

In the nineteenth century a group of nine cottages was clustered together on the west side of the turnpike road to Ludlow in an area that has long been called World's End. The road hugs the foot of the steep slope of the Long Mynd, above the marshy land which stretches across the valley. The cottages suffered by being somewhat distant from the town and tended to house a mainly transient population of labourers

One of the larger cottages housed the *Grapes Inn* which is first mentioned in 1851 when the landlord was Thomas Harley. About 1898 Martin Carter became the landlord but trade was on the decline and he worked also as a carpenter and fencer until he died in 1912. In his later years, he changed the name of the inn to *World's End Inn*. After his death it reverted to being a private residence.

Advertisement in Woolley's Guide, 1905

The Gas Works

The gas works on the east side of Ludlow Road at World's End were built in 1859 at a cost of £1000 raised by the sale of 200 shares of £5 each. The works were at first privately owned, including for a time by William Campbell Hyslop, owner of Stretton House.

The town was soon lit by gas. The first manager was James Manning who continued in that position until about 1875. As usage increased, the gas company expanded and eventually built a second and later a third gas holder on the opposite (western) side of the road. It later became a limited company but was nationalised in 1949.

After the works ceased production most of it was demolished but the gas holder was used for a time for the storage of gas, at first coal gas and then natural gas when it became available. Then, with the improved distribution of natural gas, the gasholder became redundant, was taken out of use and was eventually removed in October 1986.

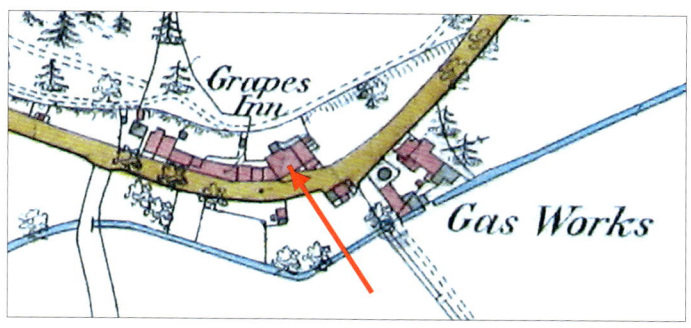

Part of the 1883 OS 25 inch map of World's End. The Grape's Inn is arrowed.

Demolition of the gas holder in 1986. [Roger Whitehead]

This photograph of World's End taken in the 1920s shows the new large gas holder on the west side of Ludlow Road. To its left is the Grapes Inn now with gabled windows on the upper floor. Woodcote can be seen on the hillside on the right with the Longmynd Hotel upper left.

113

Brockhurst School

The founder, Arthur Hazlehurst Atkinson M.A., was born in Calcutta in 1862, the son of William Atkinson who was Director of Public Instruction for Bengal. After graduating from Cambridge in 1893 he was appointed Assistant Master at Dulwich College in 1888 and was Head Master of the Junior School at Dover College from 1892 - 1901.

He built Brockhurst in 1901 and ran it as a preparatory school until he sold it to Reginald Philip Marshall M.A. about 1922. Marshall continued it as a preparatory school until the summer of 1942.

The former M.P. Julian Critchley (who went to the school in Autumn 1940) writes of it in his autobiography 'A bag of boiled sweets':

> The school was a gloomy red palatial Edwardian building set in a garden large enough for a cricket pitch. It smelt of sweat, stew, embrocation, fear and excrement.
>
> RP (R P Marshall) seemed as old as the hills. He was, at 62, tall, stooped, clean-shaven and hook-nosed with thin strands of fairish hair drawn tightly across his pink domed skull. He wore shapeless tweed suits. He had been an instructor at the Royal Naval College, Osborne. In his prime he won a reputation for running a 'tight ship'. By the early forties he had deteriorated physically and his temper was becoming alarming in the extreme.
>
> RP was a ferocious teacher of Latin in particular, inspiring so much fear that I never failed in my daily task of learning the conjunctions of verbs and the gender of nouns. We were also obliged to learn each Sunday's collect. God help those who were not

word perfect. Even away from the form room RP was a man to avoid. He was an evangelical Christian of the muscular type and a great 'swisher'.

The school was divided into four competing houses: the Trojans who were given yellow badges; the Greeks who were allocated green; the Spartans red and the Corinthians sported blue.

The food was rather good, although the weekly menu never varied and the day could be told by a glance at one's lunchtime plate."

Crichley also records that the school had an open air swimming pool:

... at the top of a slight rise in full, if distant view, of the windows of the Long Mynd Hotel across the valley. RP had believed in nude bathing but the weight of complaint from the peculiarly long sighted residents of the hotel had obliged him to kit us out with thongs.

Another old boy was R A (Rab) Butler (later Lord Butler), the politician.

In 1942 the school was bought by John Park and, in time for the Michaelmas term, moved to Broughton Hall, near Eccleshall, Staffs., keeping the name Brockhurst.

Brockhurst School dining room and (below) the chapel and one of the dormitories.

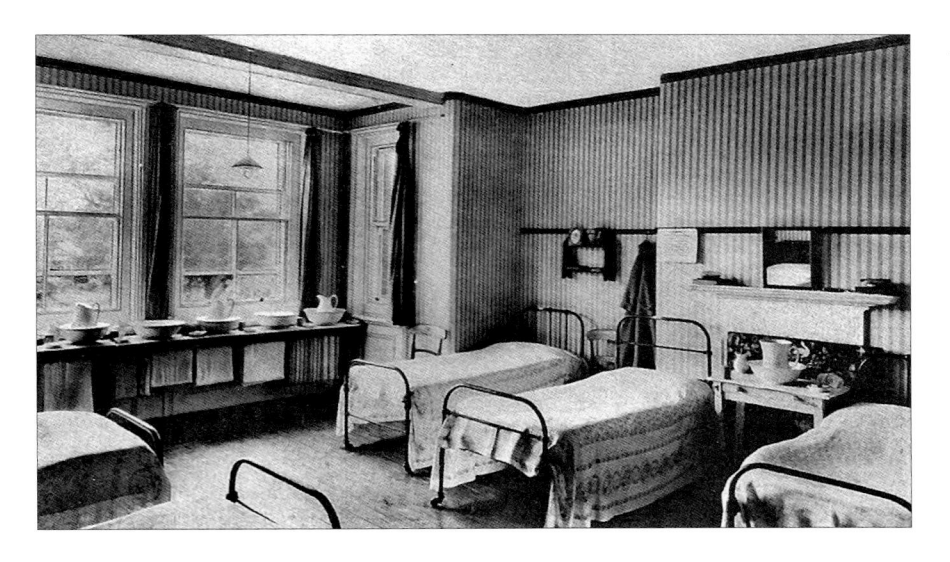

During the Second World War the Church Stretton building was taken over by St Dunstan's and was used until 1946 to provide accommodation for blinded servicemen. After their departure, the building was used as St Mary's Catholic Scholasticate by missionaries of the Company of Mary (Montfort Fathers) from 1946 to 1968.

The building has since been converted into apartments.

Les Trois and the Old Smithy, Church Street

Watercolour by Albert T Pile, early 20th century. The cottage on the right is Les Trois still recognisable today (photo below). Next to it is the Old Smithy with Park House in the distance. On the left can be seen the gables of the group of neo timber-framed houses built in 1886.

The medieval Back Lane provided a rear access to the original burgage plots to the west side of the High Street. There were only a few cottages in it, two of which still stand. A group of three has now been converted into a single residence called Les Trois. A nearby cottage, now called the Old Smithy, with it's adjacent smith's workshop was occupied by a Mr Edwards, a blacksmith, in 1838. There was another smithy in the 1860s and 70s at the corner with Cunnery Road where, in 1841, there had been a group of pig sties.

The terrace of houses called Wooddean was built about 1906 in what was the garden of Ashford House, High Street.

The Old Smithy cottage and workshop (left).

The Priory and other houses, Church Street

The Priory (right) was built in 1832 by the Rector, Robert Norgrave Pemberton. It was built on the site of an earlier house which had subsequently been divided into three dwellings. Could it be that the house is so named because the earlier building may have housed some monks or nuns?

In 1838 William and Rebecca Cadwallader were living here, but from about 1840 to at least 1863 it was occupied by Robert Hopwood, Pemberton's land agent or bailiff. Later, in 1898, The Priory was briefly a boarding house as were so many other houses in the town to cater for the many visitors to the area.

Next to The Priory is a pretty row of three cottages (pictured left), numbered 41, 43 and 45. No. 43 is named Shovel Hat Cottage. Apparently a board bearing the words 'The Shovel Hat', together with a picture of a man wearing such headgear, was found in the basement, suggesting that this may have been the site of a beerhouse or inn, albeit probably briefly. Nos. 43 and 45 (Secret Cottage) were originally one property.

This group of five neo timber-framed houses, originally called Priory Villas, was built by the Lord of the Manor, E B Coleman in 1886.

Church Street School

The school after the extension in 1893. The high windows were designed so that children should not be distracted by the outside world. Heating was provided by an open fire.

The First Schools

There was a schoolmaster in Church Stretton in 1589. Sir Rowland Hayward, who died in 1593, left £1 13s 4d a year towards his maintenance and the Rector added 20s a year in 1595 when the parish agreed to abolish the church ale. The first recorded schoolmaster was John Bowdler in 1674. Although Bonham Norton had been expected to build a school, the then master Edmund Cheese apparently taught school in the church. In 1716 the master, duly licensed, was teaching the catechism and taking his pupils to church. In 1720 Thomas Bridgman left the master 40s a year to teach four poor children to read. Eventually, in 1779, a school was built by subscription on roadside waste opposite the Hall lawn. That property is now known as Burway House (see page 22).

The Sunday School movement, which grew out of teaching the catechism on Sunday afternoons, spread very rapidly in the 1780s. In 1790 Edward Lloyd left £3 3s 0d to the trustees of the charity school who benefited from his will in other ways: half the interest on a funded gift of £100 was paid to the schoolmaster to augment his salary and half was applied towards financing two scholars aged 14 to undertake apprenticeships.

The Endowed Free School.

In 1861 the school building in Burway Road was replaced by a new building in Church Street. It was built on part of the estate left by the Rector, Rev'd Robert Norgrave Pemberton to his nephew Charles Orlando Childe Pemberton who gave the land for the new school.

The school was built in domestic Gothic style of red brick with white stone dressings. It was opened in January 1861 and cost £1000. There were three classrooms for 144 children and a 'spacious enclosed playground'. In addition, there was an adjacent school house with a garden for the schoolmaster.

The bell tower was used to call children to school. The bell would have been rung 10 or 15 minutes before the start of school.

The first schoolmaster here was Thomas Cureton and his wife Henrietta was schoolmistress. He continued in this position until about 1869 when he was appointed Registrar of Births and Deaths.

This school photograph was probably taken about 1890. The schoolmaster may be Samuel Dorrington who was appointed, with his wife Catharine, about 1865. He continued at the school until about 1892.

The school was extended in 1893 by adding a wing to provide an additional classroom. This cost £398 19s 2d and increased the accommodation to 220 pupils. The former school building in Burway Road was then sold for £119 2s 5d, the proceeds being used to help meet the cost of the new extension.

Gardening was taught from 1902 and domestic science was taught in the Silvester Horne Institute from 1918. From 1936, domestic science and woodwork classes were held in the Parish Hall and infant classes were held there from 1932 onwards.

After St Dunstan's left the town in 1946 the huts used by them in Essex Road continued in use for a time as the first secondary school until the new secondary school buildings were erected in Shrewsbury Road in 1961. The Junior pupils then moved from Church Street into the now vacant Essex Road huts until the new Primary school in Shrewsbury Road was completed in 1967.

This 1884 poster gives notice of the financial rewards for punctual attendance at school.

The Church Street school building became a Branch Library in 1968, at first using only the extension, with the rest of building left vacant. The Library moved into the renovated and altered main building in the early 1970s and the Information Centre opened in the extension soon afterwards.

Gardening was taught to the boys in the garden of the schoolmaster's house. Girls were taught how to sew a fine seam, to embroider and to darn.

A class in 1927.

Frederick J. Butler was schoolmaster for 33 years from 1892 and organist of St Laurence's Church for 55 years. He died in 1951 aged 85. This photograph was taken about 1900 and shows him with his wife Nellie. She was schoolmistress for nearly 20 years, dying in 1912 aged 46.

School House was built next to the school for the schoolmaster.

Miss Reynolds and her class.

121

The Parish Hall

Left: The old Parish Hall.

Below: The new Parish Centre was built in 1990.

The first Parish Hall was opened at Christmas 1913. It was extended in 1927 to provide extra rooms and cloakrooms. It provided the only alternative venue for social activities to the Silvester Horne Institute.

Rooms were leased to the Shropshire Education Authority for cookery and handiwork classes from 1936 and it was in that year that Church Street became one way for traffic because of worries about children's safety. The hall continued to be used by the school until 1961.

The Parish Hall, described by many as 'the worst looking building in the town' was replaced in 1990 by a new Parish Centre.

The Lodge in Back Lane

A lodge had long existed opposite the Church in Back Lane at the entrance to what is now Rectory Field. It was already there when a new drive was made, probably by the Rector Thomas Coleman in the 1810s, to run from the Rectory to the Church. The sweeping curve of the drive can still be traced across Rectory Field.

The occupants of the Lodge, at least since 1841, seemed to be retired former members of staff of the Rectory.

The Lodge was pulled down to make way for the first Parish Hall in 1913, though the gates to the drive still survive and were refurbished in 2010. (see also p 13).

Rectory Field

The path through the old lodge gates leads into Rectory Field. Once the private land of the Church (the Rectory Glebe), Rectory Field is now open to the public and is one of main tourist destinations in the town all the year round.

It is now owned and maintained by the Shropshire Council.

Shrewsbury Road

Proceeding north along Shrewsbury Road in 1838 from the corner with Lake Lane (now Sandford Avenue) there stood, on the corner, a malthouse, then the *Crown Inn* and then a farm. Just beyond the Ashbrook stream there was Ashbrook Farm and a few isolated cottages and houses.

The land shown in blue and in green on the map below on the north side of Lake Lane was owned by William Waring Belton. He put it up for sale by auction at the *Buck's Head Inn* in 1842 (see poster opposite).

The Malthouse.

In 1838 the malthouse on the corner (tithe map below, coloured green) was worked by John Belton, but when it was sold along with two small meadows four years later, John Craig was operating it. The malthouse was pulled down when *The Hotel* was built on this site in 1865 (see also pp 27 and 35).

On the corner there was a large stone with an iron ring in it. It was called 'the bullring'.

The *Crown Inn*

In 1838 John Faulkner was the landlord of the *Crown Inn*. He had outhouses, stables and a large

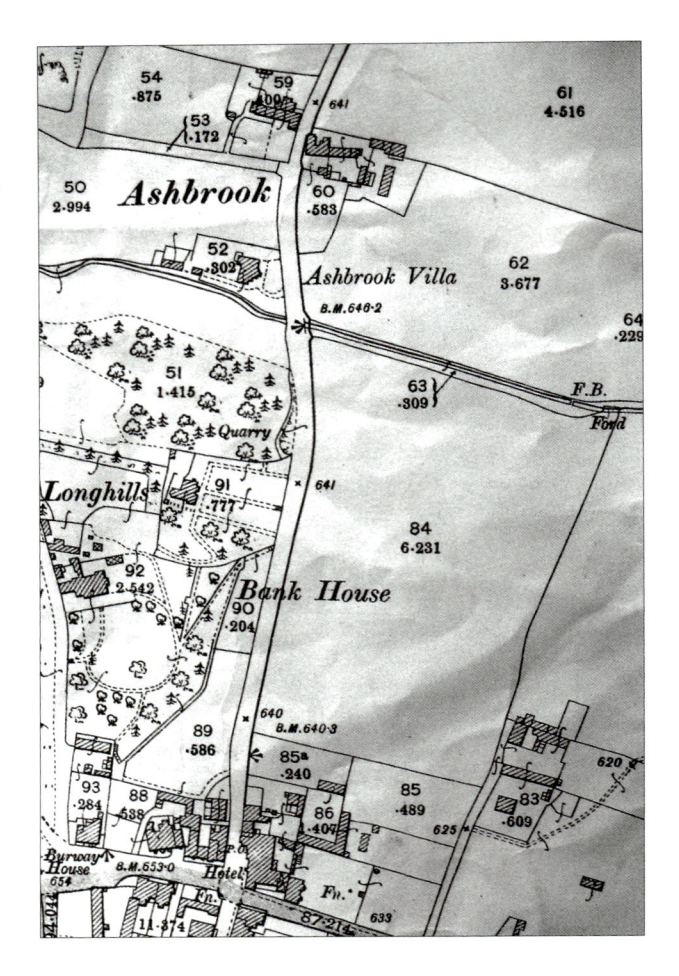

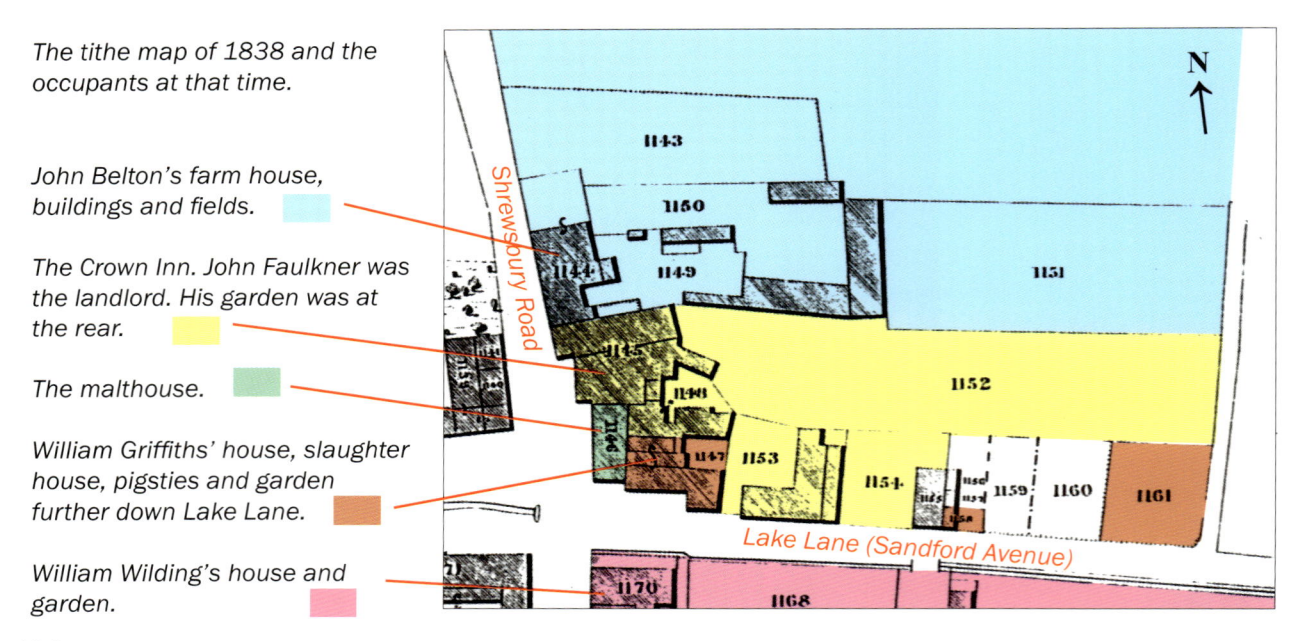

The tithe map of 1838 and the occupants at that time.

John Belton's farm house, buildings and fields.

The Crown Inn. John Faulkner was the landlord. His garden was at the rear.

The malthouse.

William Griffiths' house, slaughter house, pigsties and garden further down Lake Lane.

William Wilding's house and garden.

garden at the rear (tithe map, coloured yellow) which extended as far as a lane which is close to the route of the present Beaumont Road. The entrance to the inn stables and garden was from Lake Lane. At that time, Town Brook was still an open stream running down the south side of Lake Lane.

VALUABLE
COPYHOLD AND FREEHOLD ESTATE,
AT CHURCH STRETTON,
IN THE COUNTY OF SALOP,

COMPRISING A

MESSUAGE, MALTHOUSE, BUILDINGS,
GARDEN,
AND ABOUT

FIFTY-TWO ACRES OF EXCELLENT
MEADOW, PASTURE AND ARABLE LAND,
WITH A

THRIVING PLANTATION OF LARCH,
TO BE

SOLD BY AUCTION,

BY MESSRS. BROOME AND SON,

AT THE BUCK'S HEAD INN, IN CHURCH STRETTON,

On *Thursday*, the 28th day of *April*, 1842, at Three o'Clock in the Afternoon, in the following or such other Lots as may be agreed upon at the time of Sale, and subject to conditions then to be produced:

The Meadow Land is irrigated at pleasure, the Pasture Land excellent, the Arable Land in a high state of cultivation, and the whole is well worthy the attention of persons desirous of an eligible investment.

The Neighbourhood is good, and surrounded by the most picturesque scenery, and a Mail Coach passes to and fro daily.

The Land and Malthouse is in the occupation of Mr. JOHN CRAIG, and the House and Garden in the occupation of Mr. JOHN BELTON, on application to whom the Estate may be viewed.

Such part of the property as in the particulars is not distinguished as of Freehold Tenure, is Copyhold of Inheritance, but the fines and chief rents are very low, and no heriots are payable.

For any further information apply at the Offices of Messrs. KOUGH and SAXTON, Solicitors, Shrewsbury.

J. H. Leake, Letter-press and Lithographic Printer, Mardol, Shrewsbury.

Poster advertising the sale by auction of some of William Waring Belton's land.

The Farm next to the Crown Inn

In 1838 John Belton, as well as working the malthouse, occupied the farm next to the *Crown Inn* (coloured blue, page 124). The farm, once known as Bell's Messuage, extended as far as the Ashbrook stream to the north and to a track to the east serving an outfarm from Lake Lane. Belton's farm was described as a house with stack yard, fold, barn, two stables, two cow houses and a seven acre meadow.

The farm was sold in 1842 to Ralph Benson and rented to William Henry Bridgeman who farmed there until he went bankrupt in 1864. A very detailed inventory of his farm stock and house contents is shown in the poster opposite. Within a few years, Bridgeman become master of the Union Workhouse in Shrewsbury Road.

The Outfarm (Robinson's Buildings)

Far left: The front of no. 3 Crown Cottages faced north away from Lutwych Road.

Left: This was the more common view of the house.

The only slaughterhouse in Church Stretton until about 1860 was in Lake Lane adjacent to the malthouse at the corner with Shrewsbury Road. This was run by William Griffiths in 1838 and later by John Faulkner. Perhaps because of its proximity to the newly built *Hotel* which replaced the malthouse in 1865, the slaughterhouse was closed down and a new one built by George Robinson (who succeeded William Bridgeman at the farm next to *The Hotel*) in Shrewsbury Road.

The fortunes of *The Crown,* (later called *The Hotel*) were closely tied to that of the farm, the malthouse and the slaughterhouse. George Robinson provided post horses and carriages and supplied meat for *The Hotel*. As *The Hotel* grew over the years so did the demand for his butchery products. To satisfy this demand he built an outfarm consisting of the slaughterhouse, stables, barns and pigsties at the eastern end of his farm on Little Field.

In the 1880s he also built three cottages for *The Hotel's* catering and gardening staff which were later taken over by farm labourers. The cottages were at first called Slaughterhouse Cottages but were later renamed Crown Cottages. About 1905 Lutwyche Road was constructed. This bisected the cottages. Numbers 1 and 2 Crown Cottages still exist but no. 3 was knocked down in 2009 and replaced by public toilets and a private house.

George Robinson died in 1889 aged 79 and the main farm was then run by his sons Charles and John until it was pulled down in 1906 to make way for the extension to *The Hotel* along Shrewsbury Road. They continued with the outfarm and in 1921 Charles Robinson opened a butcher's shop at 3 High Street (see page 46).

Poster advertising the auction in 1864 of William Bridgeman's stock and household effects as a result of his bankruptcy.

Ashbrook Farm

Ashbrook Farm on Shrewsbury Road. The lane to Carding Mill Valley is in the left foreground. Watercolour by Emmanuel C Taylor, 1950. [Dorothy Beasley]

A cluster of cottages and a farm once stood where the Carding Mill Valley Road meets the Shrewsbury Road. The farm house had been extended on several occasions and there were extensive out-buildings.

In 1848 Benjamin Jones started a poultry and game business from his home at the Quarter Houses nearby. At some stage in the 1860s he moved to Ashbrook Farm from where he continued with his business. After his death in 1875 his wife Eliza continued running the farm until their son Fred took it over about 1900. A timber building facing Shrewsbury Road to the right of the farmhouse (above) was used as a shop and the range of farm products for sale was extended to include fish, game and fruit. For five years between 1905 - 1910 Fred's wife Agnes operated a hand laundry from premises in Carding Mill Valley, making use of the clean water of the Ashbrook.

Three generations of the Jones' family farmed at Ashbrook continuing into the 1940s with Fred and Agnes' son Frederick Gordon Jones running the farm. Frederick also operated a milk round using milk from the farm. Eventually the farm buildings fell into disrepair. The whole farm was sold and pulled down in 1985 to make way for the Ashbrook Court and Churchill Road housing developments.

There was a particularly good example of a bread oven in the kitchen. The walls of it were so thick that they could retain heat for long periods. Next to it

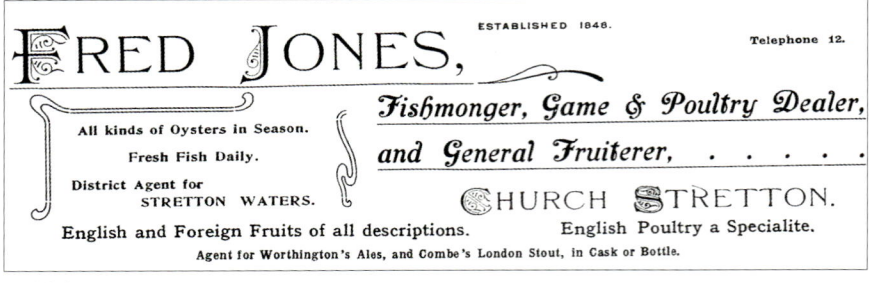

A 1905 advertisement.

was a boiler, or set pot, which had a grate underneath to heat the water in the boiler.

The farm had a horse-driven jenny or gin wheel. This consisted of an iron frame with a spindle running below ground to some gears. From the top of these gears there was a long pole to which the horse was harnessed. As the horse walked around in a circle it turned the spindle. Inside a nearby building was a long shaft with different sized wheels. Wide canvas belts were put onto the wheels to drive whatever piece of machinery was needed. The gin, together with many old implements and equipment from the farm, was donated to the Acton Scott Farm Museum where they can now be seen.

The bread oven and set pot. [David Bilbey]

The Ashbrook Farm horse gin now installed at Acton Scott Farm Museum. [Lion TV]

Hand painted glass panel, measuring 33 x 13 inches, made by Thomas J Thompson to be placed in a window probably in the farm shop to advertise Agnes Jones's laundry.
[Lesley Forbes]

Ashbrook Villa

The period 1890 to 1910 was a time when many very small private schools or academies were founded in Church Stretton. One such was run by Mrs Eliza Jones at Ashbrook Villa on the west side of Shrewsbury Road by the Ashbrook stream. This had two girls, aged 8 and 13 years, living in as boarders in 1881 together with an unknown number of day pupils. This school lasted longer than some and was in existence from 1885 to 1906.

With the rapid increase in tourism in the 1900s it became more profitable to operate Ashbrook Villa as holiday accommodation and the premises were so used until the First World War.

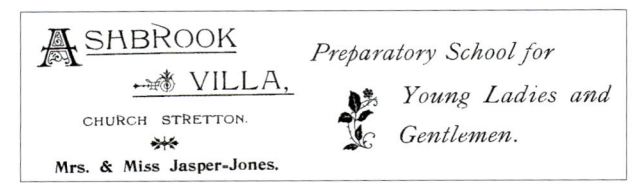

Above: 1905 Advertisement for the school.

Right: Ashbrook Villa.

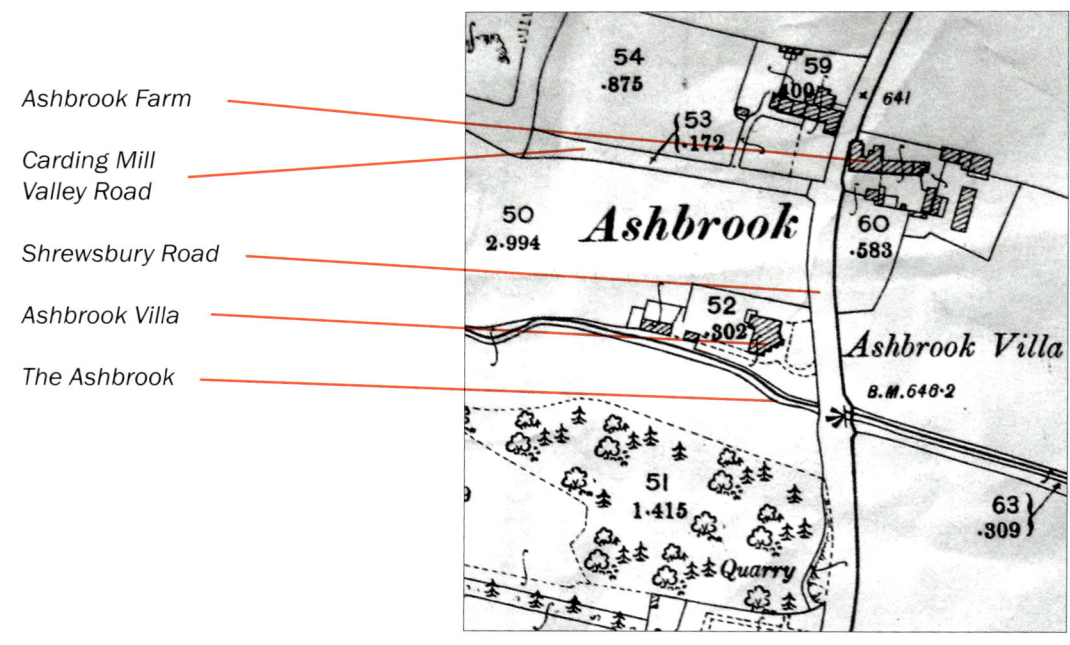

Ashbrook Farm

Carding Mill Valley Road

Shrewsbury Road

Ashbrook Villa

The Ashbrook

Part of the 1883 OS 25 inch map.

130

Denehurst Hotel

Built about 1900 the *Denehurst Hotel* may have been built as a pair of semi detached houses for private residence. However by 1901 it had become a 'boarding house and pension' complete with croquet and lawn tennis courts owned by Mrs Elizabeth Jones. It was one of three hotels opened about that time, the others being the *Hydropathic* (now the *Long Mynd*) *Hotel* and the *Sandford Hotel*, presumably to cope with an increasing number of visitors to the town. It was taken over by St Dunstan's during World War II when huts for additional accommodation were built at the rear. It was demolished during January and February 2002 following an auction sale of its contents and Denehurst Court, a development of retirement apartments, was then built on the site.

The Quarter and the Halfway Houses

Opposite the *Denehurst Hotel* were the Workhouse and the Quarter Houses which consisted of three small cottages. In 1881 Marc Donelly, a pointsman at the railway station, lived in one and his eldest son, aged 13, was a railway labourer. Richard Owen, a porter, lived in the second. He had spent part of his life abroad, his wife having been born in Halifax, Nova Scotia. One of his children was born in Madras and two others in Burma. It seems possible that he may have served in the army. A Police Constable lodged with George Millichope, a joiner, in the third cottage.

Just beyond *Denehurst Hotel* was the Police Station which had been built about 1840. Thomas Caswell was the Superintendant. George Windsor wrote at the time '*we are happily favoured here in having as our superintendant of police a gentleman much respected*'.

The Halfway Houses, now known also as Spring Bank, are situated further along Shrewsbury Road just before the mineral water works. Here were three homesteads, the first occupied by Miriam Karaton, an annuitant, the second by Charlotte Howells, a retired farmer and the third by James Mundy, a general labourer.

The Union Workhouse

The Poor Law Amendment Act of 1834 required parishes to provide indoor relief only for the poor at a level that was 'inferior to the standard of living that a labourer could obtain without assistance'. There were to be no shirkers seeking easy existence at the ratepayers' (i.e. the land and property owners') expense! Poverty was to be made painful; there were to be no incentives for idleness - those at the lower end of the income scale would be disciplined.

The workhouse was the common fate of orphans and destitute people who were nonetheless prepared to endure bitterly cold weather or near starvation before they would apply for admission into the dreaded institution. Normally husbands and wives and their children were separated from each other and even if, by chance, they happened to eat at nearby tables in the dining hall, any communication was forbidden. Meals consisted of gruel or broth and dry bread or potatoes. Once inside, the pauper was allowed to see visiting relatives only in the presence of the master or matron. Imbeciles, consumptives, syphilitics, expectant mothers and respectable souls driven there by starvation were indiscriminately lodged in bare cold wards.

Workhouses were also places where people who had no fixed abode and walked from town to town could stay for the night. If they had money and could pay for their food and bed for the night they were welcomed. If they had no money they were still given food and a bed but they had to do some work next morning. For the women this meant being in the laundry to wash sheets and bedding.

The men were put into little cells with no windows. On the floor of the cell would be a pile of stones and a hammer. To pay for their night's lodging they had to break the stones into smaller pieces that would pass through the holes in a steel plate. When they had completed this task they were free to go. It seems hard but in many cases they preferred to do that work because they hid any money that they had before they went into the workhouse so that they still had some after they came out.

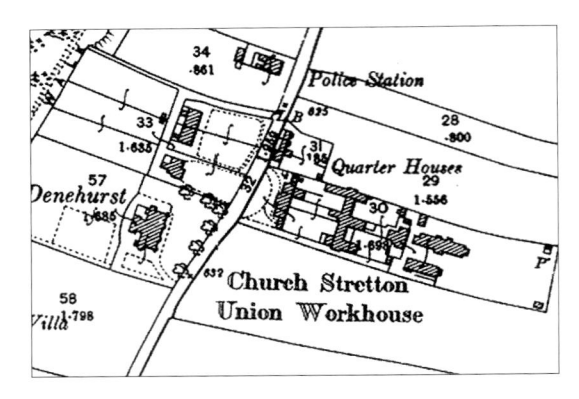

The Church Stretton Union Workhouse

To administer the Poor Law parishes were grouped into Unions. Church Stretton was the centre for a Union of 15 parishes. The workhouse was built of stone in 1838 on a field called Little Ashbrook on the Shrewsbury Turnpike road, where the Primary School now stands. It was set back from the road and had a curved approach drive to the narrow end of the buildings which were in the shape of a cross, with four wings. These, with the outer wall, formed four quadrangles. Each wing radiated from the central administrative area from where the inmates could be easily supervised. This was similar in design to the prisons of the day. The building could accommodate 120 inmates.

A drawing of the Workhouse. [David Bilbey]

Each wing housed a separate category of inmate - men, women, boys and girls, who were not allowed to meet. Each category exercised in its own yard.

Part of the workhouse just prior to demolition. [English Heritage, NMR]

Samuel Bagshaw's *History, Gazetteer and Directory of Shropshire*, 1851 described the workhouse as ' ... *in the immediate vicinity of the Longmynd Hills. The situation is remarkably dry and salubrious, and the building is admirably contrived for the convenience and comfort of the inmates.*'

The staff comprised the Master and Matron (usually man and wife) and a Schoolmistress. The first Master was John Broughall with his wife Ann as Matron. The three small stone cottages near the main entrance, traditionally called the Quarter Houses, were occupied by Institution staff until, like the work house, they were demolished to make way for the new school complex.

Over the years the number of children remained fairly constant at about half of all the inmates; women over 14 were the next largest group at 21%, including a high proportion of unmarried mothers. The percentage of old people shows a steady rise from 13% in 1841 to 30% in 1881.

The 1881 census revealed that there were 72 permanent inmates and that 12 vagrants slept there on the night it was recorded. Of the permanent residents 21 were men over the age of 63 whilst the oldest lady was 59. Seven unmarried mothers had a total offspring of twelve out of the 34 children under 13 years of age.

Children were taught by the resident Schoolmistress until 1894 after which they attended the school in Church Street.

Poor Charlotte Yapp of Wistanstow, deaf and dumb from birth, was 11 when she was admitted to the Poor House at 58/60 High Street. She was transferred to the Workhouse when it opened and was a resident there until she died aged 91 in 1917, having spent 80 years in institutions.

The workhouse was closed in 1930 after which the County Council used part of the premises as a children's home and an infirmary for mentally ill patients. The building was eventually demolished in 1959/60 to make way for the Primary School. Part of the Infirmary building was incorporated in the swimming baths as the entrance building.

All that remains of the Workhouse today. It houses the changing rooms for the swimming pool and is now incorporated into the Sports and Leisure Centre.

St Lawrence Church of England Primary School

The school from the rear, 1968.

When the Secondary School moved out of the former St Dunstan's huts in Essex Road to the Shrewsbury Road School premises in 1961 (see page 119), the 8 - 11 year olds moved from the Church Street school into the huts. The 5 - 7 year olds, who until then had occupied several rooms in the Parish Hall and one in the Silvester Horne Institute for a number of years, then moved into the vacant Church Street school premises. They stayed there until seven years later a new Primary School was built on the site of the old Workhouse, next to the Secondary School. The new School was formerly opened on 7th May 1968 by the Bishop of Hereford, Rt Rev'd Mark Allin Hodson.

Part of the former workhouse buildings sited behind the school was adapted to form the entrance and changing rooms to a new swimming pool. This was provided in two stages by public fund-raising in the late 1960s and early 1970s. The first stage to be built was an open air pool; a second round of fund raising produced enough to roof it. It is now part of the Sports and Leisure Centre built in 2010.

After the Opening Ceremony. From the left: Lt. Col. A P Sykes (Chairman, Education Committee), 10 year old Kevin Tranter who read the lesson, Ron Morris (Headmaster), The Bishop of Hereford (Rt Rev'd Mark Allin Hodson) and the Rector (Rev'd William Wilson).

The Bishop speaking at the School opening.

Below: Class rooms, 1968.

[Shropshire Star]

Bottled Water Companies

Church Stretton was never a spa because there was no spa water, only a supply of pure spring water. A guide book of 1895 stated:

Church Stretton has achieved considerable notoriety for the unrivalled excellence of its water supply and the marvellous purity of its water which is possibly the finest and purest drinking water available.

This water was exploited by two companies:

The Church Stretton Aerated Water Company

This was the first mineral water company to start operating in Church Stretton. It started in business in 1881 in part of the old Carding Mill building in Carding Mill Valley, drawing water from the nearby Long Mynd Spring. The company sold soda, seltzer, lithia and potassium waters, ginger ale and lemonade. It seemed to have ceased trading by 1906.

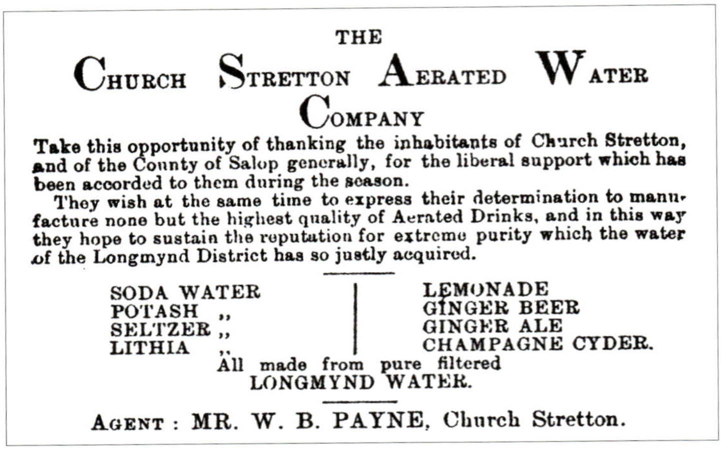

An 1881 advertisement in the Church Stretton Times.

Two rare ginger beer bottles from the Church Stretton Aerated Water Company.
[Stretton Hills Mineral Water Co. Ltd.]

The Stretton Hills Mineral Water Company

This is located in Shrewsbury Road. It was the larger of the two companies. It was opened in 1883, in a purpose built factory using the Cound Dale spring. The 1901 OS map refers to it for the first time as Cwm Dale. Perhaps the change in name was at the instigation of the mineral water company who thought it a more prestigious one.

The Company was described in 1893 as '*manufacturing every description of mineral and aerated waters, including soda water, potassium water, seltzer water, lithian water, Vichy water, quinine water, lemonade, ginger beer, ginger ale, lime fruit, juice champagne, original barm ginger beer, and puts Cwm Dale Spring pure water into pint or quart bottles*'.

During the 1880s and 1890s all advertisements emphasised the purity of this water which together with pure air were specially recommended for curing or alleviating many ailments: neuresthenia, influenza, sleeplessness, delicate children, amnesia, general debility, weak digestion, catarrh, obesity, etc.

Francis Sutton, FCS, FIC, an eminent analytical chemist of the time, expressed approval of the quality of the Cwm Dale Spring water. His comments were recorded on a stone tablet incorporated into the front wall of the works (below).

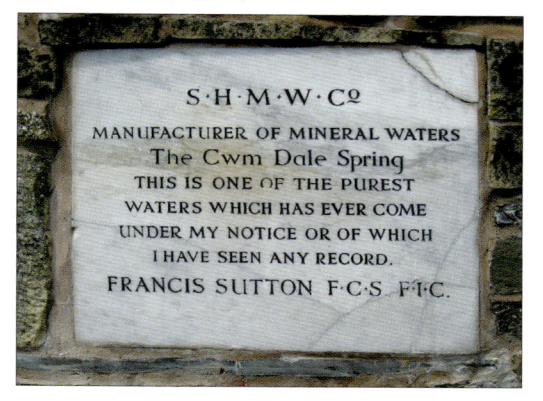

Bottle label showing the 'mountainous' Stretton Hills!

The Company was eventually acquired by Jewsbury & Brown Ltd., then by Schweppes, then by Wells Drinks Ltd. In 2003 it was owned by Well, Well, Well (U.K.) Ltd. The following year, it was taken over by Princes Soft Drinks.

In 2000 the older parts of the works were demolished and replaced with a modern industrial building which allowed production to be increased and the plant to meet modern hygiene requirements. The shape of the original frontage, shown in the illustration opposite, has been kept in the design of the new buildings.

Above: The glass bottle dates from the 1890s.

Henry Reddin was a wine and spirit merchant in Church Stretton from 1888 to 1905 and had his own ginger beer stoneware bottles personally transfer labelled.

Jewsbury & Brown owned the company from about 1926. [Stretton Hills Mineral Water Co. Ltd.]

Left: An advertisement about 1922.

At first the Company used water from the spring behind the factory, stored in a large underground settling tank built of white glazed brick holding about 70,000 gallons. The water was piped directly into the plant under gravity, any excess feeding the tap in the wall at the roadside. This source of water is no longer used. However in 1985 Cwm Dale Spring water was approved as a distinct and registered brand. To celebrate this recognition a gazebo was bought from Italy (right) and erected over the tank. This was opened in 1986 accompanied by a celebration tree planting by Percy Thrower.

To supply increasing demand for Stretton's bottled water it is now pumped from the aquifer in the Stretton valley. The company supplies water to several retailers. So that each brand can claim to have a unique water source with a distinct mineral analysis, the water is pumped from four separate bore holes located in the fields opposite.

The reputation of Cwm Dale water grew and it was widely exported. Jewsbury and Brown Ltd held Royal Warrants of Appointment to Queen Victoria, Edward VIII, George V and the late Queen Mother. To celebrate Coronation Year, 1953, the Queen Mother allowed a portrait of herself by David Jagger to be used in an advertising campaign (below).

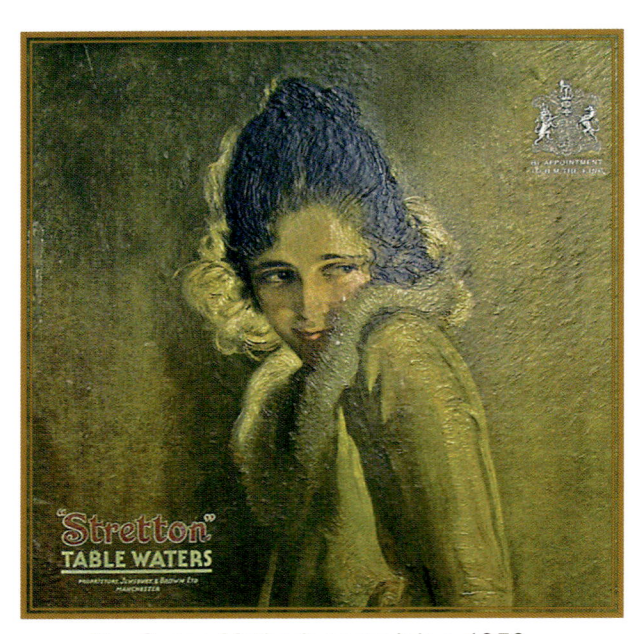

The Queen Mother's portrait in a 1953 advertisement. [Paul Miller]

Advertising plaque and metal tray. [Lesley Forbes]

The Town Water Supply and Reservoirs

A ready supply of fresh water from the Long Mynd down Town Brook Hollow and the Carding Mill Valley was probably a major factor in bringing the first settlers to the area. Later, as the settlement grew in size, wells would have been sunk to provide water to individual houses or groups of dwellings.

The Town Brook Hollow Reservoir

The first reservoir was in Town Brook Hollow.

To provide a more satisfactory water supply the Church Stretton Water Company was formed in 1857. It constructed the first reservoir in Town Brook Hollow in 1865 from which a piped water supply went to the town. Its capacity was small (about 150,000 gallons). The cost, £800, was met by the issue of 160 shares at £5 each.

By the end of the 19th century, as the town grew in size, this water supply became inadequate. So, in 1899, the Church Stretton Water Act established another water company, the Church Stretton Waterworks Company, with a capital of £20,000 raised by issuing 2,000 shares at £10 each and £5,000 of 4% debenture stock. This purchased the original Church Stretton Water Company and the separate Little Stretton Waterworks Company. It became responsible for the water supply to the three Strettons.

New Pool Hollow Reservoir

In 1901/2 this company replaced the Town Brook Hollow reservoir by a new reservoir in New Pool Hollow in the Carding Mill Valley. This had a much larger capacity of about 14 million gallons.

The reservoir contained water gathered from other side valleys further up the Carding Mill Valley, especially the Light Spout Hollow. Where this meets the main stream, an intake tank was installed from which water was piped around the hillside into the reservoir. Some of these pipes from the Light Spout Hollow can still be seen projecting above ground.

The Company installed measuring gauges at various points to ensure a minimum flow of water in the Carding Mill stream of 62,500 gallons every 24 hours. The remains of such a gauge can be seen about 30m. above the top car park and a second gauge is in the Light Spout Hollow about 50m. above its confluence with the main stream. Presumably if this showed a flow of at least 62,500 gallons per day then all the water in the New Pool Hollow reservoir could be retained.

From a height of approximately 1,000 feet above sea level, the supply of water from the reservoir would reach most of the properties in the town at that time by gravity.

This water company was aquired by the Church Stretton Urban District Council in 1912 under the Church Stretton UDC Water Act of that year.

New Pool Hollow Reservoir.

Severn Trent Water Company

In 1964 the water supply was taken over by the West Shropshire Water Board which became part of the Severn Trent Water Board and from 1990 part of the Severn Trent Water Company.

In post war years, due to the expansion of the town up the hillsides, supplies to the eastern part of the town were supplemented by water pumped from a borehole in Easthope Road. The pump did not run all the time, so the supply was spasmodic. As a result, under the building regulations of that time, houses built above a certain height had to be provided with storage tanks in the roof from which the house was supplied.

The water from the New Pool Hollow reservoir was piped direct to the houses without treatment. In the light of increased standards of purity, it was subject to analysis in the 1970s. It was found to contain biological and mineral pollutants and was declared unsafe to drink without further treatment. In 1976 over 75 people were found swimming in the reservoir during a hot spell. This hastened further the closure of the reservoir.

About that time, the water board was installing a piped water supply from Shrewsbury to villages along the A49. The original scheme terminated at Longnor. Rather than build a local purification plant in Church Stretton to treat the water from the New Pool Hollow reservoir, the Board decided it would be cheaper to extend this scheme and bring a piped water supply from the treatment works on the River Severn at Shelton, Shrewsbury, to an underground reservoir to be built into Helmeth Hill. This was completed in 1979.

This now not only supplies Church Stretton but water is pumped from this reservoir into storage tanks on the eastern side of Helmeth Hill from which the villages on that side of the hill are supplied by gravity.

For a while, both the New Pool Hollow reservoir and the new piped water supplied the town but the use of the old reservoir and the borehole was soon discontinued. Since then, to minimize maintenance costs, the height of the dam in New Pool Hollow has been substantially reduced. The reservoir is now owned by the National Trust.

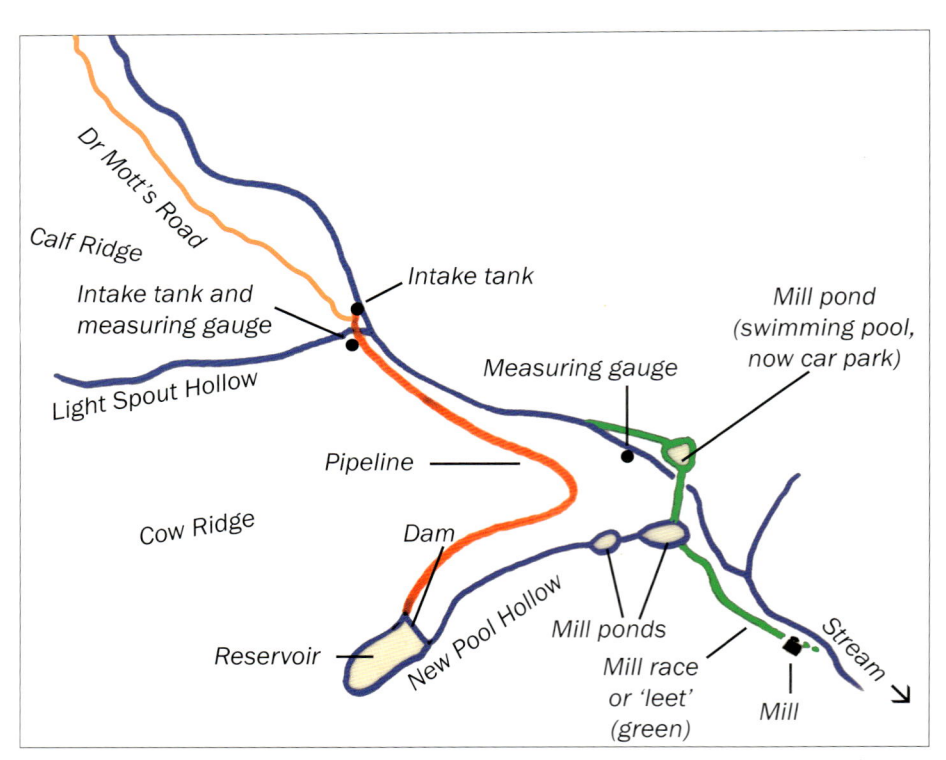

The remains of one of the measuring gauges in Carding Mill Valley.

Sketch map showing the water gathering arrangements for the Mill in the Carding Mill Valley.

Industry in the Carding Mill Valley

The Mill

Domesday Book (1086) records that there was a mill at Stretton. It is mentioned again in manorial records in 1309. It is almost certain that this was in the Carding Mill Valley and was probably a water mill for grinding corn powered by the valley stream. In 1563 the lord of the manor is recorded as selling a mill on Nash Brook to Francis Brooke who soon afterwards rebuilt it. This is likely to have been the same mill as the 'Stretton's Mill' referred to in the manorial records of the 1680s and 1690s when it worked in conjunction with a forge. The mill had belonged to the lord of the manor for nearly four centuries. It was probably approached via the track which runs down to Carding Mill Valley from Burway Gate (at the top of Burway Road).

Brooks Mill, as it was called, was an old thatched building and occupied the site on which the subsequent mill building stood. This old building, then used as a corn mill, and an old cottage were the only buildings in the valley until the mill was demolished about 1812.

A substantial new three storey mill was then erected on the site by the Rev'd George Watkin Marsh, Rector of Hope Bowdler. This was originally intended as a corn mill but as there was a carding mill (Dagers mill, later Dudgeley mill) at All Stretton, the functions of the two buildings were exchanged and the new mill in the valley became a carding mill.

The mill and mill wheel prior to demolition about 1912.

The mill stood at an angle of about 30° to the valley road and had a 16ft diameter water wheel situated at the south end of the building. The wheel was powered by water brought by leets (channels) from a series of mill pools higher up the valley. Some of these pools can still be seen and the largest was on the site of the upper car park (see map opposite).

The original function of the mill was to card wool, i.e. combing out the fibres of a fleece so that the wool can more easily be spun. It was then spun into yarn on spinning wheels by women in their own homes.

The first tenant of the mill was a Lancashire man, Ashworth Pilkington, but he was not successful and the Rev'd Marsh then worked the mill himself with the aid of his brother in law, a Mr Booth, who was a retired naval officer. He lived in two rooms in the basement, sleeping in a hammock.

The building at the right of this photo is the mill. The large building in the centre is that built by George Corfield in 1824 to house the spinning jennies and looms. It is now converted into flats.

About 1824 George Corfield of Little Stretton bought the mill. He also bought a piece of land alongside the existing mill, built a large new building facing the brook and installed hand looms and spinning jennies on the upper two floors in an open space 60 ft x 24 ft to produce cloth. The ground floor was fitted out as four cottages for employees. This is the present large three storey building facing the stream, since converted to flats.

Exactly how the mill machinery was driven using the power from the waterwheel is not known but it is possible that the two buildings were connected by an overhead shaft with belts transferring the power to the machines in the new premises.

For a number of years George Corfield, whose sisters ran the boarding school at Ragleth House (page 94), made a success of the business. However the size of the enterprise was small and eventually, due to competition from the mechanised mills in the North of England and the commercial depression of the 1830s, it failed. George Corfield died in 1837.

RICHARD WILLIAMS,

Refreshment Rooms Keeper

AND

WOOLLEN MANUFACTURER.

CARDING MILLS.

CHURCH STRETTON.

Above: An advertisement in 1888.

Below: Poster for the auction of the mill properties in 1870.

CHURCH STRETTON,
SALOP.

PARTICULARS OF VALUABLE

FREEHOLD PROPERTY

TO BE SOLD BY AUCTION,

BY

MR. EDWARD HEIGHWAY,

AT THE

Hotel, Church Stretton,

ON TUESDAY, THE 29TH DAY OF NOVEMBER, 1870,

At THREE o'Clock in the Afternoon precisely, and subject to Conditions of Sale to be then produced,

All that Substantially-built

WOOLLEN FACTORY

AND CARDING MILL,

WITH

DYE-HOUSE, WALK-MILL & DRYING FRAMES, WORKSHOP, WORKMEN'S COTTAGES, MANAGER'S RESIDENCE and GARDEN,

MEADOW & PASTURE LANDS,

Containing in the whole 7a. 1r. 37p. (more or less) situate in the MILL GLEN, about half-a-mile from Church Stretton.

Mr. Williams, the Tenant, will shew the Property, and for lithographed plans and particulars, apply to the Auctioneer, All Stretton, Salop, or to Mr. Marston, Solicitor, Ludlow.

Several other attempts were made to continue weaving but without any long term commercial success. In 1841 the mill employed ten males and two females, including two wool pickers, a sorter, two yarn stubbers, a carding engine feeder, two spinners and two flannel weavers. By 1851, in the hands of Messrs Duppa and Banks, the labour force had grown to 19.

In 1854 James Williams, who had been the manager for George Corfield, became tenant of the mill but also lost money and employed only seven workers in 1861. The scale of the business declined further and after James Williams' death in 1866 the business was carried on by his son Richard, manufacturing tweed cloth, blankets, rugs and woollen yarn with only six employees recorded in the 1871 census.

Richard Williams tried to sell the mill and the factory in 1870 (see poster) but it seems that there was no buyer. However his fortunes improved and by the 1890s he was advertising tweed and blankets and offering to provide cloth to farmers in exchange for wool. He continued to work the mill on a small scale until about 1905.

An early 1920s postcard showing the warehouse and factory converted into a hotel and café. The adjoining house, much altered, was the mill manager's house. The bungalow at the back was built on the site of the mill.

Between 1881 and about 1906 the Church Stretton Aerated Water Company operated in an extension to the front of the original mill building using water from the Long Mynd spring to produce a selection of drinks such as soda water, lemonade and ginger beer (see page 136).

The mill building was demolished by 1912 when a hotel and café was established in the old warehouse and factory. Thereafter, the café and later the Chalet Pavilion (built about 1920) became the focal point for streams of tourists who arrived in charabancs and cars. The pavilion has belonged to the National Trust since about 1978.

The old warehouse and factory was converted into flats in the late 1960s or early 1970s and called Carding Mill Court. A bungalow has been built on the site of the original mill.

Mrs. Williams,
Carding Mill,
Church Stretton,

BEGS to inform the Excursionists who visit this charming locality that she supplies TEA AND OTHER REFRESHMENTS at very moderate charges. Special arrangements made for Choirs, Schools and Large Parties. The Carding Mill is situated in the beautiful and romantic Carding Mill Valley, halfway between Church Stretton and the far-famed Light Spout.

Full Particulars on application.

THOROUGHLY RENOVATED THROUGHOUT.

Mrs Williams, wife of Richard Williams opened a café in the mill premises. This is her advertisement from 1905.

The upper mill pond was for many years used as an outdoor bathing pool by the locals, hence the sign which still stands near the spot saying *'Depth opposite this point 3 ft 10 ins'*. The pool was drained in about 1960 and filled to be used as a car park.

Before the Chalet Pavilion was built. Part of the premises of the Church Stretton Aerated Water Co. can be seen in front of the original mill.

Charabancs in Carding Mill Valley in the late 1920s.

William Ernest Gordon Pearce (pictured) bought the mill and factory buildings and much of Carding Mill Valley about 1922. He opened refreshment rooms in the Chalet Pavilion as well as in the High Street and a bakery and confectionery shop in Sandford Avenue. He continued to run the Carding Mill Valley premises until 1946 when he sold the Chalet and Chalet Pavilion, and later the rest of Carding Mill Valley, to Harold Holmes.

Right: A 1922 advertisement for the newly built Chalet Pavilion café managed by Florence Wyke.

The Chalet Pavilion — Carding Mill Valley, Church Stretton

Open Daily (Sundays included)

The best accommodation in the District for Parties.

Noted for **High Class Catering** For Large or Small Parties.

Satisfaction guaranteed.

References with pleasure.

The Pavilion is surrounded by delightful hill scenery, in the beautiful Carding Mill Valley, just off the Shrewsbury to Hereford Main Road. Easy run for Char-a-bancs, &c., up to the doors.

Lavatories and Cloak-rooms, Lock-up Cycle Store, &c. Seating accommodation for over 200.

Quotations for Hot or Cold Luncheons, Teas, &c., for Works-Outings, Private Parties, Choirs, Sunday Schools, &c., on application to **Miss Wyke, The Chalet, Carding Mill Valley, Church Stretton.**

Cwm Dale

Cwm Dale was until about 1893 called Cound Dale and must have been considered as the source of the Cound Brook which flows northwards to join the Severn at Lower Cound despite the Ash Brook in Carding Mill Valley being longer and having a greater volume water. Bilbey speculates that because of the watershed between the north and south flowing rivers in the Stretton Gap is very flat, the Ash Brook once flowed south to join the Town Brook. As a result, it would naturally be thought that the spring in Cound (Cwm) Dale was the source of the Cound Brook.

The Avenue of Lime Trees

The avenue was the brainchild of the Rev'd Holland Sandford, then Rector of Eaton-under-Heywood. He was a man of intellect who probably found life rather lonely at Eaton; the price of a comfortable country living was considerable physical and intellectual isolation. As a consequence his social life centred on Church Stretton, to which he made frequent visits.

It was because of his many journeys to and fro that he had the idea of planting an avenue of lime trees to improve the approach to Church Stretton from the east along the new road (later to be called Sandford Avenue) recently cut to replace Hazler Road as the main road east towards Much Wenlock.

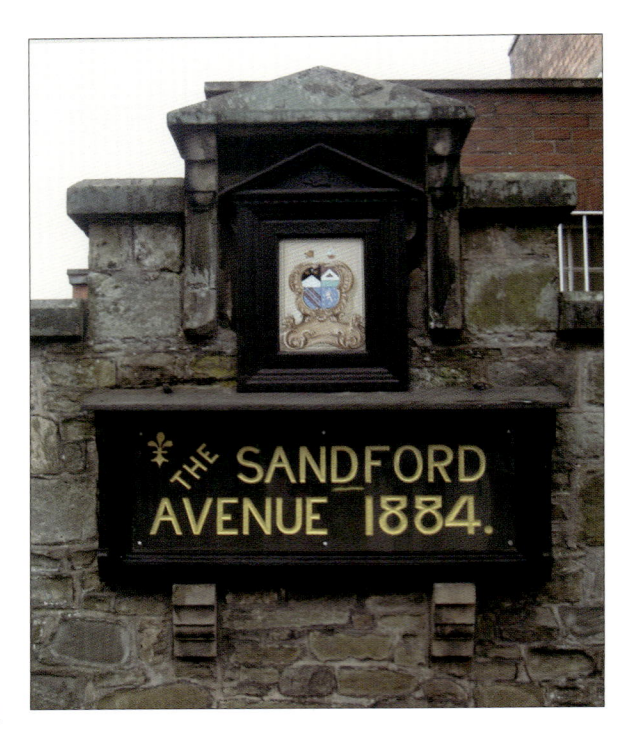

Sandford wrote to a number of local individuals offering to provide an avenue of trees from *The Hotel* to the railway station and seeking their co-operation to do so. To help him he formed a committee of local notables. Their first meeting was held in *The Hotel* on 6th November 1884.

Holland Sandford's offer was accepted and it was agreed that the trees were to be planted by George Preece, nurseryman, who lived in a house at the junction of High Street and Sandford Avenue where Lloyd's Bank now stands, with a garden extending down Sandford Avenue (see page 41).

The tree planting ceremony. Holland Sandford is holding the spade.

146

Holland Sandford plants the Prince of Wales' tree near Watling Street.

The tree planting ceremony

On the 19th December 1884 a triumphal arch with evergreens and flowers and adorned with flags stretched across the road from George Preece's house to *The Hotel*. From its centre was suspended a shield bearing on the one side the words 'Success to the Sandford Avenue' and on the other side the word 'Welcome'. The first tree was planted by Holland Sandford. Initially 83 trees were planted 15 yards apart. A celebratory banquet in honour of Sandford's gift was held in *The Hotel* later that afternoon attended by 54 men.

Over the weekend of 3rd - 4th January 1885 six of the trees were slashed with a knife. This caused the greatest indignation in the town and neighbourhood. The police were informed and promised to use their utmost endeavours to trace the miscreants. Having expressed great indignation about these 'lubberly louts', 'ruffians' and 'miscreants' who had perpetrated 'this senseless and miserable outrage', the committee resolved to offer a reward of £5 (later increased to £10) to anyone supplying information which led to their apprehension. The culprits were never found.

The Avenue extended

After the first trees had been planted, Sandford offered to extend the avenue first to Watling Street and then up the new road that had been cut to bypass the old Hazler Road. He provided another 70 trees, so bringing the total number to 153. There were at this time no houses along the new road east of Watling Street.

Sandford also hit upon the idea of having each tree planted in the name of an illustrious person. Local dignatories were written to as well as members of Royalty, the nobility, Heads of State and MPs. Many replied giving their consent, including the Prince of Wales, the Duke of York, the King of the Hellenes and President Cleveland; the Queen was invited but the reply from her equery was 'she is unable to express an opinion' which Sandford took to mean no objection.

As an expression of their appreciation of Sandford's generosity the Committee agreed to place on George Preece's garden wall an entablature which included the Sandford arms (see opposite page). Also, a small bronze plaque commemorating the planting of the first tree was placed on *The Hotel* wall. This was later moved to a slightly different position from its original on the front of John Thomas's shop but has since been stolen.

Holland Sandford was taken seriously ill in 1899. In the following March he moved into the Church Stretton Asylum for Gentlemen at Stretton House, High Street. He died in the Asylum on 23rd November 1904 aged 81 and was buried in the churchyard at Eaton-under-Heywood. However his real memorial is the splendid avenue of lime trees which is still such a major feature of the Church Stretton landscape.

The bronze plaque recording the planting of the first tree.

Electioneering in the 19th Century

Holland Sandford canvassing in Little Stetton for an election about 1890, accompanied by Edwin Corfield.

In 1432 Henry VI decreed that only owners of property worth at least forty shillings, a significant sum, were entitled to vote in elections. In Church Stretton there were only 15 such eligible voters in 1714. This law continued until 1832 when voting rights were extended to those males who rented property of a certain value. Further extensions were granted so that by 1867 up to 60% of men could vote although women still could not. Universal suffrage for those over 21 was granted only in 1928.

Election Riots in Church Stretton

In the 1868 general election serious rioting took place in Church Stretton which was one of the polling centres for the South Shropshire Constituency. Tension between supporters of the Conservative and Liberal candidates culminated in some Liberal voters being forcefully prevented by Tory agents from entering the polling booth. With a large crowd of onlookers in the streets, fighting broke out and there was much throwing of stones, sticks and mud. The result was a large number of injuries and broken windows.

13 people were arrested and charged with wilfully breaking windows including £35 worth of damage to *The Hotel*. One of the defendants was an unnamed man who occupied a 'high social position' in the County. At the Magistrates Court the prosecutor stated that 'arrangements having been made' whereby the damage sustained by his clients *(The Hotel)* would be made good and he asked that the case be withdrawn.

A separate case that day involved Thomas Lewis who appeared on a charge of breaking one pane of glass worth 1 shilling. He was fined 26 shillings. Mr Walker who appeared on behalf of the defendant then asked why the former case had been disposed of in so summary of manner, yet his client was convicted even when there were witnesses who showed that his client was charged in error.

It would appear that someone had influenced the bench of magistrates to withdraw the case and save embarrassment to a person in 'a high social position'. The scandal of the court case was reported in *The Times* newspaper. *[Ref: Election Riots]*

Ralph Beaumont Benson, Property Developer

The Benson family originated in Ulverston. The founder of the family fortune was Moses Benson (1738-1806) who was a plantation owner in the West Indies and later a ship owner and trader operating from Liverpool where he became one of the rich merchants of the city. To end his days as a country gentleman he bought Lutwyche Hall and estate in Easthope in 1806 but died shortly afterwards. Successive Bensons continued to acquire large areas of land along Wenlock Edge, including Hope Bowdler in 1828.

Moses' great great grandson Ralph Beaumont Benson (1862-1911), pictured, was of considerable significance in the history of Church Stretton. Educated at Harrow School and Balliol College, Oxford, he was for a time a Captain in the Shropshire Yeomanry. He became a County Magistrate and a member of the Board of Guardians of Church Stretton Union. He succeeded to the estate on the death of his father Ralph Augustus Benson on 18 June 1886. Four days later he married Caroline Essex Cholmondeley, a daughter of Rev'd Richard Hugh Cholmondeley, Rector of Hodnet.

He bought the manor of Church Stretton and 433 acres of land from E B Coleman in 1888. He thus became one of the chief landowners in Church Stretton. His holdings included *The Hotel*, *The Buck's Head Inn*, *The Plough Inn*, a large area of the Long Mynd (including the present golf course) and most of what we know as Sandford Avenue from *The Hotel* to the top (eastern) junction with Hazler Road near the Hazler tollhouse.

On 18 June 1901 he offered three plots in Sandford Avenue for sale by auction at *The George,* Shrewsbury. This was the beginning of the development of the western, town end of Sandford Avenue as the main shopping and commercial area of the town. In so doing Benson effectively killed off the plans of the Church Stretton Land and Building Companies to build 26 shops on the east side of Watling Street to provide facilities for their proposed housing development on that side of the town (see page 171).

In addition, Benson drew up a scheme to develop the area between Shrewsbury Road, Sandford Avenue, the railway and the Ashbrook stream (to the north) for housing, with 209 houses varying in value from £500 (on Shrewsbury Road), through £400, £350, £250 to £150 for terrace houses backing onto the railway. The proposed road layout included what is now Beaumont Road, Lutwyche Road, and (approximately) Essex Road.

The site was never developed in the way proposed though the three roads were built. Hence the names of the roads; Beaumont Road was named after Benson himself, Essex Road and Essex House after his wife and Lutwyche Road after their own house. The name of Easthope Road too has a Benson connection, being named after the parish in which Lutwyche Hall is located.

In addition, from about 1900 onwards, Benson sold plots of land for houses along the eastern end of Sandford Avenue, which had originally been cut through Benson land. This was a gradual process and usually the houses were substantial and built on large areas of ground; in a number of cases one plot was built on and the adjoining plot became the garden. Examples of these houses include The Mount, built by 1904, The Leasowes about 1905 and the White House, built for Silvester Horne in 1913.

According to the book *Stella Benson* by Joy Grant, his was not a happy marriage. Though handsome and clever, he was a solitary man, impulsive and fastidious, who disliked being touched and was intent on intellectual and religious problems which he did not share with his family. He spent a good deal of time away from his family, eventually paying little attention to them; in effect Ralph and Essex were living apart by about 1900 with only occasional visits from Ralph. He absented himself from home for long periods. On one occasion he went to Sierra Leone, adopted some black children and brought them back to Lutwyche Hall, probably to the dismay of both children and locals. Later he went to live in Poplar in the East End of London to undertake charitable work among the local poor.

During the last part of his life, Ralph Benson was mentally confused and physically feeble. He died of a brain haemorrhage on 16 October 1911 at Folkestone and was buried in Easthope Churchyard.

The Proposed Housing Development adjoining Sandford Avenue

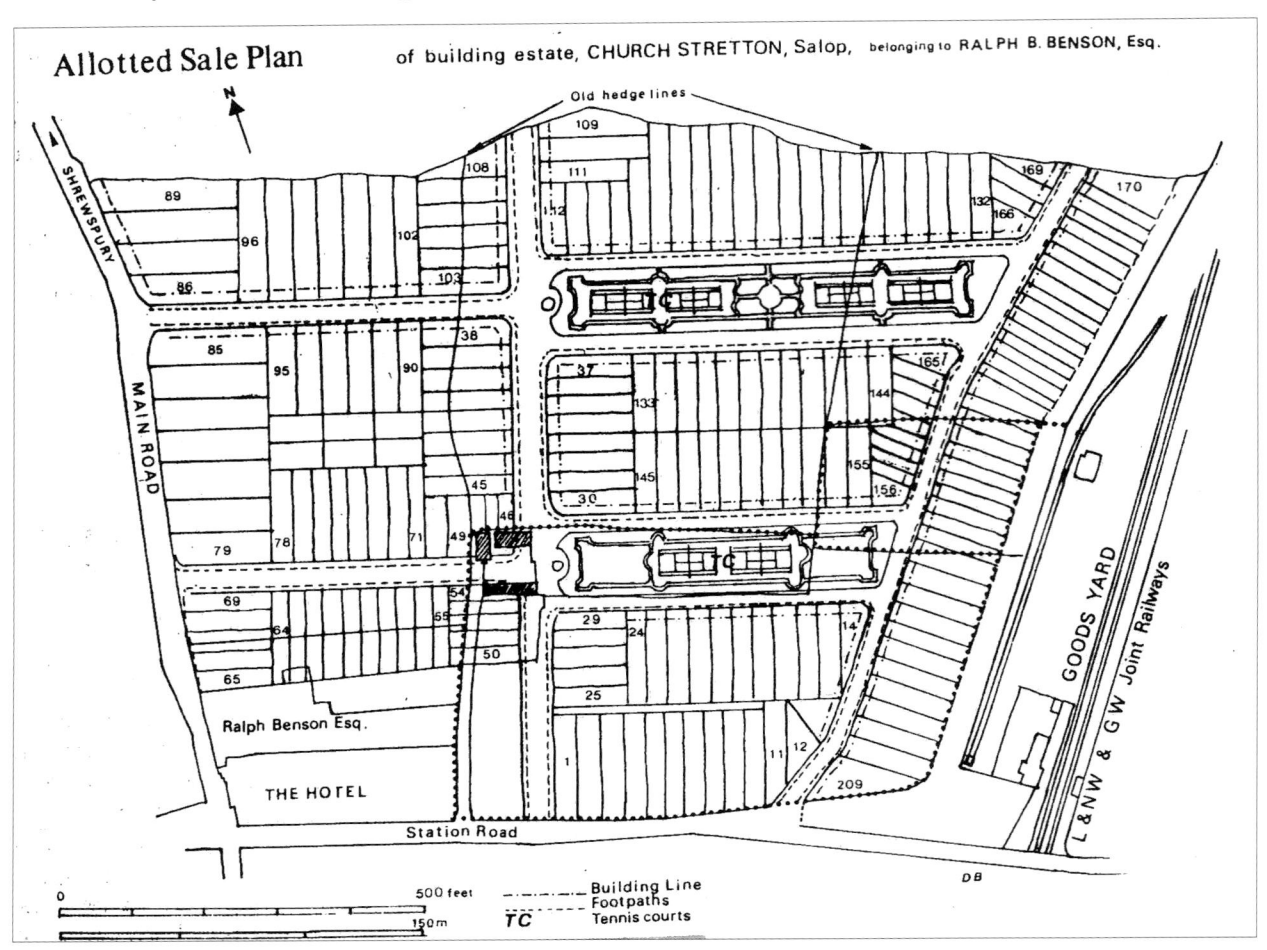

Benson's proposed housing development. The 'Main Road' refers to Shrewsbury Road and 'Station Road' is now Sandford Avenue. Note that six tennis courts were included in the plan.

The proposed road layout included what is now Beaumont Road, Lutwyche Road and Essex Road. The scheme was never carried out because in the early 1900s there was too much land available for development and not enough demand for houses at that time, especially as the plots were often large and intended for expensive houses. However, the three roads were built eventually.

The commercial development was, however, more successful. Plots along the south side of Sandford Avenue were auctioned in batches. This has resulted in the range of architectural styles for each of the shops which are well separated and gives the road its pleasing character.

The first auction in 1901 offered 61 plots around the town. There appears to have been little interest since only seven lots were sold, Only two plots in Sandford Avenue were sold and these were bought by Thomas Rich, watchmaker and cycle agent (see page 152) and Charles Simpson, a sanitary engineer. However by 1910 most of the plots had been sold and the shops built and occupied.

Although much of the area has since been developed for housing and other uses, this has been on a rather piecemeal basis and has taken place over a considerable number of years, both pre-war and post-war.

This is a view from the railway bridge of Station Road, later Sandford Avenue in the 1870s before development. Note the slip road to the station on the right which at the time was to the north of the bridge.

Sandford Avenue in 1910 showing the young lime trees in front of the shops before their removal. The newsagents board reads 'Crippen Inquest'.

Sandford Avenue Shops

Sandford Avenue about 1906, showing no. 22 built by Thomas Rich. Note Holland Sandford's lime trees remain in the garden of The Hotel on the left but those on the south side of the road by the shops have been removed.

The site of no. 22 (now Peppers and formerly McMitchell Bros) was bought by Thomas Rich, a watchmaker, who put up the first of the new buildings in Sandford Avenue in 1901 and placed the clock on the front. This development was the beginning of Sandford Avenue as the main shopping and commercial area of the town. It is interesting that in his advertisement, he still thinks of the road as Station Road, twenty years after its renaming after the Rev'd Holland Sandford. He sold his business in 1908.

T. H. Rich,
Motor &
Cycle Depot,
Station Road, Church Stretton.

Motor Cycles & Car for Hire.

REPAIRS. PETROLS. OILS.
ACCESSORIES.
ACCUMULATORS RECHARGED.

Appointed Sole Repairer to Automobile Club
and
Official Repairer to C.T.C. Resident Engineer.

CYCLES, MAIL CARTS, BATH CHAIRS
AND TRAILERS ALWAYS ON HIRE.

Practical Watchmaker and Optician
(certificated).
OCULISTS' PRESCRIPTIONS.
Spectacles to suit all sights in stock.

FURNISHED APARTMENTS:
Apply MRS. RICH, Sandford Road.

The advertisement is from Church Stretton Illustrated, 1905.

Nearly all the sites for shops were bought by 1910. They were all sold to individuals who erected substantial buildings, in most cases with attractive and individual features. This has resulted in a pleasant street of buildings.

The turnover of occupancy of shops has always been large. In many cases the nature of the shop business has continued with subsequent owners. The photographs on this and the next few pages show some of the shops that existed in the 1950s and 1960s.

Above: Edward Ross's shoe shop is now Stretton Shoes.

Right: Joseph Johnson's dispensing chemist is now Hillside Pharmacy.

Below: Douglas and Mary Somerville's bakery is now Kaboodle. [Simon Madin]

24 - 26 Sandford Avenue

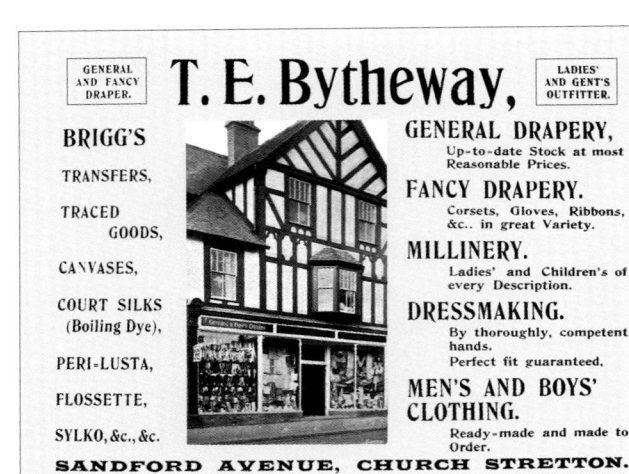

Thomas Edward Bytheway occupied the left hand of this pair of shops (no. 26) when it was built. By 1912, he had bought the site, built no. 46 further down the road and moved to those premises.

In the 1940s and 1950s Laura Ethel Bland with her two sons had a catering and confectionery shop and the Café Royal there. It is now All Seasons dress shop. Since 1986, Laura Bland's granddaughter has run the Acorn Café from rooms on the first floor.

Above: Thomas Bytheway's advertisement in Church Stretton Illustrated in 1905.

Right: Laura Bland with shop assistant Ethel Jones on her right in 1942.

Left: In the 1960s this shop still housed a branch of W H Smith and Son who had occupied the premises as soon as they were built about 1906. [Simon Madin]

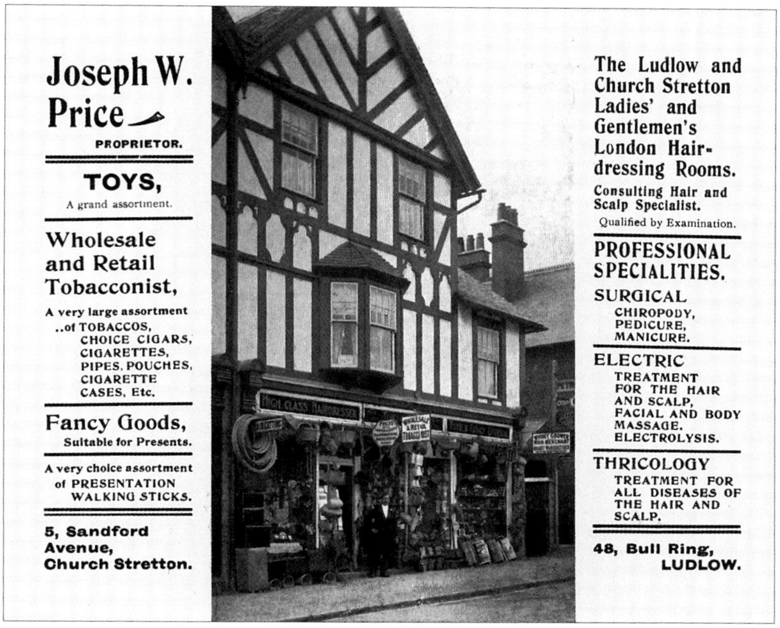

Left: The right hand of this pair of shops (no. 24) was occupied by Joseph Price. This is his advertisement in Church Stretton Illustrated in 1905.

Below: In the 1950s Harry Hampson had his hairdressing and tobacconist business here. It is now A B Optics. [Simon Madin]

Left: In the 1960s Stan Pearce had a grocery and confectionery business at no. 28, further down the street. It was part of the original Rees's Hotel (next page) which occupied the upper floor of nos 28 - 32. This shop now houses Newsworld. [Simon Madin]

William Rees's Private and Commercial Hotel, The Stretton Café

The first occupier of the corner property (now Wright's Estate Agent) was William Rees, a baker and hotel keeper. He described himself as a family and fancy bread baker as well as a pastry cook and confectioner and operator of the Stretton Café.

The elegant balcony has since been enclosed.

Top: Sandford Avenue about 1910 showing Rees's property on the corner with Easthope Road (nos 28 - 32).

Above: as it is in 2011.

Left: A 1905 advertisement.

McCartney's Maltings

For many years there were several small maltings in the town, but the scale of Robert McCartney's operations in Church Stretton eventually put the others out of business.

The large Sandford Avenue premises of malthouse, warehouse and shop (now The Antiques Market) were built about 1904 by Robert McCartney and housed Stretton's only big 20th century malting business until it closed about 1940. The east wall at the entrance to the building still shows traces of the name

R McCartney & Sons
Maltsters, Millers
Corn & Seed Merchants

The malting floors were in the main building where the grain was dampened down and spread out. When it had sprouted it was taken to the kiln, the tall tower-like building on the left (above) where it was subjected to a heating process which stopped growth and dried the malt. It was then ready for the brewing process. In the tower there still exists, on the first floor, tiles with holes in them which allowed the heat to come through and perform this drying process.

After the malthouse closed the building was used as workshops for St Dunstan's during World War II (page 190). After the war, it was rented to various businesses. The shop was occupied for a time by Messrs Coles and Francis, butchers; they sharpened their knives on the sandstone windowsill outside, the wear being still visible. They were followed by Warrener and Mason, wholesale grocers, until about 1978 when Percy Tarbuck opened the shop for the sale of greengroceries and flowers. He continued here until his retirement in 1986. Afterwards the whole maltings building became the Antiques Market.

A 1977 advertisement.

The Post Office Building, 42 - 44 Sandford Avenue

GEORGE DUNN, M.P.S.,
Chemist and Optician, POST OFFICE BUILDINGS, CHURCH STRETTON.

The Compounding of Physicians' Prescriptions is made a Speciality, and is under the direct supervision of the Principal.

Drugs of Standard Quality only used.

SPECIAL AGENT for the **Church Stretton Mineral Waters** in Syphons and Bottles.

High-Class Stationery and Fancy Goods Repository.

Bibles and Prayer Books

Leather Goods.

Photograph Frames.

Hand Mirrors

Toilet Articles.

PHOTOGRAPHIC DEPÔT and Customers' Dark-Room. FILMS AND PLATES DEVELOPED AND PRINTED.

PICTORIAL POSTCARDS. Local Views, Guides, &c., stocked in great variety. CIRCULATING LIBRARY.

This 1905 advertisement above shows the newly built PO Building with part occupied by George Dunn. It has now lost most of it's elegance. The left hand shop (below), occupied by Richard Smith from about 1946 to 1955, now houses PCB Solicitors. [Simon Madin].

Since 1609 letters have been carried in England by the Royal Mail on routes linking the major towns by horses which were changed at 'posts'. Special Royal Mail coaches were used from 1784 until the coming of the railway.

There was no regular post in Church Stretton in 1797 though a news man from Shrewsbury passed through once a week and 'generally brings the letters'.

The first record of a Royal Mail coach through Church Stretton was the Liverpool to Bristol coach in 1822, though there would have been a service of some sort between Ludlow and Shrewsbury before this date. The post was dropped at the *Talbot Inn* and delivered by the local postmaster, John Broome and later by John Haverkam.

From 1850 to 1870 the post office was part of 19 High Street occupying the premises which eventually became the Shrewsbury Old Bank and then Salts (see page 62).

In 1870 a Post Office was run by Richard Home in premises opposite the Market Hall. In 1885 it moved to 1 Shrewsbury Road and was run, until 1892, by George Windsor who was also a bookseller and stationer (see page 32).

Early in the development of Sandford Avenue, the large Post Office Building was erected and is depicted in the 1905 advertisement opposite. George Dunn had moved from the High Street and opened a large chemist and optician shop in one part with the Post Office run by Harold Gunn occupying the other. The Post Office was open on weekdays from 8 am to 8 pm and on Sundays from 8 to 10 am.

Some years later, the Post Office moved to the adjacent building (no. 46) shown below but in the late 1980s it ceased to be a Crown Post Office and was housed in the Spar store in Sandford Avenue.

The Sorting Office.

For several years after the Post Office moved into the Spar premises the sorting office remained in the rear portion of the Sandford Avenue building. In early 1990s it was moved into premises on the Mynd Industrial Estate on the A49 and is now at Craven Arms. The Post Office building stood empty for several years until it was sold and became an antiques shop.

The T E Bytheway Building, 46 Sandford Avenue

Thomas Bytheway was the first to occupy the shop at 26 Sandford Avenue (page 154) when it was built about 1904. However in 1912 he bought a plot at 46 Sandford Avenue and built the building shown here. His initials and the date are carved in the stones above the windows. He moved his drapery business here and traded until about 1923 when he retired.

Next door, no 48, was first occupied by Esther Annie Foley, a china dealer. About 1960 it housed the local Electricity Company which sold electrical appliances. It is now Shampers hairdressers.

The Post Otffice continued in this building until the 1980s. [Simon Madin]

The Regal Cinema, Sandford Avenue

In 1937 the Craven Cinemas Company owned by Mr J N Robson opened the Regal Cinema in Sandford Avenue. This was one of a chain of five cinemas he owned, the others being at Craven Arms, Ludlow, Ledbury and Tenbury Wells. Three films were shown each week at the *Regal*.

For a number of years the *Regal* functioned as a cinema only but the growing popularity of television in the 1950s and 1960s resulted in a decline in cinema going. This meant that other uses for the cinema had to be found and by the beginning of 1962 the premises were being used as a bingo club on two days each week.

The cinema soon became uneconomic and closed in September 1963. The building was demolished about 1965 and replaced by the present Spar supermarket building.

A 1937 advertisement.

Interior, showing the elaborately painted walls and the seating.

Sandford Avenue (North Side) and Beaumont Road

Other than *The Hotel* and Barclays Bank, no. 31, now Sandford Hardware, was for many years the only building on Sandford Avenue opposite the shops. The property was built by 1906 and was occupied by Richard Pryce, ironmonger, cycle agent and seller of petrol. At the rear, Harry Boulton had his fish shop which fronted onto Beaumont Road and which now houses Burway Barbers. He later moved to the High St (see page 47).

Left: Sandford Avenue about 1910 with Richard Pryce's shop and the new Barclays Bank in the background.

Left: Built about 1937 as The Stretton Garage, Arthur Morris was also a Funeral Director and had a taxi business based at these premises.

Above: The Church Stretton Urban District Council had their offices and yard in this property in Beaumont Road. It was built in 1912 and demolished in the 1970s and replaced by apartments.

Left: Tom Morris, the Council dustman in 1920s. [Ray Tipton]

Essex House, Sandford Avenue

The corner of Essex House was once a shop. The sketch by David Bilbey (below) shows how the south face originally looked.

This building was designed as offices, residential accommodation and a shop and was completed in 1907, the date being inscribed over the door. The offices, known as Stretton Chambers, were on the south side, while the shop, a greengrocers at one time, had the window shown in the drawing and another, now bricked up, fronting on to Essex Road. The east side of the building, which had its own front door and staircases, was known as Essex House.

By 1913 the whole building was known as Essex House and it had become a boarding house and private hotel. During the First World War the building became a private hospital for convalescent soldiers where Elizabeth Barnett, a commandant in the Voluntary Aid Detachment, was Superintendent. After the war it continued to be used as a boarding house run by Emily Moyle until the Second World War when it was taken over by the military. When St Dunstan's expanded from the *Longmynd Hotel,* Essex House became their offices.

Gladys and William Hardy owned the house from 1950 to 1973 and it was they who converted it into flats and gave it a new name Gladwyll.

The only changes to the exterior of the building are the removal of the rails above the bay window, the filling in of the shop windows (although the glazed brick surrounds remain) and the insertion of a new window in the west wall facing Essex Road.

The Park

The Park about 1925.

The land for the park, originally called Broadmeadow Park, was given to the Church Stretton UDC by Ralph Beaumont Benson. The site was enlarged by a further gift to the town of an additional 1¾ acres by 'The Barn Owls', an amateur dramatic group which performed in a barn attached to Stretton House.

The original site given by Benson was much larger than the present park and included what is now Coppice Leasowes, but this became a detached area when the bypass was driven through the site in 1939.

The attractive gates at the entrance were designed and made in wrought iron by M. Hermann, a Belgian refugee who lived in Church Stretton during the First World War and had a workshop and forge near the station.

Nowadays, bowls, tennis and croquet are played in the park. Recent improvements have included all-weather tennis courts, croquet green, skateboard ramp and a BMX track for young cyclists, all initiated by the Town Council.

The Railway Station

The original station. Mr Dawson, the station master, is on the right.

The arrival of the railway in the mid 19th century brought a gradual but fundamental change to Church Stretton. Road travel by horse, cart or coach remained only for local journeys.

The Shrewsbury and Hereford Railway Company was formed in August 1846 to build a line to connect with the Newport, Abergavenney and Hereford Railway at Hereford, so providing a link to the industrial and mining areas of South Wales.

To save construction costs the line between Shrewsbury and Hereford was built single track at first but with bridges and embankments, etc. wide enough to allow for later doubling of the line. This occurred in 1862, apart from the Dinmore tunnel, which was doubled in 1891-93.

A GWR Vulcan 2-2-2 loco buit in 1854, photographed in 1870 at Shrewsbury sheds.

The 27½ mile long Shrewsbury to Ludlow section was formally opened on 20 April 1852. There were stations at Condover, Dorrington, Leebotwood, Church Stretton, Marshbrook, Craven Arms and Stokesay, Onibury, Bromfield and Ludlow. The Ludlow to Hereford section was opened a year later. In the 1930s halts were provided at All Stretton, Little Stretton (1936) and Wistanstow (1934).

In 1863 the Shrewsbury and Hereford Railway became a joint L&NWR (later LMS) and GWR line and remained so until nationalisation on 1st January 1948.

View from the Sandford Avenue bridge looking northward.

The First Station

This opened in 1852. It had two platforms 170 ft long, a booking office, waiting rooms for both ladies and gentlemen, a cattle landing measuring 200 ft, goods warehouses, a coal wharf, weighing machines, turntables, sidings and from 1872, a signal box.

The station master was provided with an excellent house adjacent to the station. The first station master was Hugh Morgan. The original station buildings still survive north of the Sandford Avenue bridge.

Approaching the original station and heading south.

Celebrations for the first train

The day was ushered in by a peal of the church bells. The first official train, which contained a large number of the gentry and tradesmen from Shrewsbury, ran from Shrewsbury to Ludlow and back. It had 25 carriages carrying 300 passengers drawn by two engines belonging to the Shrewsbury and Chester Railway.

As part of the celebrations the town declared a public holiday. At 11.00, led by Dorrington's brass band, nearly all the inhabitants of the town and many hundreds from the surrounding neighbourhood proceeded down Lake Lane, soon to be renamed Station Road, to the station to await the arrival of the train. This slowly passed through at noon and was greeted by the crowds on the bridge and platform cheering and waving handkerchiefs.

Then followed an afternoon of sports and games, folllowed by tea for about 800 residents of the town and an official dinner for 70 gentlemen in the Town Hall. The meal was described as hearty and was followed by 17 toasts, the final one being the traditional 'all friends around the Wrekin'! Even the inhabitants of the workhouse were remembered, with a special meal of roast beef and plum pudding with a due proportion of ale.

The local newspaper reported that 'various rural sports took place after dinner in the Crown Meadow (between *The Hotel* and the station). These included foot races, jingling matches, etc. and much amusement and rollicking fun was created among the competitors in the different games and the spectators. The day's proceedings concluded with a public dance in the Market Hall. There were about 150 present, and the festivities were kept up until a late hour. There was sufficient food left over for next day when upwards of 60 of the aged men and labourers in the town were plentifully supplied with bread, beef and ale'.

The Goods Yard

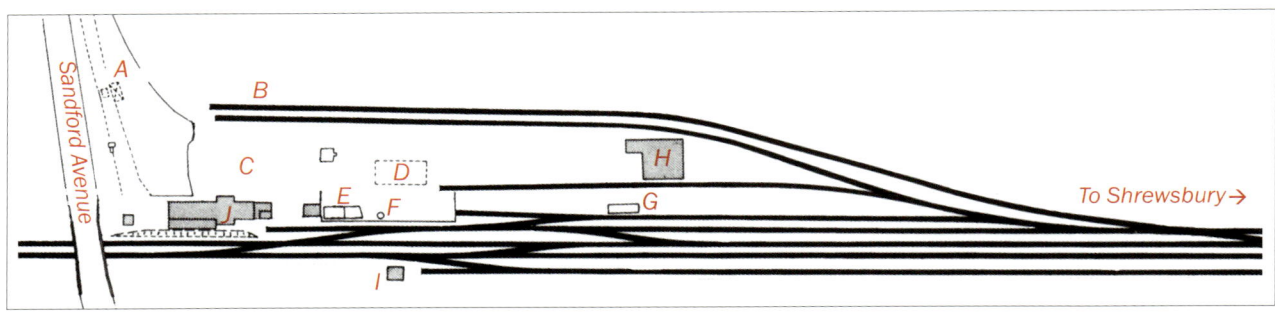

A	Weighbridge	B	Coal Yard	C	Station House Garden	D	GPO Stack Yard
E	Cattle Pens	F	Crane	G	Coal Stack	H	Goods Shed
I	Signal Box	J	Station and Platform				

The goods yard with its sidings and goods facilities was the centre for movement of goods into and out of the town. The main movement out of the town was in sheep, cattle and horses, whilst coal, building materials and manufactured goods came to the town.

Charles Hyslop, pictured here, was the main coal merchant with a sufficiently large business to warrant his own wagons.

Charles Hyslop had his own coal wagons.

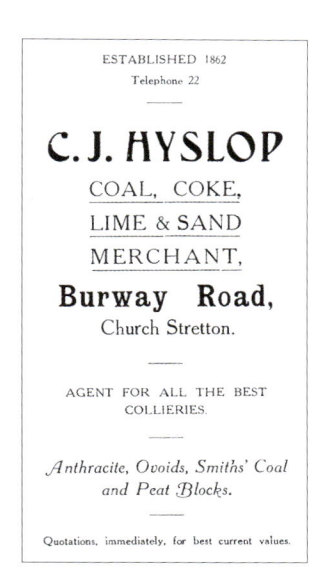

Left: The signal box controlled the line between Marshbrook and Dorrington. Demolished in March 2009, it is hoped to rebuild it in the park and open it as a railway museum.

Below left: A storage hut which was formerly the base of the water tower.

Below right: Part of the goods yard showing the cattle pens, crane and goods shed.

The second station, looking south.

The Second Station

Eventually increased passenger traffic needed longer trains and longer platforms. It was not possible to extend the platforms of the original station because to the north the entrance to the goods yard was in the way and to the south the Sandford Avenue bridge.

Consequently a second station was built to the south of the Sandford Avenue bridge and officially opened in 1914. The platforms were 551 feet long, with the main buildings on the up (west) side, waiting rooms on both platforms and a covered foot bridge over the line to link them. The lighting was by gas. Water columns stood at the end of each platform as well as one on the north side of the bridge.

In 1947 the staff consisted of a stationmaster, five clerks, four signalmen, four porters, one checker, one goods porter, two lorry drivers, two crossing keepers and ten engineering lengthmen who maintained the track.

Most of the smaller stations along the line were closed on 9 June 1958. Between Shrewsbury and Ludlow, only stations at Church Stretton and Craven Arms remain. Goods traffic to Church Stretton ceased on 19th September 1966.

Whilst passenger traffic continued, the station became an unstaffed one on 3 July 1967. The station buildings were demolished in February 1970 and replaced by a simple shelter on each platform.

After the demolition of the station buildings.

Left: The weigh bridge and hut.

Below: The goods shed, now demolished. [Eddie Conning]

Bottom: The station master's house is all that remains of the old station.

Victorian Tourism

When William McDowall arrived in Church Stretton in 1872 he stayed at Stretton House with William Hyslop, an old friend from the Dumfries area of Scotland from where other Scottish families had settled in Church Stretton in the mid 19th century.

McDowall's observations upon Church Stretton are interesting; he called it a street-town straggling irregularly over some 500 yards. He described the older tenements as quaint and queer-looking but admits that at least there were a few dainty houses of a modern type! The town was already attracting tourists drawn here in great numbers especially invalids searching for health. He was struck by the number of public-houses whose old-fashioned signs formed a feature of the town. *The Hotel*, managed by the Misses Cooper, came in for praise. He seemed to be impressed by the Long Mynd with its sheep and wild ponies and he described 'antiquarians tracing the footsteps of Claudius in the remains of Bodbury Ring' and, of course, poor old Caratacus confronting the Romans from his camp on Caradoc.

On his return home he wrote his story for the *Dumfries and Galloway Standard*, subsequently reprinting it as a booklet.

The coming of the railway in 1852 encouraged visitors to spend a day in the town and the local countryside and, from the 1870s, make use of the riding and carriage facilities provided by the Posting Establishment. Later on in that century visitors from further afield were coming to the town and staying at *The Hotel* and various inns. Visitor numbers had increased to such an extent that *The Hotel* was extended in 1899 and again in 1906 and three other hotels were built in the town in the early 1900s.

This party in a four-in-hand carriage from The Feathers Hotel, Ludlow led by Mr Goodwin is seen on the Long Mynd, June 1900. [Bernard Ford]

The Edwardian Expansion of the Town

The Church Stretton Land and Building Companies

The development of the modern town began in 1896 when a local syndicate bought about 300 acres for development. They conveyed this land to the newly formed Church Stretton Land Company in 1897. In 1899 the Church Stretton Building Company was formed at the same London address, 18, Adam Street, Adelphi, to develop the land.

A ambitious set of new roads and services were laid out on the slopes of the hills on both sides of the valley. These were named Cunnery Road, Madeira Walk (formerly known as Lover's Walk), Trevor Hill (formerly known as Rabbit Burrow and renamed after one of the Directors, G E Hill-Trevor) and Stanyeld Road (after an old field name) on the west side and Crossways, Watling Street South, Clive Avenue, Hazler Crescent and Kenyon Road on the east side. A huge number of building plots were then offered for sale.

A minimum value of the building to be erected was set on each site, e.g. in Watling Street South this was £150, in Clive Avenue and Kenyon Road it was £400, Trevor Hill, Madeira Walk and Ludlow Road were £500, Longhills was £800. None of the Kenyon Road or Brockhurst sites were sold and the proposed extensions of Cunnery Road (behind the *Longmynd Hotel* as far as Ludlow Road), Trevor Hill and Madeira Walk (dotted on the map) were never completed, though the course of these roads is still easily visible. The 1905 map below shows these roads.

Though a number of houses were built, many plots remained unsold and an auction sale of these was held in 1905. In 1908 the Land Company renamed itself Church Stretton Ltd and tried to raise £29,000 by a new share issue. In its prospectus the Company outlined plans to make Church Stretton a spa by buying and enlarging the *Longmynd Hotel* and piping water from a saline spring near Wentnor to a new Pump Room to be built in the grounds of Woodcote which the Company had contracted to buy. These plans too came to nought.

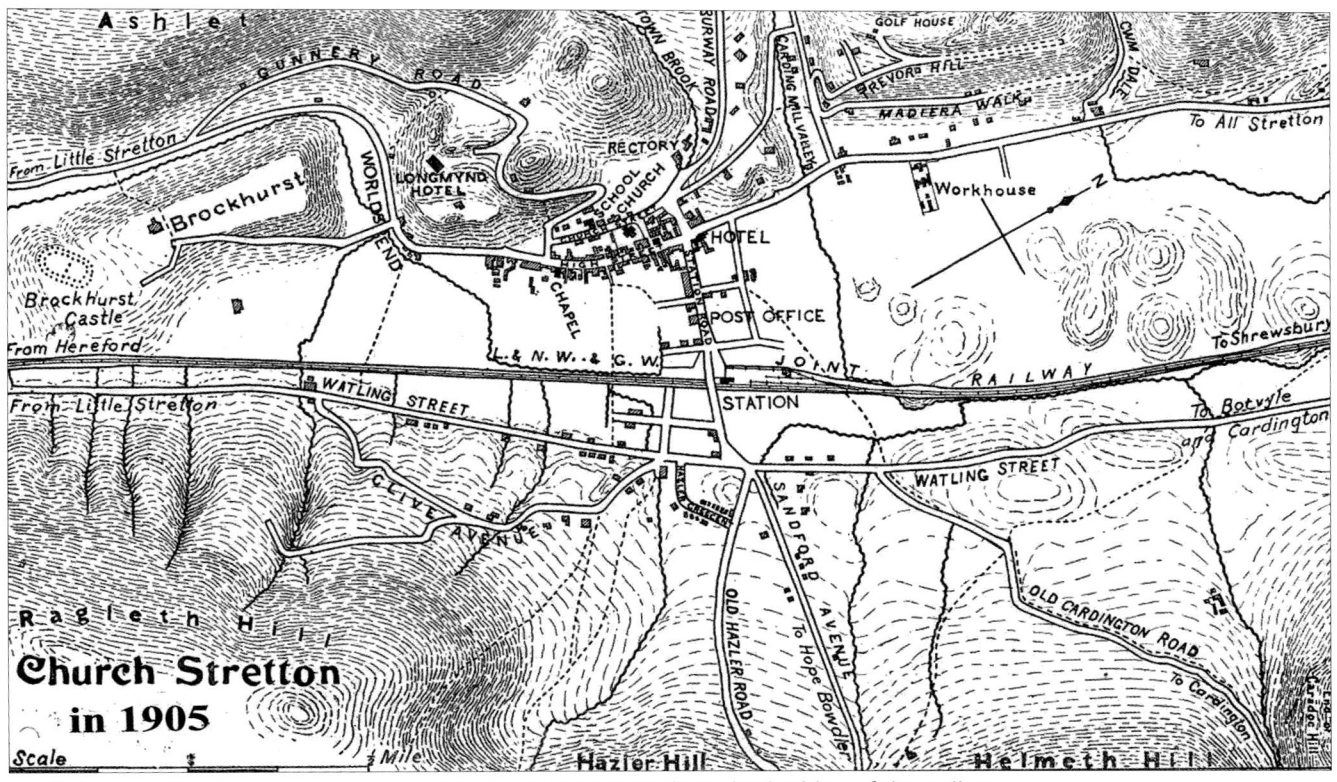

This map of 1905 shows some of the planned new roads on both sides of the valley.

> # CHURCH STRETTON, SHROPSHIRE.
>
> ## Freehold Building Sites for Sale
>
> In this Delightful Health Resort, commanding Beautiful Views of the surrounding Country, and suitable for the Erection of
>
> ## GOOD VILLAS AND BUNGALOWS.
>
> Suitable Sites for Shops and Business Premises close to the Station can also be purchased.
>
> Bracing Climate.
>
> Good Water Supply.
>
> Golf Links. Shooting and Fishing.
>
> No Law Costs.
>
> Tithe and Land Tax Free.
>
> Well-Made Roads.
>
> PAYMENTS BY INSTALMENTS EXTENDING OVER TEN YEARS (if desired).
>
> For full particulars, plans and prices of sites, apply to—
> The CHURCH STRETTON LAND COMPANY, Ltd.,
> 18, Adam Street, LONDON, W.C.;
> Messrs. BURD, SON & EVANS,
> School Gardens, SHREWSBURY;
> Or at the ESTATE OFFICE, CHURCH STRETTON.

An advertisement for the sale of building plots in Church Stretton Illustrated, 1905.

The Land Company still owned about 200 acres of building land in and around the town but the pace of development was slow and in 1909 the Company's assets were put into receivership for the sake of the debenture holders. In 1911 these assets were acquired by a new company, Church Stretton Developments Ltd., which continued in business until it went into voluntary liquidation in 1935 - 36. It was then bought by a local builder, W A Sherratt.

The new building schemes envisaged a population increase of 1,500 to 2,000 people at a time when the population of the town was only 816 (excluding Little Stretton and All Stretton) in 1901. The only extra amenities planned were six tennis courts and about thirty shops. No thought had been given to an enlarged school or the establishment of factories or other places of work and the short holiday season would not support any further working population. It was suggested that the new inhabitants would be retired people, unlikely at a time when only a minority could afford to retire and they rarely moved away from their families.

The Crossways Development

The Church Stretton Land Company also marked out the Crossways area as a major area for building. The plan of the proposed development (opposite) shows sites for 26 shops, more than were already in the town. These were meant to provide the shopping facilities for the houses which the company intended to build on the east side of the railway. The roads were to be tree lined and some had already been planted.

Sites on the east side of the railway were included for sale at the 1905 auction, though the plan shows that by that date Tower Buildings, Vernon House, the *Sandford Hotel*, the Electricity Power Station and a number of houses in Watling Street South and Hazler Crescent had already already built and the site for the Methodist Church had been sold.

Unfortunately for the Company, four years previously the Benson Estate had begun to sell plots for businesses in Sandford Avenue which were much nearer the centre of the town. Because of this and the fact that many plots remained unsold, most of the proposed shops east of the railway other than Vernon House and Tower Buildings were not built.

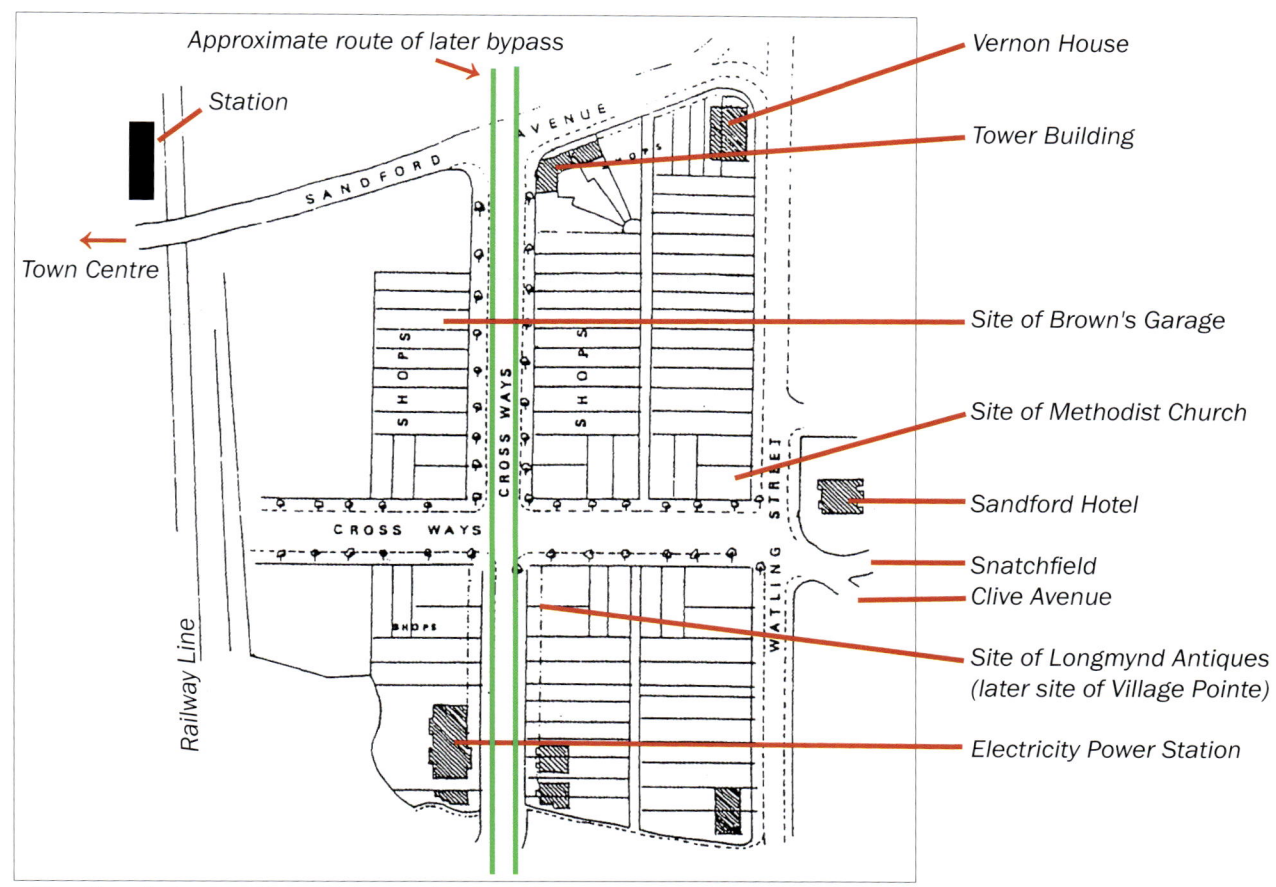

The Church Stretton Land Company's plan of the development of the Crossways area (1905).

The Electricity Power Station

The Electricity Power Station was built in 1904 by the Church Stretton Electricity Supply Co. Ltd. Electricity was generated by two gas engines using gas from the gas works at World's End. These charged a bank of batteries and supplied DC current to the town until the mid 1930s when the town was connected to the grid of the Shropshire, Worcestershire and Staffordshire Electric Power Company.

The buildings were later occupied by Express Dairies and after standing empty for some years are now used by the Stretton School of Dance and Drama.

The former electricity generating station converted for use by Express Dairies (2002).

Tower Buildings

Tower Buildings just before demolition. The advertisement for Charles Amphlett's business appeared in 1908. He took over Thomas Thompson's painting and decorating business (see page 177).

C. J. AMPHLETT, LATE THOMPSON,
Painter & Artistic Decorator,
CHURCH STRETTON.
Lettering on Wood & Glass. Stencilled work.
Special Designs for all kinds of Decorative work.
Speciality in Hand-painted Friezes.
PICTURE FRAMING.

Tower Buildings had already been erected by 1905 to a design by A B and W S Deakin said to be based on The Rows at Chester. Living accommodation was provided above the shops. The building was demolished in 1965 to allow widening of the A49 at the Sandford Avenue junction.

Telephone 34   SHROPSHIRE FARM PRODUCE   Telegrams:- SAGAR, CHURCH STRETTON.

Sagar & Co.

G. SAGAR
R. SAGAR
E. W. SAGAR
W. SAGAR

Fruit, Egg, Poultry, & Game Dealer.

The Towers, CHURCH STRETTON SHROPSHIRE.

We are out for supplying *Healthy Poultry* from a *Healthy District.* The Chicken equal to the Sussex or Surrey, perfect finish, immediate delivery. Ducklings finest quality. Selected new laid eggs. Fruit of high quality in season

Telephone: Church Stretton 2108

EATON HOUSE RESTAURANT

(Proprietress: Mrs. M. I. Pearce)

Breakfasts - Lunches - Teas

Open 9 a.m. until 7 p.m.

TOWER BUILDINGS CHURCH STRETTON

Shropshire

These advertisements from the 1908 edition of Church Stretton Illustrated show some of the businesses which operated from Tower Buildings.

The Bypass

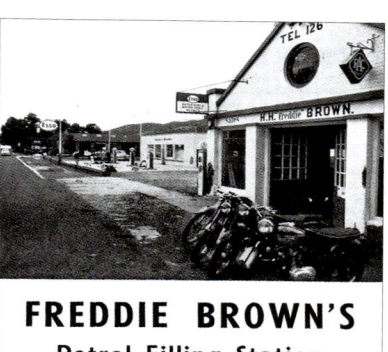

Above: The Mobil Oil filling station on the east side of the bypass at the corner with Crossways. [Bill Reynolds]
Right: This advertisement shows Freddie Brown's garage on the west side of the bypass. (1957/8).

FREDDIE BROWN'S
Petrol Filling Station
at your service
DAY AND NIGHT
(we never close)

Petrols, Oils, Tyres, Plugs, etc.

BY-PASS ROAD, CHURCH STRETTON
Telephone 126

In the mid 1950s Freddie Brown opened a business, consisting of a filling station with four pumps, a shop and a motor cycle showroom, on a site alongside the A49 near Crossways. The whole site, between Crossways, the railway station, the A49 and Sandford Avenue was at one time a market garden owned by Mr Sagar, who had a shop in Tower Buildings on the other side of the A49. Freddie Brown later erected a large building to the rear of the site alongside the railway in which he ran a tyre business. This was later owned by ATS tyres and is now part of the Longmynd Garage. About 1972 he sold the garage to Esso from whom Bill Reynolds bought it in 1981, rebuilding it in 1986.

Opposite, on the east side of the A49 at the corner with Crossways, Mobil Oils had built a filling station and workshop in the 1950s. Bill Reynolds bought this in 1986 and used it whilst his main filling station on the west side was being rebuilt. In the early 1990s, he sold the Mobil filling station which was then redeveloped to become the Longmynd Antiques shop, with an outdoor area for the display of garden and architectural antiques. In 2002 this property in turn was demolished and the block of flats named Village Pointe was erected.

Above: Longmynd Antiques had a prime site on the A49 with ample parking in front. It replaced the Mobil filling station.

Left: The Church Stretton Steam Laundry Company was operating by 1905 and continued until about 1930. It was on the site now occupied by Continental Fires. [Bilbey]

Watling Street

Watling Street South, once part of the Roman road from Wroxeter to Caerleon, had degenerated from an important route into, at best, a country lane and often into an unfenced track across fields. That it had survived for nearly two thousand years is a tribute to its designers and builders. However, as far as the inhabitants of Church Stretton were concerned, the High Street was part of the main Bristol to Chester road, whilst Watling Street was just a country lane which one crossed on the way to Much Wenlock.

The 1838 tithe map shows one house on the lane occupying a piece of land close to where Ferndale has since been built. The occupant was Edward Jones, a farmer.

By 1905, by which time the Laundry was operating, some buildings had appeared on Crossways and more houses had been completed on Clive Avenue, Hazler Crescent and Watling Street. Also in 1905 there was a determined effort to sell off the remaining building plots (see page 171).

Above: The Roman road about a mile south of the Sandford Avenue crossroads. This photograph taken before the bypass was built shows how it had become little more than a footpath eroded by a stream which had cut through the elevated road. The bypass destroyed all remains of the road south of the town.

Below: Even after houses had been built in Watling Street South, it was still without a tarmac surface as this postcard of 1906 shows.

The corner building was called Vernon House and was occupied by T Noel Jones' grocer's shop [about 1930].

From about 1906 to the early 1920s Charles Wheatley had his grocery shop in Vernon House. This photograph shows Tower Buildings in the background and Sandford Avenue leading to the railway bridge and the town centre. Vernon House was converted into flats in the early 1970s.

Thomas J Thompson was a painter and decorator as well as being a skilled painter of glass as shown by this glass panel which measures 33 by 13 inches. [Lesley Forbes]

St Milburga's Roman Catholic Church

Official returns record only one 'papist' in Church Stretton in 1676 and 1686. The next reference to Roman Catholics in Church Stretton was in 1827 when Catholics here were being served from Acton Burnell where priests were already in residence. By 1898 Church Stretton Catholics were served from Plowden but in 1907 Canon Charles Langdon, a retired priest from Plymouth, came to live at Hope Villa from where he began to celebrate mass. Unfortunately he died a year later. Mass was then occasionally offered in Tiger Hall and other houses, including the coach house at Ragleth House, by priests who were visiting the area, local members of religious orders and chaplains to Plowden Hall, the residence of a long established Catholic family about 12 miles away.

In 1923 the Bishop of Shrewsbury, the Rt Rev'd Hugh Singleton, sent Father Francis Maguire to establish a parish here and he lived in Manchester House in Churchway from where he celebrated mass. However he was unable to establish a parish and was moved to Nantwich in 1926. Once again local Catholics were looked after from Plowden.

The present church was built in 1929. It was paid for by Mrs Sarah Dutton. A resident priest, Father Edmund Bryant, a Franciscan Friar, came to live in the presbytery built adjacent to the church. The new church was designed by Frank Shayler of Shrewsbury and is dedicated to a local saint, Milburga, a Saxon princess who came to Shropshire from Kent in the seventh century, becoming Prioress of the religious community in Much Wenlock. A chapel in the church boasts a picture of the saint and an interesting wall hanging depicts Milburga surrounded by birds she is said to have prevented from gobbling up the crop grown to feed the monks and nuns under her charge.

The Methodist Church

Artist's impression of the proposed Primitive Methodist Church, School and Minister's house designed by W Scott-Deakin. The school was never built and a more modest manse was built in 1923.
Below: The Church today.

Methodism arrived in Church Stretton in 1828 when the Shrewsbury Primitive Methodist Circuit sent two men to Bishop's Castle to spread the gospel by preaching and evangelising. By 1831 they were covering an area about 15 miles around Bishop's Castle, including Church Stretton. Services were held in barns, houses and cottages. By 1857 the first chapel had been built at Wall, followed by one at Leamore Common in 1863, Little Stretton in 1867, Lower Wood in 1875 and Kenley in 1890. These chapels formed the Church Stretton circuit, with the Superintendent operating from Little Stretton.

The Church Stretton Methodist Church was opened in 1906 on a site in Watling Street South purchased for £60 from the Church Stretton Land Company. The building cost £1,300 and became the circuit church. It was refurbished in 2008.

The church did not occupy the whole of the land purchased and the Manse was erected in 1923. It was enlarged and modernised in 1998/9. A church hall was built between the church and the manse in 1956 for £2,860. This too was enlarged and joined to the church in 1994.

All the original seven chapels had closed by 1980 leaving only that in Church Stretton.

Hazler

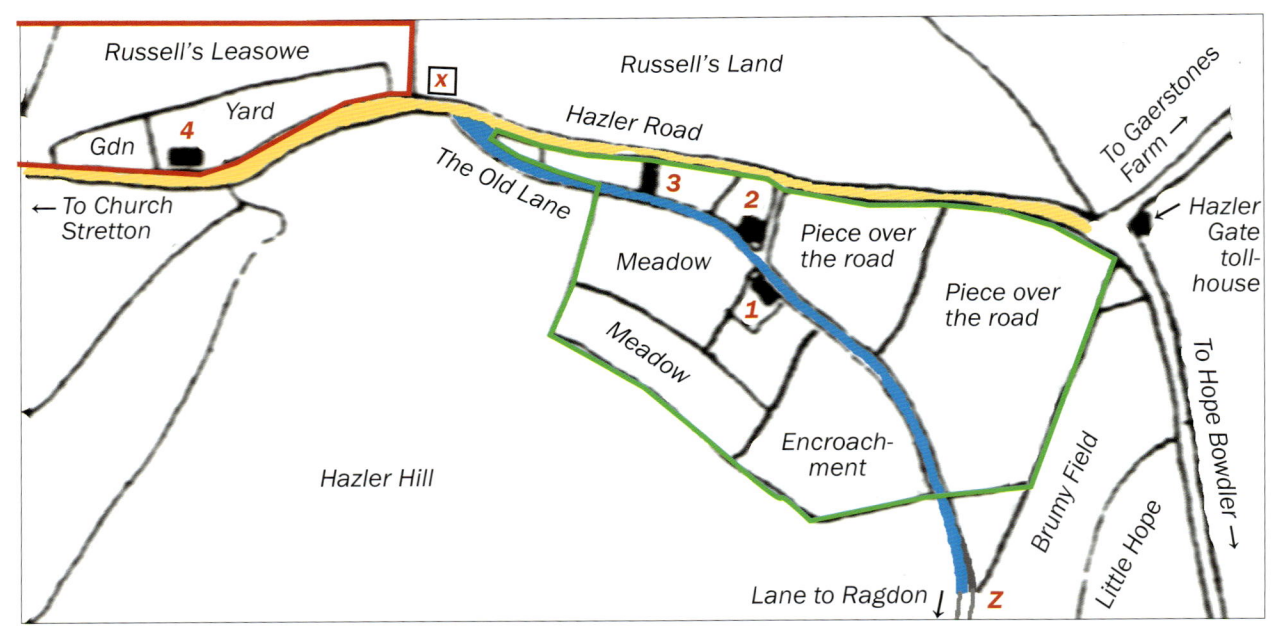

Map of Hazler based on the tithe map of 1838, showing the field names, the Hazler Road (in yellow) and the Old Lane (in blue). Building (1) is Sankey's Farm, now called Hazler Hill Farm; (2) is John Morgan's Cottage, no longer in existence; (3) is now called Foxlease Cottage and (4) is Hazler Cottage, now called Hill View. To help locate the beginning of the Old Lane, the modern property Hillgarth is marked X.

A close examination of the 1838 tithe map (above) of the Hazler Road area reveals that the cottages marked 1, 2 and 3 front onto a lane which is no longer there. It is likely that the original builders of these cottages erected them on a lane which existed at the time and which must have been the original route to Ragdon from Church Stretton, leaving Hazler Road in the vicinity of Hillgarth. The old lane fell into disuse when a new lane from point Z was made to link the lane from Ragdon to the Hazler Gate tollhouse some time in the early 20th century (it does not appear on the 1903 OS map, but does so on the 1927 map).

In 1838 the settlement of Hazler consisted of four cottages and a collection of very small fields which had probably come into existence as encroachments upon common land. The first of these houses, number 1 on the plan, was occupied by Thomas Sankey, who also owned most of the small fields enclosed in green on the map. This house has since been much extended and is now called Hazler Hill Farm. Thomas died in 1841 and the homestead passed to his son John, a weaver.

Hazler Hill Farm.

On the opposite side of this lane a few stones mark the site of Ann Hammond's cottage (no. 2) which, in 1858, was let to John Morgan while she herself lived in no. 3, now called Foxlease Cottage.

No. 4, Hazler Cottage, or Hill View as it is now called, was occupied by John Evans, a butcher and farmer who lived there until his death in 1891. His group of fields (enclosed in red on the map) stretched from near Watling Street to Hillgarth and was owned by Thomas Galliers. The cottage is first recorded in a manor court roll of 1740.

With the coming of the railway and the increase in traffic on the roads leading into Church Stretton, Hazler Road itself became inadequate especially as in bad weather it would have acted as a drain for the surrounding land. Its condition may have resembled a slightly wider version of the present Old Cardington Road. In 1855 it was replaced by a new road, known today as Sandford Avenue, as the main road to Hope Bowdler and beyond.

Above: Foxlease Cottage.

Left: Hazler Cottage, now called Hill View.

Until the 1850s the Beddoes had carried on their trade as skinners or fellmongers in the yard behind Spring Cottage in Burway Road (see page 26) but in the 1860s their son Benjamin resited the business to one of the properties at Hazler. One wonders whether public opinion had forced them to leave the centre of a town which was beginning to develop as a holiday resort where, to have one's principal hotel surrounded by four malthouses, a skinner's yard and a farm yard, no doubt posed something of a problem both for the local inhabitants and for any visitors.

Turnpike Roads out of Church Stretton

As trade between towns increased in the eighteenth century the need grew to improve the main highways over long distances. Highways were the responsibility of each parish through which they passed and their quality varied considerably; often the roads were barely more than muddy tracks.

The solution adopted was to privatise particular sections of road by an Act of Parliament which created a turnpike trust for each section. The trustees were responsible for maintaining the length of the highway with the right to collect tolls from those using the road to cover the cost of improvements.

Each trust erected turnpike gates at which a fixed toll was charged. The Act gave a maximum toll allowable for each class of vehicle or animal, for instance one shilling and six pence for a coach pulled by four horses, a penny for an unladen horse and ten pence for a drove of 20 cows. Needless to say, this upset local farmers and drovers.

The trusts also erected tollhouses beside the turnpike gate to accommodate the pikeman or toll collector. It became common for the trusts to auction a lease to collect tolls. Acts also required trusts to erect milestones indicating the distance between the main towns on the road. Users of the road were obliged to follow what were to become rules of the road, such as driving on the left.

Church Stretton Turnpikes

The main north - south road through Church Stretton was part of the Bristol to Chester road and was turnpiked in 1756 by separate Acts of Parliament for the road to Shrewsbury and the road to Ludlow. The first tollhouse northwards was near Leebotwood, and southwards at Little Stretton.

The road east to Much Wenlock was turnpiked in 1765 and proceeded via Hazler Road, The first tollhouse (Hazler Gate) was at the brow of the hill on the eastern corner of the lane leading to Gaerstones Farm.

Coaching routes via Church Stetton

One of the first regular coaches through the town was Moxey's stage wagon for heavy goods from Manchester to Hereford which passed through

Advertisement in the Shrewsbury Chronicle, 1772, inviting bids for the collection of tolls on the Church Stretton to Coleham Bridge, Shrewsbury turnpike.

weekly in each direction, changing horses at the *Talbot Inn*. Business increased so that by 1828 it was running twice weekly.

The Royal Mail coach ran daily between Liverpool and Bristol from at least 1822 until the mid 1840s, changing horses at the *Talbot Inn* which was the premier inn in the town. The black and maroon coach could carry four passengers inside and three on top. As well as the coachman there was a guard who was responsible for the safety of the mails. He had a blunderbuss, a cutlass and a brace of pistols to keep off thieves

From the 1830s an additional coach called the *Alert* ran daily between Shrewsbury and Hereford as also did the *Engineer* in later years. The journey time was reduced from 11 hours in 1802 to 6 hours in 1851. There were also local carriers operating between Shrewsbury and Ludlow who changed horses at the *Raven Inn* or the *Crown Inn*.

The opening of the Shrewsbury and Hereford Railway in 1852 resulted in a rapid increase in the amount of heavier bulk materials distributed from the railway station and a general increase in traffic on the approach roads to the town. The coaching trade collapsed but at the same time the hinterland parishes saw Church Stretton as an important trading

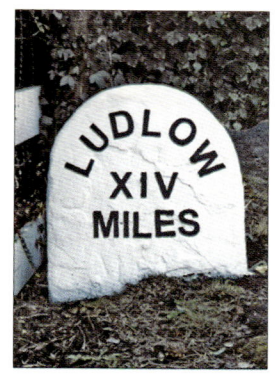

Four of the six milestones in the Parish. From the left: 1) corner of Crown Lane, Little Stretton, 2) outside Milestone, Shrewsbury Road, 3) opposite Dudgeley House, All Stretton and 4) near the top of Sandford Avenue (East). This latter, made in cast iron, may have been moved from Hazler Road when the Sandford Avenue (East) was built. The Wynstay Arms Inn in Much Wenlock is now called the Gaskell Arms. The Salop 13 stone is outside 47/49 High Street (see page 72). The Salop 14 stone which stood outside 58, Ludlow Road is missing.

centre. New carriers such as John Jones had an extensive business serving Bishops Castle, Clun and Bridgnorth through to 1885.

Hazler Road

It appears that the condition of the Much Wenlock to Church Stretton Turnpike during the 1840's was deteriorating and that the descent from the Hazler Gate tollhouse to Watling Street along the present Hazler Road was of particularly poor quality.

In 1855 the Turnpike trustees decided that a new route must be found to replace Hazler Road. They used their powers to buy land then belonging to Moses George Benson of Lutwyche Hall for £185. The new road was built from the junction with Watling Street to form the longer but less steep route over the ridge between Helmeth and Hazler Hills. The road was deturnpiked in 1875 and the tollhouse pulled down.

The new road was eventually named Sandford Avenue to commemorate the efforts of the Rev'd Holland Sandford who in 1885 extended the avenue of lime trees along both sides of the new road to the summit near the lane leading to Gaerstones Farm.

Sandford Avenue (East)

The new road allowed the land on both sides to be developed and from about 1900 individual plots for substantial houses with large gardens were sold. Development proceeded slowly; the first new buildings were The Mount built about 1904 and The Leasowes about 1905.

Looking down Sandford Avenue about 1905. Note how few houses had been built.

Housing Development on the Hazler Slopes

A number of the large houses built during the Edwardian expansion of Church Stretton found an ideal use as small private schools, often including boarding, or as holiday apartments.

The Mount

This, the first property to be built in Sandford Avenue East, was built by William Roberts about 1904 as a private residence. By 1926 Hilda Sarah Benson had opened a preparatory school for boys and girls here. By the 1950s it had become a PNEU School, which meant that it was affiliated to the Parents' National Education Union.

PNEU Schools have always been known to have a well structured and wide curriculum. The movement started towards the end of the 19th century, influenced by the principles and ideas of a renowned Victorian educationalist, Charlotte Mason. She trained students in her philosophy and methods, as well as all other aspects of education, her ideas challenging the generally accepted views of how to educate children. She believed that 'children are persons' and that teachers and parents should treat them as individuals who need to be stimulated from an early age by a broad curriculum, not simply to be trained to read, write and count. Now, these ideas may seem self-evident but they were not so at the end of the 19th century.

The Mount P.N.E.U. School

DAY AND BOARDING SCHOOL
for Girls to 12 years and Boys to 8½ years

Individual attention, extensive curriculum and happy home atmosphere in beautiful surroundings. Large gardens, delightful playground. Holiday boarders welcomed or entire charge taken if desired.

Principal: MRS. M. G. ESMOND (C.M.C.)

MODERATE FEES

Particulars on application to the Principal

Sandford Avenue, Church Stretton
Telephone: 266

Advertisement of 1957/8.

South View, SANDFORD AVENUE, Church Stretton.

Splendidly Situated.

Every Comfort

Open Country and Mountain Views.

Private Sitting-rooms.

Highly Recommended.

Moderate Terms.

Electric Light.

Sunny Aspect.

Address Enquiries to
MRS. TOON,
South View,
Church Stretton.

South View was built by Mrs Anne Toon for holiday accommodation in the 1900s. It has since been converted into a residential care home for the elderly. Advertisement of 1905.

The *Sandford Hotel* (above) was built about 1905. It boasted electric light, billiard and recreational rooms, cycle accommodation, a croquet lawn and a garage. It had a prominent position facing the station. In its early days the owner also owned Stretton House, North Pier, Blackpool. It is now a Nursing Home.

The White House was built as a private residence by Silvester Horne in 1913. After Mrs Silvester Horne left it became a private hotel but was later converted into a nursing home. A large extension was built in the garden in the late 1990s but the business ran into financial difficulties a few years later and closed. In 2003 the buildings were demolished and nine houses were built on the site, now called White House Gardens.

Another large property was Clivedon which was built by the Misses Pearson as a preparatory school by 1905.

THE WHITE HOUSE
(Proprietress: Miss F. Leech)

Ashley Courtenay Recommended

SANDFORD AVENUE, CHURCH STRETTON
SHROPSHIRE

Telephone: Church Stretton 2323

Good Food — Personal Service
Every Comfort

Surrounded by lovely grounds perfectly set among the Stretton Hills

Terms from 9½ guineas a week
Special Terms for Residents

OPEN ALL THE YEAR

Left: The White House as a hotel, from a 1969 guide book.

Right: The Clivedon school for girls, 1908.

Clivedon, Church Stretton
SHROPSHIRE

Home School for Girls
∴ and little Boys ∴

The Misses Pearson.

Housing Development on the Long Mynd Slopes

This postcard view of about 1905 shows some houses newly built on Trevor Hill. Arden House is on the far right of the picture and some houses in Carding Mill Valley Road, which were built at the same time, are shown on the left.

Arden House, which had already been built by Benjamin Blower by the time of the big 1905 sale of housing plots, is one of the best neo timber frame houses erected in Church Stretton.

Scotsman's Field, Burway Road

Scotchman's Piece was the name of a large field on the south side of Burway Road just below Burway Gate where the cattle grid is now. It was a gathering place for travelling pedlars or hucksters who were always called Scotchmen, whatever their actual nationality might have been. The name is preserved in the house called Scotsman's Field.

Scotsman's Field is an Arts and Crafts style house built in 1908 for Mrs Bertha Quick. The architect was Sir Ernest Newton who had been a pupil of Richard Norman Shaw in the 1870s. Together with other pupils of Shaw he was a founder member in 1884 of the Art Workers' Guild which aimed to unite the arts and crafts, including architecture and garden craft. In 1914 Newton was elected President of the Royal Institute of British Architects and four years later was awarded the Royal Gold Medal in recognition of his life's work.

The house and its curtilage is recognised by English Heritage to be an important example of an Arts and Crafts Movement house in Shropshire. The house is described by Pevsner as being one of two (the other being Woodcote) especially good houses of the best period of Church Stretton. An important consideration for Newton was the site of the houses he designed and Scotsman's Field stands on a slope which faces south with views across Church Stretton to the hills beyond.

He believed that a garden was an essential complement to the house plan and the gardens of Scotsman's Field were laid out according to Newton's original design for a formal garden with paved south-facing terraces and further steps and balustraded terraces leading down the terraced hillside to separate areas of garden (a tennis lawn and an enclosed area for twin herbaceous borders) defined by clipped yew hedges. A formal box-edged rose garden lies to the west of the house and from here steps lead up to a rockery. To the east lies a less formal area planted with trees including many conifers. All these features are typical of an ideal Edwardian garden.

In 1960 the house was divided into three and the garden, too, was divided. Fortunately the architects responsible for the conversion were able to subdivide the garden following the original walls and hedges. The garden is now being sensitively restored with the overall structure remaining as shown in Ernest Newton's plan of 1908.

[Photos: Shropshire Magazine]

The wrought iron grill in the Burway Road wall was designed to allow the public to peep into the gardens so that they could admire them!

Church Stretton Golf Club

The Golf Club House in 1905.

This is the oldest 18 hole golf course in Shropshire. It was originally laid out and opened in 1898 to a design by James Braid, a well known golf course designer. It was originally of 9 holes, but was extended to 18 holes in 1903. It is now just over 5,000 yards in length.

The course lay on land owned by the Church Stretton Land Co. Ltd. and the lord of the manor, Ralph Beaumont Benson, but over which the Long Mynd Commoners had grazing rights. It lies on the lower slopes of the Long Mynd, its height varying between 800 and 1,160 ft above sea level. The highest point is the 14th green at 1,160 ft. The bogey score is 82.

The Club House was built in 1899. The original entrance fee was set at one guinea and the annual subscription was also one guinea. Visitors were charged 2/- per day or 5/- per week.

In 1911 a house was built for the Professional adjacent to the Club House. The club owns the first fairway and the 18th hole and the National Trust owns the remainder of the course.

Many houses like The Links took advantage of the newly built golf course to open as guest houses. This house was built by the Misses Preston about 1909.

Church Stretton during World War II

Military vehicles parked on the bypass.
[Imperial War Museum]

Though the bypass was nearly finished in 1939, it was used during the war as a vehicle park for lorries, tanks and guns. In the first weeks of the war many of the larger buildings in the town, especially the hotels, were requisitioned as accommodation for members of the armed services. Later on, many of these were released for use by St. Dunstan's as their need for accommodation and training facilities for blinded servicemen and women increased.

Civilians were organised too. An ambulance and ARP (Air Raid Precautions) unit was formed in 1939 as was a Civil Defence Unit. A Home Guard Unit was formed in 1940 with its headquarters in the Golf Club House.

Each year from 1941 onwards, a week of special fund raising events was held nationally to 'buy' weapons for one of the services. In Church Stretton each week's campaign usually started with a march up Sandford Avenue to the Square. Senior officers of one of the services would take the salute and a local dignatory made an inaugural speech. A military band led the parade followed by contingents from the WAAF, Air and Army Cadets, Home Guard, Royal Observer Corps, Fire Service, Civil Service, St John's Ambulance Brigade, Scouts, Guides and Rangers.

Money was raised in various ways with dances in the Silvester Horne Institute and a fête at St Dunstan's. There were also whist drives and a golf competition between a Forces team and the Home Guard. The Women's Institute held an Olde English Fair and a Repertory Company would present a play at the Institute. These were preceded by house-to-house canvassing and advance sales of raffle tickets. There were also side-shows and competitions, games and amusements, fortune tellers and refreshments.

Taking the salute.

The Remembrance Day service in 2005. The War Memorial records the names of 51 Strettonians who lost their lives in the 1st World War. 35 further names were added after the 2nd World War. [John Corfield]

St Dunstan's in Church Stretton, 1940 - 1946

Outside McCartney's malthouse, the present Antiques Centre.

After the fall of France in mid 1940 St Dunstan's, the rehabilitation and training centre for blinded service men and women located at Ovingdean near Brighton, had to move away from the south coast to a safer location. They chose to move to Church Stretton.

The training centre and the hospital initially moved to the *Longmynd Hotel*. Huts were put up in the grounds, on the lawn and tennis courts, and the garages were converted into workshops. Later the hospital was transferred to Tiger Hall. Brockhurst, the former preparatory school, and the *Longmynd* and *Denehurst Hotels* were used for accommodation with more huts in their grounds.

The St Dunstaners were of many nationalities, British, Poles, French, Dutch, Americans, Canadians and South Africans and included some civilians, e.g. police, ambulance drivers, fire fighters and those wounded in armament factory accidents.

Belmont, in Cunnery Road, was used for the accommodation of blinded girls and servicewomen who were trained in domestic work, including cooking, washing, ironing, and sewing along with typewriting and Braille. There was plenty of time allowed for the traditional crafts including weaving and leather work, metal and plastic model making, basketry, carpentry, rug-making and string-netting. Training was given in physiotherapy including anatomy, with the help of a skeleton affectionately known as Clarence.

McCartney's premises in Sandford Avenue were taken over as an industrial training centre. Here the men were trained to operate capstan lathes, drills, routers, presses and learn the skills of re-upholstery with something of the normal factory atmosphere and background noise. In addition, some huts built for the use of the Army on land between Essex Rd, Lutwyche Road and Sandford Avenue were taken over and used for a number of purposes.

Over 700 blinded service men, women and civilians were trained here during the war. Two large additional huts were erected, one a lounge and recreation room, the other a cafeteria.

A dramatic society flourished and numerous music groups and bands were formed. Dancing was the most popular indoor entertainment. All this musical activity led to bigger and better concerts and soon a concert party was formed and the 'St Dunstan's Fol de Rols' took the stage.

A relief map of the surrounding countryside and a model of the buildings of the Training Centre were made to help the men and women orientate themselves. To assist blinded men and women to get about independently, wires on posts were erected from the *Longmynd Hotel* down Cunnery Road and through Rectory Fields down to the gate opposite the Parish Church for guidance and guiding wires were placed along the footpaths.

Some of the greatest achievements were the annual summer fêtes held to support the big national money raising campaigns such as War Weapons Week (May 1941), Warships Week (March 1942), Wings for Victory (1943), and Salute the Soldier (1944). Very large sums of money were raised locally, e.g. for Wings for Victory Week in 1943 over £60,000 was raised.

A group of servicemen with Matron Postlethwaite (3rd from left) outside Tiger Hall.

Training at a lathe.

The Princess Royal (Princess Mary, Countess of Harewood) talking to a serviceman learning boot repair. She visited Church Stretton in December 1943.

191

Shropshire Artillery Volunteers

The 1st Shropshire Artillery Corps was formed in 1860. In 1880 it amalgamated with the Staffordshire Artillery Volunteers to become known as the 1st Shropshire and Staffordshire Artillery Volunteers. In 1902 it became the 1st Shropshire and Staffordshire Royal Garrison Artillery (Volunteers). Finally in April 1908 it was formed into the Shropshire Royal Horse Artillery. It was initially based at the Drill Hall, Coleham, Shrewsbury, but sub-units were formed at Wellington and Church Stretton.

The Long Mynd was used for training the Volunteers in artillery practice, manoeuvres and carbine drill (a short rifle carried by cavalry and the mounted artillery). The Long Mynd ranges were used only during the summer months with the guns being pulled up by teams of horses, some of which

Wives would often accompany Officers at camps, staying with their husbands at The Hotel.

were hired from the Church Stretton Posting Establishment in Burway Road. Blacksmiths were reported to have done well shoeing horses and mending broken limber chains at exorbitant prices.

The Volunteers used the railway to travel from Shrewsbury to Church Stretton. Men, horses, food and all their equipment arrived by specially chartered trains and the band often played as they marched through the town before going up to the gun platform, the band preceding the gun teams, watched and accompanied by many townspeople. Their camps brought trade to the town and the glamour of military bands playing in the evening outside the officers' mess in *The Hotel*.

The Volunteers' Band also played at local functions such as the Church Stretton Flower Show.

About 1865 a gun platform was established on the Long Mynd to the southwest of the Devil's Mouth off Burway Road. This consisted of four brick bases on which naval-type cannons were placed, looking towards Ashes Hollow, Little Stretton. Eventually, as guns become more manoeuvrable, the bases became unnecessary and were broken up.

On one occasion the Volunteer gunners overshot their target and shelled Minton. Fortunately they used solid practice shot which damaged some buildings, but no one was hurt. The terrified villagers sent a horseman *post haste* to the Church Stretton police to report the matter and a police constable immediately rode up to the gun platform to tell the gunners. Unfortunately, in 1880, a man from Little Stretton was killed in a similar incident.

The Battery was originally commanded by Col. William Field, at one time joint owner of *The Hotel*, which became the Officers' Mess during annual camps and weekend training. Officers would often be accompanied by their wives who stayed there and would visit them in the field. In the evening the regimental band, with the men in their navy blue uniforms, white belts and pill box hats, would play outside *The Hotel* for the officers and their wives who were dining inside.

Gunnery practice with an Armstrong breech loader.

The drill hall was in the *Lion Inn* yard and contained a 32 pounder gun for drill purposes. This was stored in Lion Meadow. Later, when Capt. William Campbell Hyslop was in charge of the Stretton Battery, the guns were moved from storage on Lion Meadow to the grounds of Stretton House which were also used by the gunners for drill. For manoeuvres and carbine drill, they established a range in fields on the north side of Brockhurst near the gas works.

Several summer camps for the Volunteers were held in fields behind Ashbrook Farm and also below Caradoc and Helmeth hills near the present Battlefield Estate.

After the turn of the century the ranges were no longer used, but a drill hut, used later by the Shropshire Royal Horse Artillery, stood between the railway station and Stretton Forge. This was demolished in the 1960s when the units amalgamated with the Territorial Army.

The King's Shropshire Light Infantry (KSLI)

The Artillery Volunteers were not the only military unit to use the area for exercises and manouvres not possible in more built up areas. At least once, in July 1909, the 1st Battalion of the King's Shropshire Light Infantry, consisting of several hundred men, set up camp in a field on the Shrewsbury Road opposite Carding Mill Valley Road. Their leaving parade through the town must have created great excitement as they marched down Sandford Avenue to the railway station to return to their barracks in Copthorne, Shrewsbury.

The KSLI marching down Sandford Avenue in 1909. Notice Richard Pryce's ironmongery and cycle agency shop in the background (now Sandford Hardware) and Harry Boulton's first fish shop at the rear.

Above: The 1st Battalion KSLI Scouts.

Right: The 1st Battalion KSLI camp off Shrewsbury Road. Note the regular lines of tents!

Two of Stretton's Literary Figures

Hesba Stretton

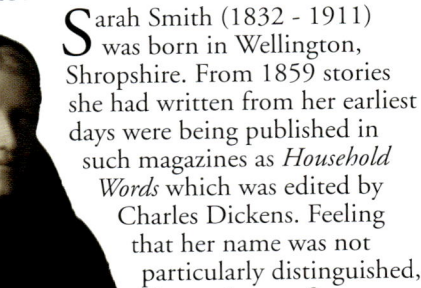

Sarah Smith (1832 - 1911) was born in Wellington, Shropshire. From 1859 stories she had written from her earliest days were being published in such magazines as *Household Words* which was edited by Charles Dickens. Feeling that her name was not particularly distinguished, she made up a first name from the initials of the five siblings Hannah, Elizabeth, Sarah, Benjamin and Ann. Her Uncle James had property in All Stretton and he bequeathed Caradoc Lodge to his niece, Ann. It was here that Sarah spent much of her time and she also came often to Cloverley in Farm Lane. It is not surprising that she took 'Stretton' as her pen-surname.

Hesba Stretton wrote many books but in 1867 her story about a girl waif, *Jessica's First Prayer,* brought her instant and overwhelming fame. It fast became a best seller, was translated into most European languages and many Asiatic ones and sold over 1,500,000 copies. Through all her writing, her strong Christian faith and her concern for children, especially the waifs and strays of the great cities, are constant themes.

Her concern did not end with writing; she was instrumental in founding the London (later National) Society for the Prevention of Cruelty to Children as well as campaigning for the abolition of serfdom and slavery world wide and raising money for famine relief in Russia. It is said that Tsar Alexander II was so impressed by *Jessica's First Prayer* that he ordered it to be sent to every school in Russia but his successor, annoyed by her support of an oppressed religious group in Russia, revoked that order and directed that every copy should be burnt.

One of the lancet windows in the south transept of the Parish Church (right) is dedicated to the memory of Hesba Stretton and depicts the figure of Jessica dressed in a green gown. A plaque below honours this major social reformer and best-selling author, now an almost forgotten figure.

Malcolm Saville

[Malcolm Saville Society]

Although born and raised in Sussex, Malcolm Saville (1901 - 1982) has always been closely associated with this area of Shropshire, following the success of his series of *Lone Pine* stories which were set on and around the Long Mynd and the Stiperstones. The books were published between 1943 and 1978 and over a million copies were sold.

The Saville family first came to South Shropshire in 1936 and Malcolm was very taken with the area. When war came the family was evacuated to Cwm Head at the southern end of the Long Mynd. His first children's book, *Mystery at Witchend*, is a thrilling story of German spies in the Shropshire hills. Nineteen further titles followed in the *Lone Pine* series and he wrote over ninety books (both fiction and non-fiction) in his career. Although many of his books are now out of print, his influence still brings many visitors to the area to see the sights and to relive their childhood memories.

The attraction of Malcolm Saville's books, as opposed to his more famous contemporary Enid Blyton, was that he set his stories in real places and encouraged his readers to come and explore them for themselves. With the detailed description of the countryside, the wildlife and the atmosphere, the reader can almost feel the wind blowing in the trees, hear the sound of the ravens and feel the warmth of the sun or the cold chill of the Long Mynd mist. He had the ability to immerse the reader right into the story and place as if really there.

Malcolm was a deeply religious man. This comes through in his books with the deep sense of loyalty between the various characters, Their constant struggle to fight evil or injustice is cleverly woven into the story. He uses his personal beliefs and his deep love of the countryside as a base line without forcing his views onto the reader, so that the reader has to find those hidden depths for himself.

There is a Malcolm Saville Society, formed in 1994, which seeks to promote the life and work of the author.
[Based on an article by Guy Hawley and Robert Smart]

Church Stretton in the 1950s

This aerial view of the town was taken in 1952 and shows many features and buildings which no longer exist. As a result, the town centre is now much more built up than shown here, with housing developments on the *Hotel* gardens, in Beaumont Road, McClintock Place, King's Court, Queen's Court, St Dunstan's Close, St Laurence Close, Mayfair, etc. Some notable buildings, e.g. the second railway station, the cinema, and the market hall have disappeared, whilst others such as the original Parish Hall, have been replaced. The overall effect is a considerable change within the original road layout. Social change is reflected in the current provision of car parking, not necessary in 1952.

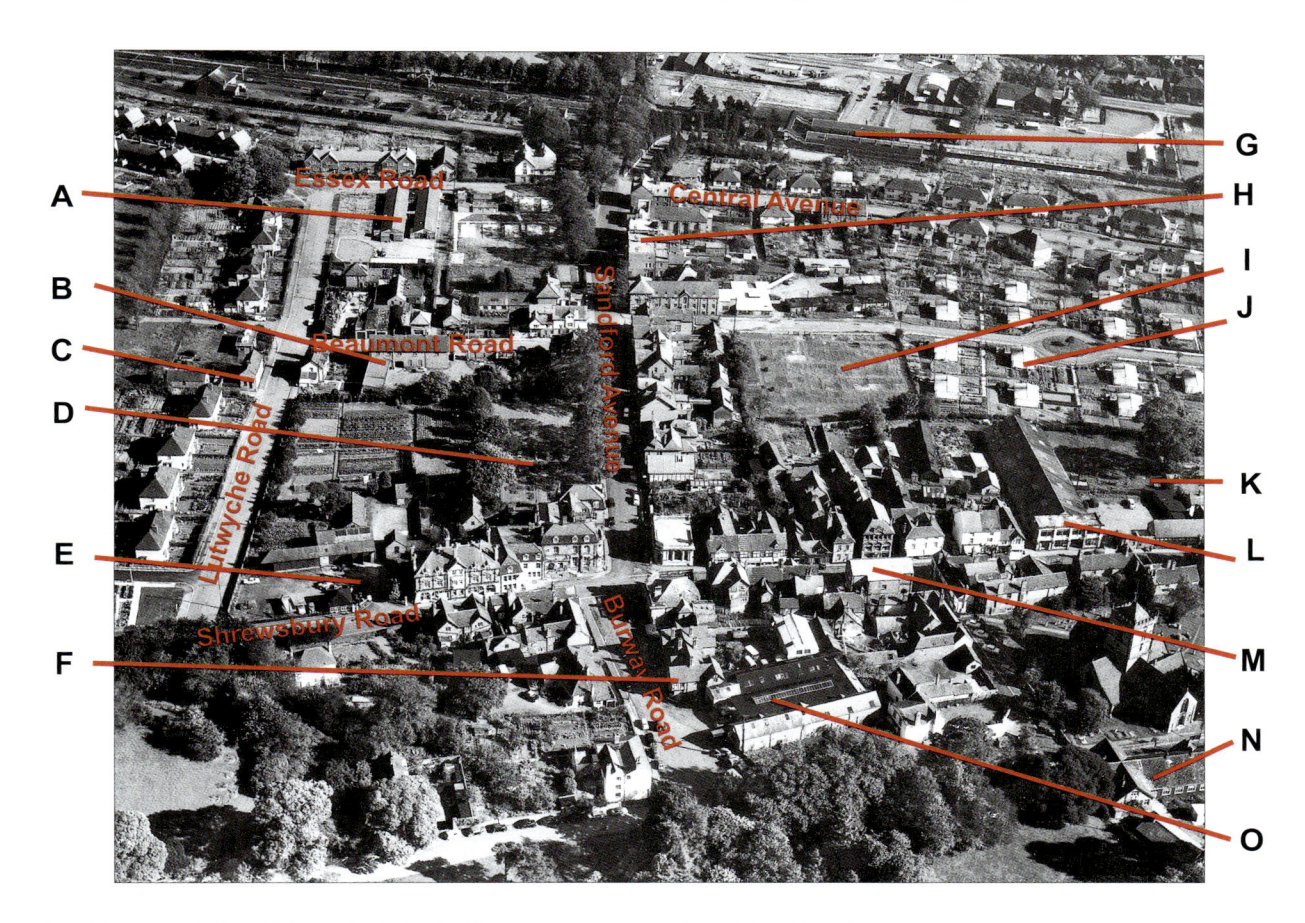

- A   The remaining St Dunstan's huts, then used as the secondary school.
- B   The UDC offices and yard.
- C   No. 1 Crown Cottages
- D   The gardens of The Hotel
- E   Wiggins Garage next to The Hotel
- F   Beaconsfield
- G   The second Railway Station
- H   Regal Cinema
- I   Lion Meadow
- J   Prefabs
- K   Buck's Head yard and bowling green
- L   James' Garage
- M   Market Hall
- N   The first Parish Hall
- O   Central Garage, formerly the Church Stretton Posting Establishment.

An Expanding Population

From an original settlement in Anglo Saxon times of a few houses possibly clustered around the Town Brook, increasing prosperity brought an increase in the population and the emergence of a larger and more ordered town with a market area. The houses of the more prosperous merchants, traders and artisans fronted the market area, with workshops and smaller houses filling in the burgage plots which led off the main road.

> **Population figures** can be difficult to interpret particularly as parish and township boundaries change. There is also ambiguity in some of the early figures as to whether they refer to the whole parish or just Church Stretton township (excluding All Stretton, Little Stretton and Minton).
>
> 1086 140 - 175 population
> 1327 Lay subsidy tax paid by 38 households (11 CS, 11 AS, 6 LS, 10 M)
> 1667 Poll tax paid by 489 'men, women and children'
> 1672 Hearth Tax paid by 98 householders (37 CS, 29 AS, 12 LS, 20 M)
> 1676 434 adults in the parish
> 1792 166 houses in the parish (87 CS, 42 AS, 26 LS, 11 M)
>
> From 1801, figures are based on the census for the whole Parish or Registration District, though the boundaries may vary:
>
> 1801 924 population (199 families)
> 1811 944
> 1821 1,226
> 1831 1,302
> 1841 1,604
> 1851 1,676
> 1861 1,695
> 1871 1,756
> 1881 1,683
> 1891 1,707
> 1901 1,749 (816 CS, 635 AS, 298 LS/M)
> 1911 2,435 (1455 CS, 671 AS, 318 LS/M)
> 1921 2,652 (1671 CS, 663 AS, 318 LS/M)
> 1931 2,637 (1704 CS, 728 AS, 290 LS/M)
> 1951 3,513 (2580 CS)
> 1961 3,640 (2707 CS)
> 1971 3,514
> 1981 3,945
> 1991 4,184
> 2001 4,186 (1,933 houses)

People from outlying hamlets were attracted to the increasingly prosperous town, more houses were built and services such as a larger market, a public hall, schools, the railway and more churches appeared during subsequent centuries. The increase in the number of wealthy business people in late Victorian and Edwardian times followed by an increase in visitor numbers from nearby crowded industrial towns to enjoy the fresh air of Church Stretton brought with it a gradual expansion of house building. This continued at a steady rate until World War II with many houses being built near the town centre, in Central Avenue, Lutwyche Road and Essex Road and on the lower slopes of the hills.

After the war a renewed surge in population was associated with further major housing developments at Ashbrook and Brooksbury in the early 1960s, Battlefield and Ragleth estates in the late 1960s followed by the Stretton Farm Estate, the Churchill Road development, Swain's Meadow and a considerable number of smaller schemes (see opposite). In recent years, many gardens of large houses have been sub-divided to enable further houses to be built, a process of infilling which could radically alter the older residential areas.

In parallel with the housing expansion there has been modern industrial development on the former sidings area around the original railway station to the north of Sandford Avenue where Polymer Laboratories (now Agilent Technologies) erected three large factory buildings to become one of the largest employers in the town. A small factory estate (Mynd Industrial Estate) on the A49 on the site of the former Swain's goods yard has provided further employment opportunities.

The expansion of population after the war has brought with it improvements in public services including new buildings for the police station, a fire station, a primary school with associated swimming baths, a secondary school, medical and health centres, the library, the Mayfair Centre and very recently a sport and leisure centre for school and community use.

A large supermarket, initially Morris's and now the Co-op, has been built on waste ground between High Street and Easthope Road.

The age distribution of residents is such that over 36% are over 65 years old (2001). House prices have risen so much that it is difficult for young people to afford to buy property in the town, despite several schemes to provide affordable housing. Nevertheless, Church Stretton remains a market centre with several hundred people commuting into the town to work. The Church Stretton School (secondary) has some 740 students and St Lawrence C of E School (Junior and Primary) has about 230 children, in both cases drawing from a large catchment area.

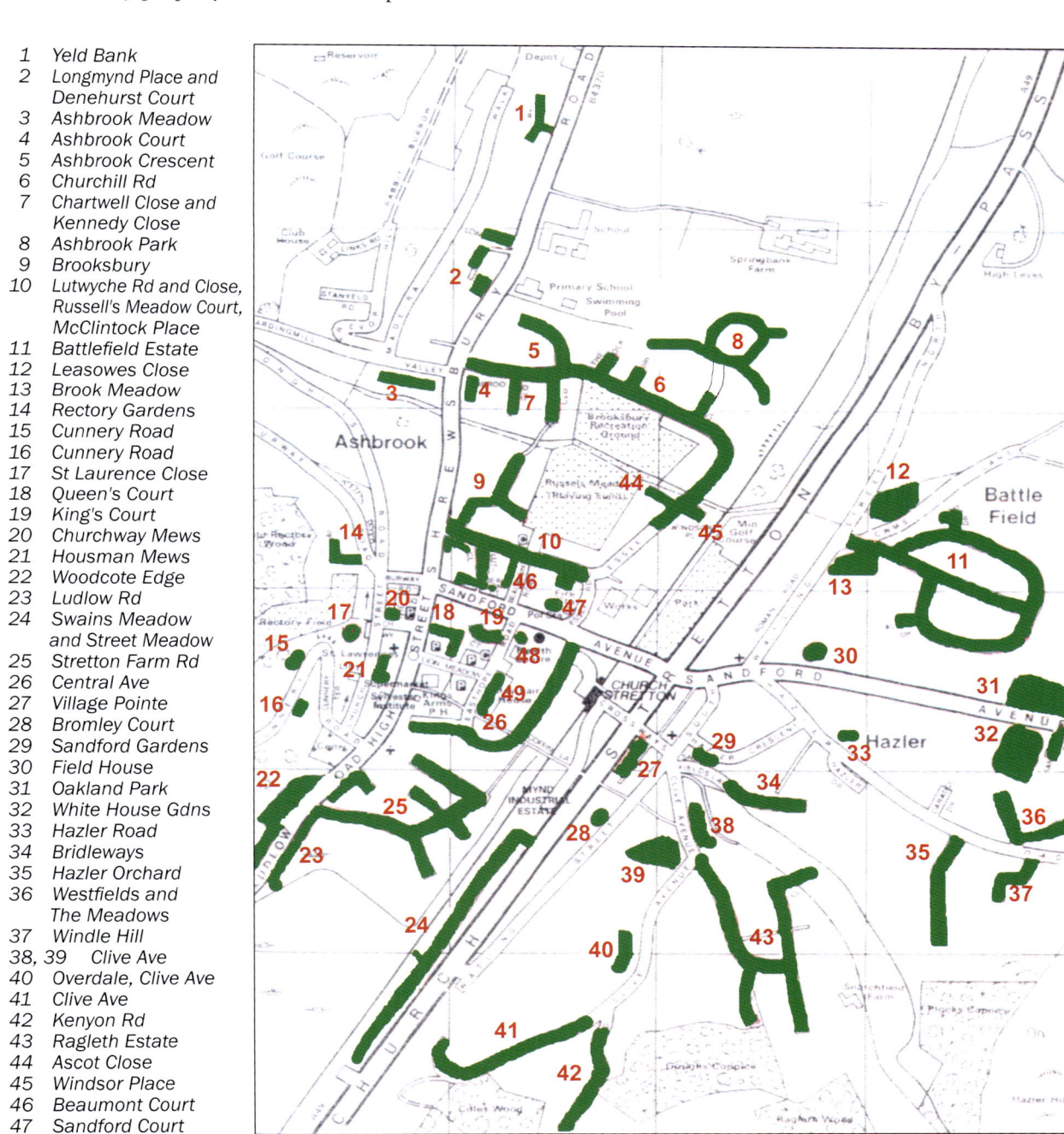

1 Yeld Bank
2 Longmynd Place and Denehurst Court
3 Ashbrook Meadow
4 Ashbrook Court
5 Ashbrook Crescent
6 Churchill Rd
7 Chartwell Close and Kennedy Close
8 Ashbrook Park
9 Brooksbury
10 Lutwyche Rd and Close, Russell's Meadow Court, McClintock Place
11 Battlefield Estate
12 Leasowes Close
13 Brook Meadow
14 Rectory Gardens
15 Cunnery Road
16 Cunnery Road
17 St Laurence Close
18 Queen's Court
19 King's Court
20 Churchway Mews
21 Housman Mews
22 Woodcote Edge
23 Ludlow Rd
24 Swains Meadow and Street Meadow
25 Stretton Farm Rd
26 Central Ave
27 Village Pointe
28 Bromley Court
29 Sandford Gardens
30 Field House
31 Oakland Park
32 White House Gdns
33 Hazler Road
34 Bridleways
35 Hazler Orchard
36 Westfields and The Meadows
37 Windle Hill
38, 39 Clive Ave
40 Overdale, Clive Ave
41 Clive Ave
42 Kenyon Rd
43 Ragleth Estate
44 Ascot Close
45 Windsor Place
46 Beaumont Court
47 Sandford Court
48 St Dunstan's Close
49 Mayfair Court

New roads and plots where post-war housing development has taken place (excluding infilling).

References

Election Riots, *The Times*, 23 Dec 1868; *Shrewsbury Chronicle*, 27 Nov 1868 and 25 Dec 1868.

Hannaford, H R. *Shropshire County Council, Archaeology Service Reports* No. 235 (2004) and 267 (2009).

Hardwick, W. William Salt Library, *Hardwick Mss.* [350/5/40].

Moran, M. *Trans. Shrops. Arch. Soc.*, 2001, pp 48 - 53.

Morgan, R, Private communication (Glamorgan Archives); J Wright, *English Dialect Dictionary*, vol 3, p 495, 1902; Richard Morgan, 'Place-names in the Northern Marches of Wales', in *A Commodity of Good Names*, p 204, Oxbow (2008).

Index

Acton Scott Farm Museum 129
Aerial view of town 194
Allen's Coppice 108
Alliance Insurance Company 104
Almshouses 86
Amber Room 88
Angela's hairdressing salon 72
Anglo Saxon settlement 1
Anthony's hairdressing salon 72
Antiques Market 27, 157
Arden House 186
Artillery Volunteers 192
Arts and Crafts Style House 187
Ash Brook 145
Ashbrook Court 128
Ashbrook Farm 124, 128
Ashbrook Villa 130
Ashford House 91
Ashlett Cottages 3, 85
Ashlett House 82, 84, 85, 89
Asylum 102
Atkinson, Arthur Hazelhurst 114
Aust Ferry 45

Back Lane 6, 122
Bakewell, Dr Samuel Glover 101
Bank House 15, 18, 19
Bank House Lodge 19
Barclays Bank 161
Barnett, Dr Horatio 74
Barn Lane 49
Barn Owls 105, 163
Barn Theatre 105
Barn, The Old 70
Bathing pool 144
Beaconsfield 29
Beastleech 80
Beaumont Road 149

Beddoes 27, 28, 30, 181
Bell's Messuage 36, 126
Belmont 190
Belton, John 124
Belton, William Waring 124
Benefaction board 87
Benson, Caroline Essex 42, 43
Benson, Moses 149
Benson, Ralph Beaumont 42, 67, 101, 149, 163
Berry's 6, 7, 49
Berry's Messuage 48
Besom Inn 23
Black and White Cottage 98
Black death 52
BMX track 163
Bodbury Ring 1
Bolinbrooke 5
Botefelde, John 66
Boulton, Harry 47, 161, 193
Bowdler, John 118
Bowling green 68, 163
Box pews 81
Bridgman, Wm Henry 126, 127
Bright's Messuage 60
Bright, Thomas 60
Bristol Road 45
Britannia Inn 89
British Legion 105
Broadmeadow Park 163
Brockhurst 93, 190
Brockhurst Castle 2
Brockhurst School 114
Bronze Age 1
Bronze plaque (Sandford) 147
Brook Cottage 26, 28
Brooke, Francis 15, 18, 141
Brooks Mill 2, 141

Brook Street 1, 26
Broome, John 159
Broome, Margaret 32
Brown, Freddie 175
Brown, Lancelot (Capability) 14
Bryant, Rev'd Charles 84
Buck's Head Inn 66
Buck's Head Yard 68, 70
Bullring, The 124
Burgage plots 3, 4, 6, 7
Burway Barbers 161
Burway Gate 141, 187
Burway House 22, 118
Butler, Frederick J 121
Butler, R A (Rab) 115
Bypass 175, 189
Bytheway, Thomas 154, 159

Caer Caradoc 1
Camden 2
Capital and Counties Bank 84
Caradoc Motors 68
Carding Mill Court 143
Carding Mill Valley 1, 139
Cardington Road, Old 30
Car Rally 40
Carter, Martin 112
Central Boarding House 49
Central Garage 29
Chalet Pavilion 143, 144
Charlton, John 87
Childe, Richard 56, 63
Children's Home 133
Cholmondeley, Caroline Essex 149
Church clock 79
Church Street School 118
Church Stretton Aerated Water Co. 136, 143

Church Stretton Building Co. 149, 171
Church Stretton Electricity Supply Co. Ltd 173
Church Stretton Entertainments Ltd 105
Church Stretton Fish Bar 65
Church Stretton Furniture Centre 68
Church Stretton High School for Boys 84
Church Stretton in 1838 44
Church Stretton in the 1950s 194
Church Stretton Land Co. 149, 171
Church Stretton Ltd 171
Church Stretton School 119, 197
Church Stretton Times 33
Church Stretton Town Council 87
Church Stretton UDC 139, 161
Church Stretton Water Act 139
Church Stretton Water Co. 139
Church Stretton Waterworks Co. 139
Churchyard 11
Clayton, Rev'd Henry 12
Clee Hill Electrics 6, 7, 63
Clive Avenue 171
Clivedon 185
Coach House, The Old 95
Coaching inn 100
Coaching routes 100, 159, 182
Coffin Lane 75
Coleman, Mrs Anne 67
Coleman, Rev'd T B 13, 15, 67
Coles and Francis, Butchers 157
Collegiate School 22
Coneyborough 108
Congregational Church 96
Cook, Lucy 83
Copper's malthouse 27, 35
Coppice Leasowes 163
Corfield, George 142
Corfield, John 30
Council in the Marches 5
Cound Brook 145
Cound Dale 136
Craig, John 56, 124
Craven Cinemas Co. 160
Critchley, Julian 114
Crocker's 88
Croquet 163
Crossways 171

Crossways Development 172
Crown Carpets 29
Crown Cottages 46, 126
Crown Inn 35, 124
Cunnery, The 16, 108
Cunnery Road 92, 108, 171
Curio Shop, The 88
Cwm Dale 145
Cwm Dale Spring 136
Cycling 88

Dagers Mill 141
Dappled Duck, The 75, 76
Dead man's fair 24
Deakin, A B and W S 174
Deakin's Field 48
Demesne 2, 52
Dendrochronology 66
Denehurst Court 131
Denehurst Hotel 131, 190
Diamond Jubilee (1897) 85
Diamond Villa (Cottage) 93, 96
Dixon, Rev'd Henry 19
Domesday Book 1, 8
Dorrington, Samuel 119
Drill Hall 193
Dr Mott's Road 74
Dudgeley Mill 141
Dumfries and Galloway Standard 170
Dunn, George 158, 159
Duppa and Banks 142

Early settlements 1
Early Stretton Township 1
Easthope Road 149
Edwardian Expansion 171
Edward II, King 5
Edwards, Charles 65
Edwards, Stan 72
Eight The Square 57
Election Riots 148
Electricity Company 159
Electricity Power Station 172, 173
Emmaus Chapel 10
Endowed Free School 118
Entablature, Sandford 147
Entertaining Elephants 70
Essex House 74, 157, 162
Essex Road 149
Essex Road huts 119, 190
Evans, Andrew 89
Everall, Richard 89

Express Dairies 173
Fairs 24
Faulkner, John 124
Ferndale 176
Films 105
Fire engine 29, 104
Fire hooks 89
Fire marks 28, 49
Fire of 1593 5
Fishponds 2
Folly at Tiger Hall 109
Fountain 42
Four-in-hand carriage 170
Foxlease Cottage 181

Gaerstones Farm 182
Gambier, James 19
Gas works 113
General election, 1868 148
George, George 63
Gladwyll 162
Glover, Edward 46
God's Acre 11
Golden Jubilee (1887) 42
Golf Club 188
Gooch, Drs Horace and Winifred 95
Goulder family 10, 37
Grapes Inn 112
Great Elmith 16
Green Dragon 49
Greengates 80, 81
Greenhills Cemetery 11
Grounds, Douglas 11
Grove, The 74, 83
Guardians of the Poor 87
Gunn, Harold 33, 159

Halfway Houses 131
Hall 13, 15
Hampson, H 155
Handbook to Church Stretton 33
Hannett, Frank 74
Hannett's 73
Harman and Carey 58
Harries, Rev'd William 12, 19
Haughton, Richard 80
Haverkam, John 159
Haverkam, William 100, 101
Hawkes, Thomas 86
Hayles's messuage 81
Hazler 180
Hazler Cottage 181

199

Hazler Crescent 171
Hazler Gate 182
Hazler Hill Farm 180
Hazler Road 180, 183
Hazler Tollhouse 182
Hearth Tax 5, 15
Heath Church 8
Hermann 163
Hermitage 11, 14
High Street 45 - 105
Hillgarth 180
Hillside Pharmacy 153
Hill View 181
Holiday resort 35
Hollybush Café 26, 30
Holmes, Harold 145
Home Guard 189
Home, Margaret 32
Home, Richard 57, 159
Horne, Charles Silvester 90
Horne, The Hon. Mrs Silvester 90, 185
Horse Engine 129
Hotel fire 10, 36
Hotel, The 35, 38, 148, 170
Housing development 150, 196, 197
Housing, post war 196
Housman, A E 36
Housmans 64
Hughes, John 56
Hydropathic Hotel 110
Hyslop, Charles 166
Hyslop, David 27, 29, 30
Hyslop, W Campbell 103, 104, 106
Hyslop, William 102

Ice house 14
Industrial Training Centre 190
Information Centre 120
Institute Cottage 86
Insurance House 73, 74
Iron Age 1

James' Garage 68
Jessica's First Prayer 195
Jetty construction 99
Jewsbury & Brown Ltd 137
John, King 2, 3, 52
John o' th' Inn 66
Johnson's Dispensing Chemist 153
Jones, Benjamin 128
Jones, Fred and Agnes 128

Jones, Joseph 92
Jones, T Noel 177
Jubilee Building 83, 89
Jubilee Fountain 42

Kaboodle 153
Kenyon Road 171
King's Arms 75
King's Arms (Lion) Inn 48
King's Court 48
King's Shropshire Light Infantry 193
Kinnoul Villa 96
Kough, Samuel H 74

Ladies' Academy 94
Lake Lane 21
Land and Building Companies 171
Land and Building Company 149
Laundry, Agnes Jones' 128
Laundry, The 175
Laura Heathjohn 33
Leasowes, The 183
Leighton, Frances 15, 18
Leighton, Lord, of Stretton 19
Leland, John 15
Les Trois 116
Lewis, Fred 65
Lewis, Mary 89
Lewis, Thomas 32
Lewis, William Henry 34
Library 53, 87, 120
Light Spout Hollow 139
Limes, The 74
Lime trees 41, 146, 147
Links, The 188
Lion Inn 7, 48
Lion Meadow 48, 68
Little Elmith 16
Little Stretton Waterworks Co. 139
Lloyd's Bank 41, 46, 84
Lockup 87
Lodge on Back Lane 122
Lodge on Ludlow Road 108
Lone Pine stories 195
Longhills 19
Longhills Road 25
Long, Mary, café 87
Long Mynd 1, 139, 141, 170, 192
Longmynd Antiques 175
Longmynd Hotel 108, 110, 171, 190
Lover's Walk 171

Lower House 100
Lower Living, The 60
Ludlow Road 108, 113
Lutwyche Road 126, 149

Madeira Walk 171
Mainwaring, Rev'd John 6, 12, 14
Malthouses 26, 27
Manchester House 178
Manor of Stretton-en-le-Dale 1, 2
Market Halls 52, 53
Markets 2, 52
Market Square 3, 56 - 61
Marston, Samuel 80
Masonic Hall 80
May Fair 52
McCartney, Robert 19, 27, 50, 56, 157
McCartney, Robert E 19
McCartney's Estate Agency 56
McClintock, Dr John 74, 83
McDowall, William 170
Medlicott family 62
Methodist Church, The 179
Midland Bank 42, 43
Milburga, St 178
Milestones 72, 183
Mill, Carding Mill Valley 141
Miller and Evans 56
Millichope Hall 20
Mills, Jonathan 48
Minerva 64
Mop Fair 24
Moran, Madge 66
Morgan, Sam 88
Morris, Arthur 161
Morris, Christopher 88
Morris, Tom 161
Mott, Dr Charles 73, 74
Mount, The 183, 184
Mund's House 82
Mynd Court 19

Narrows, The 73, 75
Nash Brook 141
National Trust 143
New Pool Hollow Reservoir 139
Newsworld 155
Newton, Sir Ernest 187
Nicholls, Richard 80
Norfolk Lodge 19
Norgate, C E 83
Norman architecture 8

Norman Manor 1
Norton, Bonham 15, 55, 81
Norton, Sir George 15
Nunn, Rev'd Preston 91

Oakham Dingle 21
Officers' Mess 192
Old Barn 70
Old Coppers Malt House 37
Old Rectory 12
Old Smithy 116
Oswell, A E Lloyd 93
Outfarm (Robinson's Buildings) 126
Over Field 15
Overseers of the Poor 86
Ox Leasowe 16

Parish Centre 122
Parish Church 8 - 11
Parish Hall 122
Parish Poor 86
Park, The 163
Park Cottage 17
Parker, Barry 106
Park House 16
PCB Solicitors 158
Pearce, Stan 155
Pearce, William Edward Gordon 145
Pemberton, C O Childe 18, 118
Pemberton, Rev'd Robert 6, 13,
    14, 18, 19, 20, 108, 109
Peppers 152
Pevsner 35, 94, 106, 187
Philips, Edward 49
Phillips, Arthur 84, 89
Phillips, John 60
Phillips, Thomas 82
Pie-Powder, Court of 52
Pile, Albert T 116
Plague 52
Plough Inn 3, 50, 56
Police Station, Shrewsbury Rd 131
Poor House 86
Poor Law Amendment Act 86, 132
Poor Law Unions 86
Population 6, 196
Port Way 1
Posting Establishment 29, 30
Post Office 27, 32, 62, 159
Post Office Building 158
Post Office, Old 32
Precious Bane 80
Preece, George 41, 46, 146

Price, Dennis 65
Price, Joseph 155
Princes Soft Drinks 137
Princess Royal 191
Priory, The 20, 117
Priory Villas 117
Private Mental Hospital for Ladies
    (The Grove) 83
Proffit, Anne 93
Proffit, John Edwin 64
Proffit, Thomas 56, 64
Prosser's Yard Field 80
Protestant Church 10
Pryce, Richard 161, 193
Pryll Cottage 1, 23

Quäck, Emil 19
Quarter Houses 128, 131, 133
Queen's Court 65, 68
Queen's Head Inn 80
Queen's Stores 80
Quick, Bertha 187
Quintessence 87

Rabbit Burrow 171
Ragleth House 94
Railway 6, 164
Railway, First Station 165
Railway, Goods Yard 166
Railway, Hyslop Coal Merchant 166
Railway, opening 166
Railway, Second Station 168
Raven Inn 60, 61
Rectory 12
Rectory Field 14, 30, 123
Rectory Wood 13, 14
Reddin, Henry 63, 137
Red Lion Inn 48
Rees's Hotel 156
Regal Cinema 160
Remembrance Day 189
Reservoirs 21, 139
Reynolds, Bill 175
Rich, Thomas 152
Roberts, W J 57
Robinson, Charles E 46, 126
Robinson, Elizabeth 61, 64, 65, 75
Robinson, George 35, 126
Robinson, John 56, 60, 61, 63
Robinson's Buildings 46, 126
Robinson's shop 46
Roger de Montgomery 2
Roman Catholic Church 10, 178

Roman road 176
Roman settlement 1
Ross's Shoe Shop 153
Royal Exchange Assurance Co. 49
Royal Mail coach 100, 159, 182
Ruabon brick 18
Ruscoe, Harry 72, 74

Salop Fire Office 28
Salop Infirmary 20
Salt, Henry 62, 84, 85
Salt's 6, 7, 62
Sandford Art Gallery 37
Sandford Avenue 146, 150
Sandford Avenue (East) 183
Sandford Avenue Shops 152 - 161
Sandford Hardware 161
Sandford Hotel 51, 172, 185
Sandford, Rev'd Holland 41, 146,
    147, 148
Saville, Malcolm 195
School attendance notice 119
School House 121
Scotchman's Piece 187
Scotsman's Field 187
Screen, Chancel 10
Secret Cottage 117
Settlement Act 86
Severn Trent Water Company 140
Shampers Hairderssers 159
Sheela-na-gig 9
Sheep and pony fair 24
Sheep sales 81
Sheep Sales Field 48
Shepwardine 78
Sheriff of Shropshire 2
Shingles, Miss Susannah 16
Shovel Hat Cottage 117
Shrewsbury and Hereford Rly Co
    164
Shrewsbury Old Bank 32, 62
Shrewsbury Road 124 - 138
Shropshire Artillery Volunteers 192
Silvester Horne Institute 86, 90
Simpson, Charles 150
Simpson, Elizabeth 64
Skateboard ramp 163
Skin Yards 26
Slaughterhouse 46
Slaughterhouse Cottages 126
Smith, Gaius 63
Smith, R O 158
Smith, Sarah (Hesba Stretton) 195

Smith, W H 154
Smithy 116
Somerhey 93
Somerville's Bakery 153
Sorting office 159
South View 184
Spa 110, 171
Spar Supermarket 160
Spice Corner Restaurant 57
Sports and Leisure Centre 134
Spring Bank 131
Spring Cottage 26, 28, 30
Spring Terrace 26
Square, The 56
Stanyeld Road 171
Station 164 - 169
St Dunstan's 27, 117, 119, 162, 190, 191
Stella Benson 149
Stephen's messuage 30
St Laurence Church 8, 81, 87
St Lawrence CE Primary School 134, 197
St Mary's Catholic Scholasticate 115
St Milburga's Church 178
Stretton Café 156
Stretton Chambers 162
Stretton-en-le-Dale, Manor of 2
Stretton Farm 102
Stretton Galleries 88
Stretton Garage 161
Stretton Gazette 74
Stretton, Hesba 195
Stretton Hills Mineral Water Co. 136
Stretton House 102 - 104
Stretton School of Dance and Drama 173
Stretton Shoes 153
Stretton's Mill, Carding Mill Valley 141
Studio Restaurant 79
Sun Alliance Insurance Ltd 28
Sunday School 118
Suters Close 16
Sutton, Francis 137
Swan and Malt Shovel Inn 30
Swan Inn 30
Swimming baths 134

Talbot Inn 35, 100
Talbot Meadow 11
Tarbuck, William and Percy 65, 157
Temperance Hotel 88
Temperance Refreshment Rooms .88
Tennis 163
Thompson, Thomas J 177
Thursdays Corner 93
Thynne 66
Thynne family 15
Tiger Hall 108, 109, 190
Times, The 148
Tipton's 84
Tithe 45, 61, 71
Tithe apportionment map 7, 97
Tithe barn 12, 16
Tithes 6
Tolls 182
Top Gear 77
Tourism, Victorian 170
Tower Buildings 172
Town Brook 1, 21
Town Brook Hollow Reservoir 139
Town Hall 52, 53
Townshend, Sir Henry 53
Trades 6
Tranter, Kevin 134
Trevor Hill 171, 186
Tudor Cottage 98
Turnpike Roads 45, 182

Unwin, Raymond 106

Vermont 109
Vernon House 172, 177
Victoria Court 109
Victoria House 89
Victoria, Queen, Golden Jubilee 42
Village Pointe 175
Volunteers' Band 192

Walters House 86
Waring, Thomas 81
War Memorial 189
Water (Bottled) Companies 136
Water Supply 139
Watling Street 1
Watling Street South 171, 176
Webb, Captain Matthew 74
Webb, Mary 78, 80
Well's Messuage 91
West Shropshire Water Board 140
Wheatley, Charles 177
Wheel-pit 63
White House 185

White House Gardens 185
Wilding, William 49
Wilkes' Messuage 79, 80
Wilson, Rev'd William 134
Windsor, George 32, 33, 159
Windsor, George (Laura Heathjohn) 33
Wine Vaults 64
Witting, David and Sylvia 70
Woodcote 106, 113, 171
Wooddean 116
Wood, Henry 62
Wool fair 24
Workhouse 132, 133
Working Men's Club 105
World's End 112
World's End Inn 112
World War II 27, 189
Wright, Sampson 83
Wright's Estate Agent 156

Yapp, Charlotte 133
Ying Wah 79

Zrinyi, Arthur Edward 16
Zrinyi, Demetre de Stourdza 16